R/γ

001

D1381573

OXFORD MEDIEVAL TEXTS

General Editors

V. H. GALBRAITH   R. A. B. MYNORS
C. N. L. BROOKE

THE CARMEN DE
HASTINGAE PROELIO
OF GUY
BISHOP OF AMIENS

Bibliothèque Royale de Belgique, MS. 10615–10729, fol.
229^v, col. ii, vv. 519–66

Reproduction of lines from the manuscript of the *Carmen de
Hastingae Proelio* (actual size), describing the last stages of the
battle, culminating in the death of Harold, and the night pursuit
led by Eustace of Boulogne

THE CARMEN DE HASTINGAE PROELIO

OF GUY
BISHOP OF AMIENS

EDITED BY

CATHERINE MORTON

AND

HOPE MUNTZ

OXFORD
AT THE CLARENDON PRESS
1972

Oxford University Press, Ely House, London W. 1

GLASGOW NEW YORK TORONTO MELBOURNE WELLINGTON
CAPE TOWN IBADAN NAIROBI DAR ES SALAAM LUSAKA ADDIS ABABA
DELHI BOMBAY CALCUTTA MADRAS KARACHI LAHORE DACCA
KUALA LUMPUR SINGAPORE HONG KONG TOKYO

PRINTED IN GREAT BRITAIN
AT THE UNIVERSITY PRESS, OXFORD
BY VIVIAN RIDLER
PRINTER TO THE UNIVERSITY

PREFACE

In preparing this edition of the *Carmen de Hastingae Proelio*, we have been greatly indebted to the assistance and lively interest in our research of many institutions and even more medieval scholars, and the number of friendships here and abroad that our questions to them have brought about has been a happy accidental product of our work.

Our thanks must go first to the Delegates of the Oxford University Press and the Editors of the Oxford Medieval Texts for their generosity in accepting this edition and in allowing the text and translation of the *Carmen* to be accompanied by historical analysis and commentaries greater in length than is usual in this series. We are also most grateful to Messrs. Chatto & Windus Ltd. and Charles Scribner's Sons, Hope Muntz's publishers, for allowing this work to be offered to the Clarendon Press.

Space does not permit more than a brief listing of the many libraries and societies to which we owe so much. We thank: the Rare Book Room of the University of Virginia, Charlottesville; the New York Public Library; the municipal libraries of Rouen, Alençon, Boulogne, Amiens, and Abbeville; the Public Record Office, London; the Bodleian Library, Oxford; the library of the Fitzwilliam Museum, Cambridge; the library of the Society of Antiquaries of London; the library of Karl-Marx Universität, Leipzig; the municipal library of Berlin (DDR); the Seminar-bibliothek and Stadtbibliothek, Trier; the Archives Nationales, Bibliothèque Nationale, and École des Chartes, Paris; the Royal Historical Society; the Kent and Sussex Archaeological Societies; the Battle and District Historical Society; and the National Central Library of London, together with all of the many libraries from which we were privileged to borrow books through its services.

In like manner, we can give but a summary list of the scholars and friends who have encouraged and aided us in so many ways; we are most grateful to: R. E. Latham, Esq. and Mrs. Katherine Thomson of the Committee for a Medieval Latin Dictionary, London; Mmes Bautier and Gilles of the Comité Français Du Cange; Professor Franz Blatt of Aarhus University, General

Editor of *Novum Glossarium*; Dr. Otto Prinz of Munich University, General Editor of *Mittellateinisches Wörterbuch* (for lexicographical and philological information and help); Father Petrus Becker, O.S.B., of St. Eucher-Matthias Kloster, Trier; Mgr. Heinrich Moritz, Rektor, St. Nicholas Spital, Bernkastel-Kues; Dom Emile Van de Vyver, O.S.B., of the Abbey of SS. Peter and Paul, Dendermonde; Professor Francis Wormald of London University; Mr. N. R. Ker of Oxford University; Dr. R. Laufner, Direktor, Stadtbibliothek, Trier (for palaeographical information and help in tracing the history of the manuscripts); Brigadier C. N. Barclay, C.B.E., D.S.O.; Brigadier Kenneth Leader, O.B.E., M.C.; Lt.-Col. C. H. Lemmon, D.S.O.; Major G. L. M. Welstead; Patrick Thornhill, Esq.; the late Clement Chevallier, Esq. (for military and topographical data); Professor Bernhard Bischoff of Munich University; Mlle Raymonde Foreville, Directeur de Recherches, Institut de Recherche et d'Histoire des Textes, Paris; Professor Dorothy Whitelock and Mrs. Marjorie Chibnall of Cambridge University; Dr. J. M. Wallace-Hadrill of Merton College, Oxford; Dr. Johanna Stuckey of York University, Toronto; Mlle Simone Bertrand, Keeper of the Bayeux Tapestry, and her staff; Miss Anne Roper, C.B.E., J.P., Archivist of Hythe, Kent; Miss Elizabeth Eyres; Miss Phyllis Abrahams; the late Father Conrad Walmsley, O.F.M.; Miss Celia Walmsley (for information and assistance historical, linguistic, ecclesiastical, etc.); the late Miss Elfrida Raufer; Miss Audrey Bamberg; Miss Jean Adamson; Mrs. Winifred Bryher; Miss Elizabeth Muntz; Mr. Denis Butler; Mr. and Mrs. Norman Denny; Mr. and Mrs. William Collier; Mrs. Francesca Desborough; Dr. Vincent Desborough; Miss Margaret Dixon; Mrs. Evelyn Webster (for many kindnesses and good offices).

We wish to call out for special thanks four libraries without whose courtesy and assistance this edition could not have been prepared: the Bibliothèque Royale de Belgique, which possesses both the unique manuscript of the *Carmen* and the fragmentary later copy, gave us every facility both for study and collation of the text and for tracing the chequered history of the manuscripts themselves. We are deeply grateful for the patience with our interminable questions shown by our good friend Mlle Marguerite Debae of the Cabinet des Manuscrits and the help that she gave us in so many ways. We thank the Trustees of the British Museum for giving us permission to use its great library, without which scholarship would be difficult indeed, and particularly thank P. J. Fitzpatrick Esq. of the Reading Room for his help in obtaining books. We are also much indebted to the London Library, whose generous policy of loans has made it so much easier for us to work at a distance from London, and to Miss Wells and Miss Terry of the Kent County Library, for their friendly co-operation in securing for us the most unlikely books. Our profound thanks to them all.

We wish to express here our deep gratitude and obligation to Professor Frank Barlow of Exeter University, to whose penetrating and original work on the Conquest and the *Carmen* we owe so much, and who has been the kindest of friends and colleagues. We are greatly indebted, too, to the generosity of Dr. L. J. Engels of Groningen University, himself the author of a distinguished study of the *Carmen*, both for allowing us to quote his brilliant interpretation of certain passages, and for his selfless postponing of further research on the *Carmen* until our edition should appear. Finally, we thank most warmly our editor, Professor C. N. L. Brooke, for the perceptive scholarship that he has brought to our book and for the great courtesy that he has shown it and us throughout. The ultimate responsibility for the content of this edition rests, however, with ourselves.

CATHERINE MORTON
HOPE MUNTZ

CONTENTS

LIST OF PLATES

Reproduction of lines from the manuscript of the *Carmen
de Hastingae proelio*   *Frontispiece*

PLATES

(between pp. 82 and 83)

List of plates, reproduced here by kind permission of the Phaidon Press
and by courtesy of the Victoria and Albert Museum (Photographic
Department), from Sir Frank Stenton's edition of *The Bayeux Tapestry*
(1957). English sub-titles have been added for reference. These are not
translations of the Latin captions.

LIST OF MAPS

INTRODUCTION

AUTHORSHIP AND DATE OF THE *CARMEN*

ALTHOUGH the manuscripts of the poem commonly known as the *Carmen de Hastingae Proelio* bear neither title nor ascription, it has generally been assumed, since their discovery, to be the work of Guy, bishop of Amiens (1058–75), written before 11 May 1068. Whilst this assumption is incapable of absolute proof, the few objections that have been raised to it can be shown to be either based on error or invalid in themselves. It is possible as well, in our opinion, to demonstrate that the poem was composed before 1072, that is, sufficiently earlier than the *Gesta Guillelmi* of William of Poitiers for the latter to have made use of it in his own work (written *c.* 1073–5), and that it was written by a man whose background and attitudes, where these appear, are wholly in accord with what is known of Guy of Amiens.

The fact that Guy of Amiens, uncle of Guy, count of Ponthieu, wrote a verse account of the Norman Conquest is known from two mentions of it by Orderic Vitalis: 'Guido etiam praesul Ambianensis metricum carmen edidit, quo Maronem et Papinium gesta heroum pangentes imitatus Senlacium bellum descripsit; Heraldum uituperans et condempnans, Guillelmum uero collaudans et magnificans';[1] 'In clero qui ad diuina ei (sc. reginae) ministrabat; celebris Guido Ambianorum praesul eminebat, qui iam certamen Heraldi et Guillelmi uersifice ediderat.'[2]

Somewhat later, Robert of Torigny, perhaps following Orderic, described it: 'Edidit preterea de eadem materia opus non contempnendum Guido, episcopus Ambianensis, heroico metro exaratum.'[3]

Their citations leave it doubtful whether Orderic or Robert had actually seen the poem; certainly after their time it vanishes from sight for almost 500 years. Guy's work is next mentioned by André Duchesne.[4] The great bibliographers of the eighteenth century

---

[1] OV, pp. 184f. (ii. 158).   [2] Ibid., p. 214 (ii. 181–2).
[3] Interpolation to *GND*, p. 264.
[4] 'Guidonis Ambianensis Episcopi, de Cõquestu Angliae per Guillelmum Normannorum Ducem. Lib. M.S. citatur ab Orderico Vitale' (*Bibliothèque des auteurs qui ont escript l'histoire et topographie de la France* (Paris, 1618), p. 144).

have nothing to add save information about Guy himself and the fact that his poem had apparently been lost since the twelfth century.[1]

In November 1826, Georg Heinrich Pertz discovered in the Bibliothèque dite de Bourgogne two manuscripts of a poem on the Norman Conquest (one a copy of the first sixty-six lines of the other), beginning:

> Quem probitas celebrat sapientia munit et ornat·
> Erigit et decorat L. W. salutat·

Pertz immediately thought of the lost poem of Guy of Amiens, and read the initials in the second line as standing for *Lanfrancum Wido*. Henry Petrie, who came to Brussels to transcribe the poem, thought that *L*. might stand for *Lanfrancus*, as Lanfranc himself had been said by Sigebert of Gembloux to have written on the Conquest, but Pertz adhered to his reading,[2] and Petrie eventually accepted *W*. as the author.

Petrie remained, however, cautious in identifying *W*. He entitled the poem *De Bello Hastingensi Auctore W*. in his *Monumenta Historica Britannica*, suggesting in a footnote that it was not unlikely that this was the poem written by Guy of Amiens.[3] In his notes for the preface to the *Monumenta*, edited by T. D. Hardy, Petrie explained that he considered the proem of the *Carmen* too fulsome to have been addressed by a bishop to an abbot, even an abbot as distinguished as Lanfranc.[4] Hardy himself accepted this reservation as valid.[5]

Yet, on the whole, Pertz's identification of the *Carmen* with the poem written before 11 May 1068 by Guy of Amiens was accepted for over a hundred years without serious challenge. In 1944, however, G. H. White attacked this assumption. He argued that, in listing the four knights who killed Harold (vv. 540–4), the

---

[1] e.g. P. Leyser, *Historia Poetarum . . . Medii Aevi* (Halle, 1721), pp. 342 f.; J. A. Fabricius, *Bibliotheca Latina Mediae et Infimae Aetatis* (Hamburg, 1735), iii. 370–2; *Histoire littéraire de la France* (Paris, 1747), viii. 29–32; J. Lelong, *Bibliothèque historique de la France* (Paris, 1771), iii, no. 39,647.

[2] *Archiv* vii (1839), pp. 2 f.   [3] *MHB*, p. 856.

[4] Ibid., p. 95.

[5] *Descriptive Catalogue . . .* i. 671–2 (no. 1,269). Of the other early editors, William Black, who prepared a version of Petrie's text for *Appendix C to a Report on Rymer's Foedera*, thought both initials to refer to the author; Francisque Michel called the poem *Carmen . . . Widonis*, but thought the poet insufficiently vehement against Harold to be certainly Guy of Amiens (*CAN* iii. v); and J. A. Giles simply followed Michel's text.

author of the *Carmen* called one of them simply, *Pontiui nobilis heres*. Guy of Amiens, uncle of the reigning count, would have known the name of his heir, and would certainly not have omitted it in recounting what was for him the climax of the battle. Therefore, White claimed, the *Carmen* could not be the work of Guy of Amiens.[1] In 1950, White put forward yet another argument against Pertz's identification: the close similarity between many passages in the *Carmen* and the *Gesta Guillelmi* showed, he said, that the poem was derived from William of Poitiers's work, and hence could not have been written by Guy.[2] White's theories have been largely ignored by continental historians, but have had a considerable effect in England. Professor D. C. Douglas, for example, reversed his earlier opinion of the *Carmen* as a most valuable source for the Battle of Hastings[3] to one of caution in its use and suspicion as to its authenticity.[4]

Other objections that might be raised to Guy's authorship are: that the poem is in elegiacs, apart from the first twenty-five lines, not in the hexameters (*heroico metro*) which Robert of Torigny says Guy used; that Queen Mathilda is not mentioned in the poem, a surprising omission, were it the work of her chaplain; and that it is not Bishop Guy's own family, that of Ponthieu, that is eulogized, but Eustace II, count of Boulogne.

We shall now consider these objections in the order in which they have been raised. The poet's obsequious address to Lanfranc is not out of place when one remembers his position of pre-eminence as a scholar and teacher[5] and his place as William's chief counsellor, a point that cannot have been unimportant to a writer seeking William's favour. As for Michel's qualification, that he thought the poem insufficiently vehement against Harold, this has never been taken seriously. The poet allows the king's ability and

---

[1] In 'The Companions of the Conqueror', *The Genealogists' Magazine* ix (1944), pp. 422 ff.
[2] Published in 1953 as 'The Battle of Hastings and the Death of Harold', *The Complete Peerage* xii, Appendix L, pp. 36 ff.
[3] 'Companions of the Conqueror', *History* xxviii (1943), p. 138.
[4] *William the Conqueror* (London, 1964), pp. 200 and 398.
[5] Cf. A. J. Macdonald, *Lanfranc* (Oxford, 1926), pp. 25 ff.; F. Barlow, 'A View of Archbishop Lanfranc', *JEH* xvi (1965), p. 175. Verse 10 of the *Carmen* may refer to this aspect of Lanfranc's work. The word *lucifer* (v. 3) may also be significant; William of Malmesbury uses it of Lanfranc (*GR* ii. 329), and he is frequently likened to a light in the dark ignorance of the times, e.g. OV, p. 250 (ii. 210) and his epitaph (Giles, *Scriptores*, p. 175).

eloquence, but has a low opinion of his integrity. King Harold is condemned as a villainous ruler (v. 129), a fratricide (vv. 134–8), a perjured usurper (v. 261), and a treacherous opponent (vv. 130, 279–80). The writer lays much emphasis on his great personal prowess (vv. 533–4, 543–4), but this tribute is paralleled in descriptions by Tudor apologists of Richard III (otherwise for them a monster of iniquity) as well as in contemporary accounts of Gilles de Rais. The more valiant the evil man, the more resounding the victory over him by the just.

As to the first of White's objections to Guy as author of the *Carmen*, that the noble heir of Ponthieu is not identified, the phrase, *Pontiui nobilis heres*, cannot, grammatically, stand alone, but must modify one of the four named killers of Harold. We think that the man in question is *Hugo*, for a Hugh, count of Ponthieu witnessed a royal charter in 1084 (see Appendix D, pp. 116–20).

White's second contention was that the *Carmen* was based on the *Gesta Guillelmi* of William of Poitiers, and hence could not be the earlier work of Guy. Professor Raymonde Foreville, however, has shown[1] that it was William of Poitiers, essentially a propagandist rather than a historian, who carefully altered earlier material less favourable to the duke.[2] But as Foreville, in common with most continental scholars, had never questioned the priority or authorship of the *Carmen*, she considered it sufficient to adduce a great number of parallel passages to illustrate William of Poitiers's borrowing, without analysing the significance of the different manner in which the materials were treated in the two works.[3]

More recently, Dr. Sten Körner, examining certain parallel passages (including those cited by White), agreed that one writer had copied the other, but argued that the much greater bias in favour of William found in the *Gesta Guillelmi* showed it to be the later text: 'At a number of points in the chronicle, it is evident that GdeP has enlarged upon and heightened the account in the *Carmen* in the same way that he made use of the Jumièges chronicle.'[4] The examples that Körner himself adduces are chiefly ones in which the *Gesta* multiplies the statements of the *Carmen*: (1) in the *Carmen*,

[1] *GG*, pp. xxii ff.

[2] Ibid., p. xlvii. Professor Foreville has been kind enough to inform us and allow us to quote, that she has seen no evidence to cause her to change her opinion about the order in which the *Carmen* and *Gesta* were written.

[3] Ibid., pp. xxxv ff.

[4] *The Battle of Hastings; England and Europe 1035–1066* (Lund, 1964), p. 98.

William loses two horses (vv. 476, 507), in the *Gesta*, three (*GG*, p. 198); (2) in the *Carmen*, Harold has 500 ships (v. 319), in the *Gesta*, 700 (*GG*, p. 180); (3) in the *Carmen*, one feigned flight takes place (vv. 421–4), in the *Gesta*, three (*GG*, p. 194). Köhler, he remarks, has commented severely on the unlikelihood of the last *Gesta* story;[1] a general who had just barely stemmed a rout of his troops would be most unlikely to tempt fate by simulating others. Körner is therefore of the opinion that William of Poitiers seized upon the description in the *Carmen* of a feigned flight (which in the *Carmen* is an instance of French ingenuity) and the account of the halting by the duke of a headlong flight of his Normans (v. 444); these he has deftly transformed into a deliberate and repeated tactic of Duke William.

The examples presented by Körner and his arguments from them, although strongly indicative of an earlier date for the *Carmen*, have not established it beyond question and show nothing as to the authorship. There are, however, a number of passages which are not parallel, and in which it is the omissions of one or the other writer that are of significance. These show clearly that the author of the *Carmen*, confessedly writing in hope of the duke's favour (vv. 26–38), cannot have been following William of Poitiers, unless we are to assume that he deliberately altered his model to the duke's detriment. More than this; there is evidence that the *Carmen* was written at least before 1072 and very probably before the autumn of 1067.

Only the author of the *Carmen* mentions that Saint-Valery is in Vimeu and halts his narrative to extol the people, showing an intimate knowledge of the place and local history.[2] He is alone, too, in telling us that the duke was weather-bound there for a fortnight (v. 54), and depicts him frequenting the saint's church above the harbour, making vows and lavishing offerings (vv. 56–7). The veering of the weathercock alternately transports William and reduces him to tears of despair (vv. 58–61). In the *Gesta* no adversities can shake the duke (*GG*, p. 160); yet in describing William's

[1] G. Köhler, *Die Entwicklung des Kriegswesens und der Kriegführung in der Ritterzeit von Mitte des 11. Jahrhunderts bis zu den Hussitenkriegen* (Breslau, 1886), i. 39, n. 3.

[2] See below, p. 2 n. 2. The reference to the valour of the men of Vimeu has dramatic irony; they had driven back the Viking invasions. It was in Vimeu on 3 August 881 that Louis III and his Franks defeated the Northmen at the famous battle of Saucourt, still celebrated in song in the eleventh century. William's Norman panegyrists may have preferred to omit reference to Vimeu.

despair, the poet addresses his hero in person (vv. 61–2): 'Effusis lacrimis . . . desolatus eras.' It is remarkable that the *Carmen* lacks the famous story found in the *Gesta* (loc. cit.) that the wind changed when the relics of the saint had been borne from the church to be venerated by the army. The poet can only report that at last (*tandem*) God took pity on the duke, as on St. Peter sinking in the waves, and sent fair weather (vv. 64–71). If this writer knew the *Gesta*, therefore, we must accept that—contrary to all medieval practice—he suppressed a story exalting the merits of the local saint.[1]

In his famous account of the battle, William of Poitiers, a former knight, laments the strength of the English position.[2] Twice he asserts that the enemy seized the hill because they dared not meet the duke on level ground (*GG*, pp. 186, 248). He omits, however, to explain why William, the commander on the spot, allowed the English to gain a tactical advantage so damaging to the attackers. The *Carmen* alone answers this not unimportant question; and answers it in terms which suggest the reason for the *Gesta*'s silence:[3]

> Ordine post pedites sperat (dux) stabilire quirites,
> Occursu belli set sibi non licuit . . .
> Ex inprouiso diffudit silua cohortes,
> Et nemoris latebris agmina prosiliunt.

(vv. 341–2; 363–4)

It is easy to see why this episode would have been censored by the duke's chaplain, but not why an aspiring rival, noting the discretion of the *Gesta*, should have intruded it.

---

[1] *GG*, p. 160: 'Sacris supplicationis adeo decertavit (dux), ut corpus etiam acceptissime Deo confessoris Gualerici, contra praepedientes et pro secundo vento, extra basilicam deferret; concurrente in eadem humilitatis arma concione profecturorum cum ipso. Spirante *dein* aura expectata . . .' This episode is not in William of Jumièges. Silence here and in the *Carmen* suggests that no immediate change of weather followed the veneration of the relics, but that William of Poitiers adroitly implied a miracle by using the ambiguous adverb *dein*. The story is inflated by later writers in the normal medieval manner.

[2] *GG*, p. 188: 'Angli nimium adjuvantur superioris loci opportunitate . . .'

[3] *GG*, pp. xlvii–xlviii: '. . . *l'Histoire de Guillaume le Conquérant* ne comporte seulement le panégyrique du souverain . . . mais . . . des silences voulus sur certains épisodes défavorables . . .' William of Jumièges (*GND*, p. 135) neither describes the terrain nor says who took the offensive, omissions which may well be significant. The *Carmen* says unequivocally that the English seized the hill by a tactical surprise. Perhaps because it is intentionally veiled in rhetoric, this statement appears to have escaped notice. We believe it to be important evidence of the very early date of the *Carmen*. For an analysis of the remarkable information given in the poem and comments on the evidence of the *ASC*, *BT*, and later sources see below, pp. 73–83.

There are several such anomalies in the battle, if the *Carmen* be the later work: in it, the main body of the English attack after the feigned flight (vv. 439–43), in the *Gesta*, they are the ones attacked (*GG*, p. 194); the papal banner (*GG*, p. 184) is not even mentioned in the *Carmen*; the *Carmen* has William call for aid to kill Harold (v. 535), whereas William of Poitiers assures us that he would not have feared to meet him in single combat (*GG*, pp. 198 f.).

According to William of Poitiers, Queen Edith fervently supported William's cause with her prayers (*GG*, pp. 166 f.). The *Carmen*, on the other hand, says that she reluctantly submitted to him under siege (vv. 631–5). That Edith probably did not support William is borne out by his total absence from the *Vita Aedwardi* and by the almost wholly English composition of her own court after the Conquest.[1] Yet, why did the author of the *Carmen* even suggest opposition from her, if he was following the *Gesta*? A similar question is raised by the description in the *Carmen* of William's remarkable offer to Ansgar (vv. 687–90), which finds no place in the *Gesta*.

All of these points are readily explained if William of Poitiers, following the *Carmen*, altered its material to the greater glory of his duke and his nation. But one can do more, we think, than point to the difference in the intensity of the propaganda; there is evidence that shows the *Carmen* to have been written before the *Gesta*.

The two archbishops who assist at William's coronation are both metropolitans (vv. 803–4) and are described as *honore pari* (v. 804). This was the position of Canterbury and York before the accord of Winchester in 1072.[2] We have thus a *terminus ad quem* for the *Carmen* antedating the *Gesta Guillelmi*. (William of Poitiers, writing after 1072, anachronistically makes Stigand *totius Britanniae episcoporum primatem* (*GG*, p. 252) and *pontifex metropolitanus* (*GG*, p. 216), while Aldred is only *Eboracensis archiepiscopus* (*GG*, p. 220) and *primas Eboracensis* (*GG*, p. 270).) No work composed after the accord and, furthermore, addressed to Lanfranc, could have spoken of two archbishops of equal dignity. William of Poitiers, on the other hand, has modified the status of

---

[1] Cf. *VE*, p. 100, citing F. H. Dickinson, 'The sale of Combe', in *Proc. of the Somerset Arch. and Nat. Hist. Soc.* xxii (1876), pp. 106–13.

[2] Cf. the coronation of Edward the Martyr, as described by a monk of Ramsey *c.* 1000: 'Duo metropolitani Doroberniensis et Eboracensis . . . Aedwardum . . . promoverunt in regem' ('Vita Sancti Oswaldi' in T. Gale, *Historiae Britannicae, Saxonicae, Anglo-Danicae Scriptores* xv (Oxford, 1691), p. 413).'

the two in conformity with the accord, which purported to antedate the primacy of Canterbury on written authority.[1]

The author of the *Carmen* omits to name either archbishop or to give a clear indication of which anointed and crowned William. Had the poem been written after Stigand's deposition in 1070, there would have been no reason not to credit this to Aldred of York, as the *Gesta* does (*GG*, p. 220). There is no hint in the *Carmen* of any cloud in Canterbury's title to his office, whereas William of Poitiers makes it clear to his readers on first introducing Stigand that he was an anathematized outcast (*GG*, p. 146). William of Poitiers also explains, however, that Stigand's influence with the people was such that King William thought it best to wait until a papal legate could depose him (*GG*, p. 234). The silence of the *Carmen* about the archbishop of Canterbury strongly argues that it was written before 1070, by an author well aware of Stigand's uncanonical position, but aware, too, that it was thought unwise, as yet, to move decisively against him.

There is, moreover, evidence that the poem may well have been written early in 1067. Barlow has recently drawn attention to the emphasis by the poet on the contribution to William's cause made by Boulogne and Ponthieu.[2] Eustace of Boulogne is, in fact, the second hero. We know, however, that he and William quarrelled soon after the victorious campaign, and that, at some time between March and December 1067, when William was in Normandy, Eustace landed an invasion force at Dover. As a result of his rebellion, he temporarily lost his lands in England, and he and William were not reconciled for several years.

Yet, in describing William's march on Dover in 1066, the author of the *Carmen* characterizes the port in terms that would have been an insulting reminder to Eustace and an impolitic one to William, had the former's invasion already taken place:

> Hinc hostes cicius Anglica regna petunt.
> Set castrum Douerę, pendens a uertice montis,
> Hostes reiciens, litora tuta facit.   (vv. 604–6)

---

[1] Cf. the similarity between his language and that of the accord itself (Canterbury Cathedral, Cartae Antiq., A. 2): '. . . ostensum est · quod eboracensis ecclesia cantuariensi debeat subiacere · eiusque archiepiscopi ut *primatis totius britannie* . . . in omnibus oboedire . . . cantuariensis *metropolitanus* . . .'

[2] 'The Carmen de Hastingae Proelio', *Studies in International History presented to W. Norton Medlicott*, ed. K. Bourne and D. C. Watt (London, 1967), p. 46.

The poet is clearly sympathetic to Eustace, who is on more than one occasion described as coming to William's aid. That the poet was also capable of discretion, we know from his silence about Harold's detention in Ponthieu (or his apprehension there by Duke William), described by every early Norman source for the Conquest. We think it most unlikely that the man who preferred to pass over Count Guy's humiliation at the hands of the duke and who wrote of Eustace and William as 'comes et dux' composed this passage after Eustace had experienced the fate of other *hostes* at Dover.

The objections that we have raised ourselves can also be refuted. Orderic says that Bishop Guy imitated Statius and Virgil in hymning the deeds of heroes,[1] but not that he actually wrote in heroic verse. Robert of Torigny, from whom this statement comes, may have seen the proem, which is in hexameters, or (and we consider this more likely) he misunderstood what Orderic had written. There is, in fact, no reason to assume that either chronicler had read the poem.

Queen Mathilda may have been mentioned at the end of the *Carmen*; the author never introduces a character until he is required by the plan of the work, and the poem, as we have it, is incomplete. On the other hand, there is no evidence that Guy of Amiens was more than a temporary chaplain to the queen, a distinguished cleric appointed to add lustre to her entourage for the coronation. In that case, her absence from the poem is easily understood, as Guy is said to have finished and published it before he attended her in England.

The most serious objection might seem to be that the author of the *Carmen* emphasizes the role in the battle of Eustace II of Boulogne, and barely mentions Hugh of Ponthieu, a member of

---

[1] Cf. *GG*, p. 200 (William has just been compared to the heroes of epic): 'Scriptor Thebaidos vel Aeneidos . . . ex actibus hujus viri aeque magnum plus dignum conficerent opus vera canendo.' William of Poitiers continues by saying that, while the versions of poets are unreliable, his is the unvarnished truth. We think it curious that both the *Gesta* and Orderic should mention Statius and Virgil in this connection, when the obvious parallel is Lucan. The *Pharsalia* was at least as popular as the *Aeneid* and *Thebaid* in the Middle Ages, and, like Guy of Amiens's poem, recited the deeds of historical persons rather than those of legendary heroes. Is it possible that we have in this passage of the *Historia ecclesiastica* an unnoticed echo of the *Gesta*, and that Orderic, in describing Guy's poem, remembered the strictures of William of Poitiers and knew to whom they referred?

his own house, if he be Guy. Such modesty is completely foreign to the practice of medieval chroniclers, whether in verse or in prose. On the other hand, it must be pointed out that no other early account mentions Hugh of Ponthieu (or anyone else of Ponthieu) at all. The circumstances under which the *Carmen* must have been composed go some way toward explaining this apparent anomaly.

Guy of Amiens was writing very shortly after the events that he describes. Eustace, the leader of a large force, inevitably played a much greater role in the battle than was possible for a brother or son of Guy of Ponthieu. While the bishop could give full credit to Eustace, toward whom he had reason to feel gratitude,[1] perhaps even pardonably exaggerating his exploits, he could not manufacture heroic deeds for Hugh at a time when the knowledge of what had been done and by whom was still fresh. It is, perhaps, significant that the heir of Ponthieu is mentioned only as one of those who killed Harold. This would have been a safe role to give him, for the confusion about the English standard would have made it almost impossible to determine exactly who had participated.[2]

It may be objected that Guy has invented heroic deeds for Eustace himself, whose reputation is not such as to sustain them. Certainly, William of Poitiers gives a poor account of him during the pursuit,[3] but it must be remembered that he is writing after Eustace had rebelled against William, and that Eustace, like Harold, the brother-in-law of Edward the Confessor, must have been to some extent a dangerous ally. And too, as so often, William of Poitiers contradicts himself; in detailing the subversive negotiations of the men of Kent with Eustace, he says: 'Nam quia Normannos odere (*sc.* qui Cantium inhabitant), cum Eustachio pridem sibi inimicissimo concordavere. Eum bellandi peritum atque in praelio felicem *experimentis* cognoverant.'[4] Here it must

---

[1] There is no actual evidence that Eustace II and Guy of Amiens were in any way related (cf. below, p. xxxi, and see genealogical tables nos. IV and V). Our information on the tenth- and eleventh-century counts of Boulogne and Ponthieu is extremely sparse. The fact that William of Talou and his wife (the niece of Guy of Amiens) sought refuge after the siege of Arques with Eustace II of Boulogne, rather than with the king of France, may indicate some tie of blood of which we are ignorant. On the other hand, Eustace's very hospitality could easily explain Guy's vindication of him; Guy had no reason to love the Normans.

[2] *RR*, vv. 8859-60.

[3] *GG*, p. 202 (William of Poitiers inadvertently lets slip that Eustace was, in fact, leading the pursuit).

[4] Ibid., p. 266.

be assumed that we have the actual opinion of the men of Kent, and that the author has forgotten his earlier denigration of Eustace as a warrior.[1]

In the *Carmen*, Eustace's role is noble, but not incredibly so, and none of his deeds is extraordinary. He rescues William, but with a large attending force (v. 520); he gives him his own horse, but with another awaiting him (vv. 523–4); he aids in killing Harold, again with many others (vv. 535–50); he pursues the fleeing English night-long, while the duke rests, but here narrative ceases, there is only rhetoric (vv. 563–6).

We consider it probable that Guy of Amiens, writing after the estrangement between William and Eustace, but before the latter's attempted invasion, is simply reminding the duke of the count's services.

Certainly, only a native of Ponthieu would be so eager to refute the charge of wrecking often laid against his nation (vv. 50–1), or would bother to give such a precise, almost affectionate description of the setting of Saint-Valery. The odd phrase '(aqua) Quę uallat portum' (v. 49) becomes clear only when one has looked down from the headland at the estuary of the Somme. Nor is there any reason to assume that Guy of Amiens and Guy of Ponthieu were on good terms, simply because they were uncle and nephew. The former was the beloved scholar and patron of the Abbey of Saint-Riquier,[2] the latter its insatiable depredator.[3] It is, further, possible that the bishop had acted as regent of Ponthieu in the youth of Count Guy (presumably while his nephew was Duke William's prisoner).[4] For a former regent and his ward to be later on bad terms is by no means uncommon.

Professor Frank Barlow has kindly given us permission to quote from an article in which he has made the first full analysis of the authorship of the poem since the discovery of the manuscripts:[5]

The second line of the prologue, written in hexameters [he begins], ends with 'L. W. sălūtāt'; and it was conjectured that this stood for 'Lanfrancum Wido salutat'. Although it is unlikely that all the possible

---

[1] The *Battle Abbey Chronicle*, which has no known connection with the *Carmen*, and the French writer Benoît de Saint-Maure give a similar account of the role of Eustace and his French; cf. below, Appendix B, ii, pp. 95 f.

[2] Hariulf, p. 274.   [3] Ibid., p. 239.

[4] Notice of Guy, bishop of Amiens in the 'Nécrologie de l'église d'Amiens' (xi Kal. Jan.), ed. Canon Roze, *Mem. de la Soc. des Antiquaires de Picardie* xxviii (1885), pp. 265 ff.   [5] See p. xxii n. 2.

alternatives were considered, an investigation of these produces no obvious substitutes. If we are to scan the line, and it scans only when the initials are extended,[1] we need one name in the nominative and the other in the accusative case, for *saluto* invariably takes a direct object. As the final syllable of the second name (W.) must be short, that name must be the subject, for it is virtually impossible to find an accusative singular which scans. In which case we are, for practical reasons, confined to the forms 'W . . a' or 'W . . o' (the short 'o' permissible at least since Ovid: *Nāzŏ*, common in Juvenal, and usual in eleventh-century verse). Accordingly, since it is unlikely that the author was a woman, we are probably limited to Wādă, Wāzŏ, and Wīdo.[2] This finding allows the following possibilities for 'L . . . em' or 'L . . . um': *Lambertum, Lanfrancum, Lanzonem, Letoldum, Ludolfum, Leobertum, Lietardum,* and possibly some other Germanic and Old English names (e.g. *Leofricum*). We must, therefore, allow that it was not unreasonable to expand W. to *Wido*; and, even though the choice of *Lanfrancum* is on metrical grounds even more arbitrary, there is something to be said in its favour. W. asks L. to improve and protect his poem, and describes his correspondent as 'renowned for his goodness and wisdom' and 'the morning star who with his learning has dispelled the darkness of the world'. These phrases fit Lanfranc of Pavia, abbot of Caen . . .[3]

Barlow continues by pointing out that Bishop Guy was connected by blood or marriage to most of the men involved in the question of the English succession: Guy of Ponthieu, Eustace of Boulogne, Edward the Confessor, and William himself. 'He would have known the political, social, and military world that he was describing.' As to his qualifications as a poet, he would have had the necessary skill and interest as a distinguished scholar of Saint-Riquier, a house which, as Barlow reminds us, had had close ties with England during Edward's reign, and held lands there.

[1] We inquired on this point of Dr. Bernhard Bischoff of Munich University, who kindly confirmed that: (1) the initials themselves would not scan; (2) it was normal in this kind of address that they be expanded to names that did scan; and (3) he agrees completely with the traditional 'Lanfrancum Wido': 'Eine andere Ausfüllung scheint mir unvorstellbar' (letter of 20 Oct. 1968).

[2] We would add as possibilities *Walo*, a common name in the tenth to eleventh centuries; *Wato* (a Guaton was actually abbot of St. Valery in 1066); and *Wigo* (a name cited by Froumund the hermit before 1051, *P.L.* cxli, col. 1287).

[3] It may be of some interest that Guy of Amiens calls himself 'W.' in at least one charter ('Cartulaire du chapitre de l'église cathédrale d'Amiens', in *Mém. de la Soc. des Antiquaires de Picardie; Documents inédits* xiv (1905), p. 8). Lanfranc, too, occurs as 'L.' in the autograph manuscript of the *Gesta Pontificum* of William of Malmesbury (*RS* lii. 38): 'quantae prudentiae L. esset'.

After discussing most of the objections to Guy's authorship that we have treated above, Barlow sums up in its favour, 'No anachronism has been found in the *Carmen*, and there is no clear evidence for any *terminus a quo* but 1066 . . . The onus of proof seems to lie upon those who would dispute an early date for the poem.' He adds that there are clear pointers to Guy's authorship, such as the treatment of Saint-Valery and Eustace of Boulogne, who 'is allowed the importance that his lineage and position merited, but which Norman writers were inclined to mark down'. What Barlow calls 'the rather detached tone of the poem' (verging to our mind into acidity at times), he attributes to the resentment that Ponthieu traditionally felt toward Normandy: 'Guy's grandfather had been established at Abbeville to withstand the Normans; the counts had usually joined the royal army against these barbarians; and two of the bishop's nephews had been killed and a third captured and imprisoned while on campaign against Normandy.'

Barlow, however, does not believe that the date given by Orderic for the poem is correct. Because of the reference to Lanfranc in the proem as *tutissima nauis*, he thinks that it was Lanfranc himself who was to carry the poem across the sea to William. As Lanfranc is not known to have visited England before assuming the archiepiscopate of Canterbury in 1070, Barlow suggests this year as the date of composition of the *Carmen*. He considers that a later date fits well with the emphasis in the poem on the contribution of Ponthieu and Boulogne to the Conquest. Eustace of Boulogne, by his revolt, had forfeited his English lands; the house of Ponthieu had received none. It is therefore possible, Barlow thinks, that Bishop Guy appealed to Queen Mathilda on behalf of both his nephew and his neighbour; crossed with her in 1068 to plead their cause; and, finally, wrote the *Carmen* to press home the gratitude owed them by William.

This thesis is well argued by Barlow, but we cannot agree. For one thing, if Orderic's account of Guy's poem be accepted, so also must his date for it be, in default of clear evidence that it is wrong. For another, had Guy written the poem as a last appeal, having already received a hearing and an office from the queen, it would be curious, to say the least, that she be not mentioned by him early in the poem.

Lanfranc is called a ship in the proem, but he is also a safe haven, oarsman, the morning star, and a teacher. Nautical metaphors were popular throughout the Middle Ages, in most un-nautical settings. So, Folcard, in the introduction to his *Life of St. John of Beverley*, alludes to the earlier unhappy state of his monastery as follows: 'Turbato siquidem fluctuantis coenobii mei pelago . . . perperam comparato saeculari potentatu exturbatum, a carina monasteriali fluctibus immersit ponti, jamque irruentibus vicissim et volventibus undis . . . nec ulla spes emergendi esset . . .'[1] Earlier, Hrabanus Maurus, addressing Grimold, abbot of Saint-Gall, had exhorted him to be his anchor, sailing, and shore (as well as his strong support, native land, city, and surcease for a soul afflicted with care), despite Grimold's inland location.[2]

To the arguments that we have put forward above (pp. xxi ff.) for an early date of composition, we would add here the fact that *L.*, accepted as Lanfranc by Barlow, is not even hinted to be an archbishop-elect. Had the proem, to say nothing of the rest of the poem, been written when Lanfranc was sailing to take up the primacy of England, surely this high ecclesiastical office would have been included in the list of *L.*'s attributes.

We agree that the *Carmen* is connected with the estrangement of Eustace of Boulogne from William, but we suspect that Eustace would have been brought in by name earlier (for instance at the muster at Saint-Valery), had the sole purpose of the poem been his vindication. It is unlikely that Guy could have drafted much of the poem, at least in its present form (and it bears no indication of re-working), before the arrival in the spring of English hostages, for even the preliminaries to the battle are apparently based on eyewitness accounts from both sides (e.g. vv. 169 ff.). William and Eustace may well have quarrelled as early as December 1066, but it was Eustace's attempted invasion of Kent that made relations between them finally impossible, and we have given our reasons for thinking that the poem would not have been written after the invasion (above, pp. xxii f.).

The news of William's success is said to have reached Normandy in January 1067, when the newly crowned king sent home thank-offerings to churches.[3] News of the quarrel may have come then; Eustace himself may have returned to Boulogne with English hostages and a grievance against William. In the opinion of Dr. L. J. Engels of Groningen University, who has made a study of

---

[1] In *RS* lxxi, i. 240. Translated in *VE*, p. liv.
[2] *Carmen VI, MGH, PLAC*, ii. 169 f.   [3] *GG*, p. 226.

the *Carmen*, it was probably written for King William's triumphant home-coming in Lent 1067.[1] It is undeniable that poetic tributes would have been thought appropriate on such an occasion; the *Carmen* may, therefore, have been composed within six months of the battle of Hastings.

To summarize what we know of the author of the *Carmen*: he was French; his name was one of two syllables, beginning with W; he was well-born;[2] he was conversant with the sea and with warfare;[3] he was attached to Eustace of Boulogne; he was knowledgeable about and defensive of Vimeu; he was tactless at times in his references to William, whether deliberately or not;[4] he was writing earlier than William of Poitiers; and he shows fluent skill in writing verse.[5] All of these criteria fit Guy of Amiens perfectly, and they fit no other person known.

It is perhaps worth recalling, in this connection, that the lost manuscript of the *Gesta Guillelmi* also lacked an ascription. It was identified as the work of William of Poitiers from the known use of the *Gesta* by Orderic Vitalis[6] and other chroniclers. The *Carmen* has been shown to have been used by William of Poitiers, and the only verse treatment of the Conquest known for certain to have been earlier than the *Gesta* is that of Guy of Amiens. Therefore, unless two men with almost identical backgrounds and prejudices both wrote poems on the Conquest, Guy must be accepted as the author of the *Carmen*. We consider the cumulative evidence for his

[1] *Dichters over Willem de Veroveraar: Het Carmen de Hastingae Proelio*, Inaugural Lecture, University of Groningen (Groningen, 1967), p. 17.

[2] His point of view is that of an aristocrat (cf. v. 356), and he has clearly had his account of the battle from knights. He is careful to inform his readers whenever one of his characters is of royal or noble descent.

[3] Cf. the description of William's voyage (vv. 81–103) with that in the *GG* (pp. 162 f.), in which only the duke's ship has a light and William heroically, but impractically, outstrips his fleet. Cf. also the description of the battle, and especially v. 374. No other source mentions the immediate strengthening by Harold of his wings, the move of a prudent and experienced general.

[4] Cf. vv. 334, 617–19, 723–4, 751.

[5] It is perhaps only coincidence that the sole work in verse known without question to be Guy's, his epitaph on Abbot Enguerrand of Saint-Riquier, begins with the same word as the *Carmen*:

Quem tegit hic tumulus lectissimus Angelirannus . . .

(Hariulf, p. 216). While examples of *quem* as the initial word of a poem occur sporadically in medieval literature, it is not at all common.

[6] OV, p. 260 (ii. 218): 'Contextionem eius de Guillelmo et eius pedissequis breuiter in quibusdam secutus sum, non tamen omnia quae dixit nec tam argute prosequi conatus sum.'

authorship too strong to be rejected without clear proof to the contrary, and this has, at the time of writing, not been adduced.

THE AUTHOR AND HIS FAMILY

Like so many of their contemporary fellow nobles, the counts of Ponthieu were *noui homines* who had risen to power with the Capetian dynasty, and, to make matters worse, Abbé Le Sueur's claim that neither the name nor the county of Ponthieu existed before the tenth century is but little exaggerated.[1] Until the time of Charles the Simple, it varied in size and name, frequently formed part of an ephemeral greater province, and was administered (if at all) by royal delegates. Thus, little evidence exists upon which to found a history of the family of Guy of Amiens, for few documents survive from the tenth century, and later inflated genealogies purporting to connect his line with earlier counts of Ponthieu or with the house of Flanders and Boulogne are completely untrustworthy.[2]

According to Hariulf, our only witness to his existence, a certain *Hugo miles* was chosen by Hugh Capet, then not yet king, to be advocate of the abbey of Saint-Riquier and castellan of Abbeville; he also received Hugh Capet's daughter, Gisla, in marriage.[3] Nothing is known of Hugh the knight's origins, nor is the date at

[1] C. Ducange, *Histoire des Comtes de Ponthieu et de Montreuil*, ed. A. Le Sueur (*Mém. de la Soc. d'Émulation d'Abbeville*, sér. 4, viii (1917)), pp. i–iii. A hereditary countship existed from the first half of the ninth century.

[2] Cf. J. Delaîte, *Les Comtes de Dammartin en Goële et leurs ancêtres du VIIIᵉ au XIIᵉ siècle* (Liège, 1911), pp. 29–36. The county was held from 949 until his death in 965 by Arnold the Elder of Flanders, a supporter of King Lothar. (The last count of the earlier line and his young son had died in 961.) Later genealogies of new houses such as that of Ponthieu (and of Boulogne) tried to endow them with antiquity and invented alliances with the great families of the tenth and eleventh centuries. Works based on these, such as *L'Art de vérifier les dates* and its successors, were little questioned until the end of the last century, when careful appraisal of documentary evidence and contemporary narrative sources showed most of them to be completely useless for the early period. Cf. E. Rigaux, 'Recherches sur les premiers comtes de Boulogne', in *Bulletins de la Soc. Académique de l'Arrondissement de Boulogne-sur-Mer* v (1894), pp. 151–77. It is upon his study and that of Delaîte that the genealogical tables nos. IV and V are largely founded.

[3] Hariulf, p. 205. Hariulf, however, is inaccurate on events of the preceding century. Cf. J. Laporte, 'Étude chronologique sur les listes abbatiales de Saint-Riquier', in *Revue Mabillon* xlix (1959), pp. 101–36. Saint-Riquier was a great abbey and teaching-house founded in the early seventh century and re-endowed under Charlemagne; it lies near Abbeville. The *advocatus* of an abbey was a lay person charged with the administration of its lands and its protection against attack.

which he received his fief ascertainable save within broad limits.[1] Hariulf claims that he never took the title of count, and that his son and successor, Enguerrand I, did so only after killing the count of Boulogne in battle and marrying his widow,[2] but, as Prarond shrewdly observed, the nephew of the reigning king of France would hardly have needed such an alliance to assume the comital style.[3] If the story be true, the marriage took place before 1027, for in a charter of 1024–7 Enguerrand witnesses as *comes*.[4] On the other hand, he is erratic in his title: in 1035 he witnesses as *comes*, but in 1043 merely as *advocatus*.[5] It is quite possible that Hariulf has emphasized the counts' advocacy of his abbey at the expense of their secular title.

The count of Boulogne killed by Enguerrand I must have been Arnold II, and his death took place after 1023, for in that year his brother and successor, Eustace I, was not yet count.[6] It is, there-fore, clear that Enguerrand I had had an earlier wife, the mother at least of his heir, for Enguerrand II and his youngest brother Waleran, killed in battle in 1053 and 1054, can hardly have been the grandsons of the former countess of Boulogne.[7] Furthermore, Enguerrand I, who died *c.* 1045 and at a great age, according to Hariulf, is hardly likely to have waited until he was in his forties to ensure the succession.[8] He had four sons in all: Hugh II, his

---

[1] After 965, when Arnold the Elder died, and before 987, when Hugh Capet assumed the crown. Probably before 980, by which date the abbey of Saint-Valery-sur-Somme had been restored and the bones of Saint Riquier returned to his abbey (from which Arnold the Elder had translated them to Ghent).

[2] Op. cit., p. 230. He does not name the count or his wife.

[3] Marquis Le Ver, *Chronique de Centule*, ed. E. Prarond (*Mém. de la Soc. d'Émulation d'Abbeville sér.* 4, iii (1899)), lv.

[4] Brunel, i and ii, p. 2.   [5] Hariulf, p. 193 f.

[6] Cf. E. Rigaux, op. cit., p. 162, and Balderic of Thérouanne, *Chronique d'Arras et de Cambrai*, iii. 43, ed. Le Glay (Paris, 1834), p. 305.

[7] Enguerrand II had married before October 1049, when he was excommuni-cated for incest by Leo IX, and had two daughters at the time of his death in 1053. Cf. T. Stapleton, 'Observations on the History of Adeliza, sister of William the Conqueror', in *Archaeologia* xxvi (1836), pp. 358–60. Prarond (op. cit., p. lvi) suggested that Enguerrand I's children must have been by a first wife. The countess of Boulogne is not, as often said, Adela or Adelvia of Ghent, wife of 'Baldwin II of Boulogne'. These names, those of Baldwin the Bearded of Flanders and his wife, have been interpolated in the genealogy of Boulogne. See genealogical table no. IV.

[8] Hariulf, p. 230. Guy, abbot of Forest l'Abbaye, was not, as Ducange (op. cit., p. 48) said, the brother of Enguerrand I. Ducange has misread Hariulf (pp. 205 f.); the abbot was the brother of Abbot Enguerrand of Saint-Riquier.

successor;[1] Guy, bishop of Amiens;[2] Fulk, abbot of Forest l'Abbaye;[3] and Robert, known only from two charters of Count Guy I, in which he is identified as, 'Robertus, patruus meus'.[4] It is possible that Guy and Fulk were sons of the second marriage. Guy was a student under Abbot Enguerrand of Saint-Riquier, who held that office between 1017 and 1045; he seemingly became an archdeacon only *c.* 1045,[5] and was a bishop only in 1058. The description of Fulk given by Hariulf in the years 1042 to 1045 is that of an ambitious and headstrong youth.

We know hardly more of Hugh II than of his predecessors. He was associated with his father in charters as early as 1035;[6] married at some date unknown Bertha of Aumale;[7] and had by her four sons[1] and a daughter who married William of Talou, count of Arques, a younger son of Richard II of Normandy.[8] Hugh II died 20 November 1052, 'post expletum tempus vitae';[1] as his sons were all full-grown, he must have been born *c.* 1010 at the latest.

Guy of Amiens's elder nephews were thus Enguerrand II and Guy I, counts of Ponthieu from 1052 to 1053 and 1053 to 1100 respectively.[9] Waleran, the fourth of Hugh II's sons, we know only from Wace and Benoît de Saint-Maure.[10] He was killed at the battle of Mortemer in 1054. Hugh, count of Ponthieu, signed the royal confirmation of the foundation charter of Saint-Nicholas-des-Prés at Ribemont in 1084, and we have conjectured that he was the third of Hugh II's sons (see Appendix D, pp. 117 f.).

Guy I had a son, Enguerrand, who predeceased his father,[11] and two daughters, Agnes (or Anna), his heiress, and Mathilda.[12] The former carried the county to Robert of Bellême. The line also

---

[1] Hariulf, p. 230.   [2] Hariulf, p. 282.   [3] Hariulf, pp. 204 f.
[4] Brunel, viii (p. 12) and ix (p. 17).   [5] Hariulf, pp. 216, 234.
[6] Hariulf, p. 193.
[7] Stapleton, op. cit., p. 350 f.
[8] Orderic Vitalis, interpolations to *GND*, p. 160.
[9] The idea that Guy I was the son, not the brother of Enguerrand II (Ducange and Le Sueur, op. cit., pp. 62 ff.) depended on one charter, which Brunel has shown to be a forgery (Brunel, pp. 651 f.).
[10] *RR*, vv. 4927–8; Benoît, vv. 37658 ff.   [11] Brunel, vi (pp. 7 f.).
[12] Brunel viii (p. 14) names both; xii (p. 25) only Agnes, who there signs as 'comitissa' in her father's lifetime. It is worth noting that the daughters of Enguerrand II appear not to have been treated as heirs, despite the fact that William of Normandy's sister was their mother. That Hugh signs as count of Ponthieu in 1084 would seem to show that Enguerrand, the son of Guy I, was dead by then, and that Hugh was heir presumptive. By the time that Guy I died, there remained, in so far as can be determined, no males whatever of the house.

continued through the daughters of Enguerrand II, for Judith, married to Earl Waltheof, had a daughter, Mathilda, who carried the descent of *Hugo miles* into the royal house of Scotland.

For our information about the author of the *Carmen* himself, we must rely almost wholly upon Hariulf, a handful of charters and diplomas, and the documents bearing upon the quarrel between the bishops of Amiens and Fulk, abbot of Corbie. Guy of Amiens was one of the most brilliant students at the Abbey of Saint-Riquier under Abbot Enguerrand,[1] and became successively canon of Amiens cathedral and one of the two archdeacons of the diocese.[2] His predecessor in the episcopate of Amiens, Fulk II,[3] was caught up in the emerging struggle between the secular clergy, dominated by the political contentions of the great feudal families, and the reforming popes, with their bias in favour of monastic houses, which they often rendered exempt from episcopal jurisdiction. In 1049, Fulk II sent Archdeacon Guy as his emissary to Rome, to present his complaints against Fulk, abbot of Corbie (1048-95), who had acquired privileges for his house from Leo IX that displeased and disquieted the bishop.

The outcome of Guy's mission was inconclusive, and we know nothing of his activities during the next nine years. It is possible, however, that for a time during this period he held the regency of Ponthieu. The necrology of the cathedral of Amiens states that Bishop Guy held for a time the government of Ponthieu.[4] While there may have been a confusion between Count Guy and Bishop Guy, it is equally possible that the latter was regent at the time that the former was a prisoner in Normandy.

In 1058, Fulk II went to Fécamp with Letzelin, bishop of Paris, to negotiate peace between Henry I of France and William of Normandy. Fulk died soon after his return, having nominated Guy as his successor. The designation was endorsed by the chapter of Amiens, for an inscription survives describing the translation on 12 July 1058 of the body of St. Paschase Radbert to Corbie, the abbey he had once headed, and adding, 'auctor fuit Wido presul

---

[1] Hariulf, p. 202.

[2] There were two archidiaconates, Amiens and Ponthieu, the latter including Vimeu.

[3] Son of Drogo, count of the Vexin, and Godgifu of England, sister of Edward the Confessor. He became bishop in 1036. Hariulf (p. 252) describes him as more given to hawking and hunting than to the cure of souls.

[4] See above, p. xxv n. 4. Guy was said to have succeeded 'iure hereditario'.

Ambianensium, primo ordinacionis sue anno'.[1] In the next year, Guy, in the company of clerics and nobles including his brother, Fulk, abbot of Forest l'Abbaye, and his nephew and namesake, Guy I of Ponthieu, attended the coronation on 23 May 1059 of the young Philip I.[2]

Between 1060 and 1063, the old quarrel between the bishops of Amiens and the unfortunate abbot of Corbie flared up again. In spite of a series of papal and royal privileges that Fulk of Corbie had obtained, limiting severely the rights of the see of Amiens over his abbey, Guy demanded certain goods belonging to the house, and offered in return not to try to exercise administrative authority over it in the future. In the presence of Baldwin V of Flanders, then regent of France, Fulk handed over forty pounds of silver, but Bishop Guy did not keep his part of the bargain. He summoned the monks of Corbie to meet him at Amiens; when they refused to come, he excommunicated them. Abbot Fulk appealed to Baldwin V for support, and was upheld by a conclave of bishops and abbots assembled by the regent at Cambrai. Bishop Guy thereupon convoked a synod (which he had no authority to do), and demanded the attendance of Fulk of Corbie. Fulk sent a lay proxy in his stead, but Guy refused to recognize him, and excommunicated Fulk. At this point, Gervase, archbishop of Rheims, intervened, and summoned both parties to appear before him. Guy refused. The archbishop then asked him to rescind his excommunication of Fulk. Guy again refused, and Fulk thereupon appealed to Alexander II. The pope wrote to Guy, expressing in strong terms his astonishment and anger at the bishop's actions, particularly as Fulk had been ordained by Leo IX himself. He demanded that Guy make restitution and amends at once, and directed that the archbishop of Rheims or his nominee carry out Guy's episcopal functions as they affected the abbey. Guy was warned that failure to obey would result in his suspension, interdiction, and excommunication.

Guy made a verbal submission (but seems not to have returned any property to Corbie), and was suspended from his duties. In a papal bull to Gervase of Rheims, Alexander II confirmed the privileges of Corbie, and asked Gervase to see that the papal

---

[1] J. Corblet, 'Sur une inscription du XIe siècle provenant de l'abbaye de Corbie', in *Bulletins de la Soc. des Antiquaires de Picardie* ix (1867), pp. 79 ff.

[2] Bouquet xi, pp. 32 f.

verdict was enforced. Although Guy was summoned to Rheims and told of the pope's decision, Alexander had to write repeatedly between 1064 and 1067, demanding the interdiction of Guy, unless he restored two altars that he had seized from Corbie and took Fulk again under his protection.[1]

Papal displeasure did not hinder Guy from ruling the see of Amiens, or from witnessing a number of documents between 1060 and 1067, even including one at Corbie.[2] In the year of the Conquest itself, he even presented an altar to Corbie, and officiated at the raising of the chapel of Saint-Martin at Picquigny to the status of a collegiate church. He died on 21 December 1075.[3]

THE HISTORICAL IMPORTANCE OF THE *CARMEN*

We have already set forth the evidence for the priority in date of the *Carmen* over any other account of the Norman Conquest, together with our reasons for accepting it. Admittedly, the earliest account of an event need not be either the most nearly accurate, or the most nearly complete, but even could the poem be shown to be at variance with known fact (as against accepted assumptions), its closeness in time to the events that it describes and the light that it would cast on the contemporary attitude to these events would lend it great interest and no little historical importance.

It is, however, possible, we consider, to show that in addition to the *Carmen*'s priority in date the poem is also a source at once fuller than the *GND*, more honest and reliable than it or the *GG*, and more explicit than the Bayeux Tapestry. Its neglect in comparison with these other early sources apparently stems from two disadvantages: firstly, it was discovered only in 1826 and not published until 1840, that is to say over two hundred years after the accounts of William of Jumièges and William of Poitiers had first been printed, and over a century after the first reproduction of the

---

[1] Many of the documents in this quarrel survive. Cf. *Gallia Christiana* x and A. Fliche, *Le Règne de Philippe Ier, roi de France* (Paris, 1912), pp. 479 f.

[2] The royal confirmation of Baldwin V's restoration of the abbey of Saint-Menge to Saint-Étienne de Chalons on 4 August 1065.

[3] See above, p. xxv n. 4. The year is not given. Hariulf (p. 273), our source for Guy's death, places it in the same year as that of Abbot Gervin of Saint-Riquier, but gives the latter as on Tuesday, 3 March 1074, an impossible date, as Tuesday did not fall upon 3 March in that year. The indiction he gives is wrong, too. Tuesday, 3 March occurred in 1075, which is probably the year of both Gervin's death and Guy's, the more so in that Guy's successor had not yet been consecrated as late as October 1076. Cf. also *Gallia Christiana* x. 1165D.

Bayeux Tapestry had appeared. There was, therefore, among scholars, a feeling (most clearly expressed by Thierry)[1] that, apart from such matters as the siege of London, wanting in the other three sources, it could add little to the known outline of events. Secondly, the *Carmen* is in verse, and there has been a tendency since the nineteenth century (which has become immeasurably stronger in the twentieth) to regard verse as a vehicle of expression inherently emotional and subjective, suitable for special pleading, but upon which one cannot place the reliance that one can on bald prose. This, however, is to overlook the fact that almost all medieval chronicles are subjective pieces of special pleading to some degree and some of the most extreme examples in quite bald prose. Any appraisal of the intrinsic merit of an account must therefore be founded on its contents, not its form.

But the contents of the *Carmen* have also been called in some question, even by those who have not doubted its authenticity as the work of Guy of Amiens. It has several rhetorical passages, two of them quite long, which interrupt the narrative, and which are apparently no more than a device to allow the poet to display his art and vent his emotions. Certainly, the rhetoric is a device, but a carefully calculated one: it is employed at all the points in the story (save one) at which the duke finds himself embarrassed or threatened.

As the *Carmen* opens, William is weather-bound; Guy therefore intrudes a passage of four lines (vv. 34-7), which owes something to Ermoldus Nigellus,[2] emphasizing that the English could not prevent his claiming his ancestral kingdom, nor could the sea, nor the rocky shore, nor the imminence of winter. The reader is thus reassured that the hero of the poem will triumph over the obstacle of weather. William, however, lacking this foreknowledge, despairs and weeps. Another short rhetorical passage at once reassures the reader again: God, ruler of sky and sea, who made St. Peter to walk upon the water, will not fail the duke (vv. 64-7). And the weather then clears.

The next insertion in the narrative is much longer, for, while weather must change in time (and had it not done so in time for William, he would have lost little more than face—and money); the danger that confronted him when Harold seized the ridge com-

---

[1] *Histoire de la conquête de l'Angleterre par les Normands*, 3ᵉ éd. (Paris, 1830), i, p. vi.   [2] Ermoldus ii. 127-8.

manding his exit from the peninsula in which he had based himself (see Appendix B) was an immediate one to his life, not merely his *amour propre*. To minimize the shock to the reader, and to gloss over the failure in generalship which allowed the newly arrived Harold the higher ground, Guy carefully separates the statement, for he, William, perceived the presence of enemy formations not far off and saw the forest glitter, full of spears (vv. 343–4), from the embarrassing explanation: *Suddenly* the forest poured forth troops of men, and from the hiding-places of the woods a host dashed forward (vv. 363–4), by an apostrophe of eighteen lines to Mars, in which William, the 'Iulius alter' of v. 32, is again likened to Caesar, and Pompey's defeat recalled to foreshadow Harold's. By this reminder of William's ultimate victory, the impact of the surprise is so effectively diminished that it has escaped notice.

A similar, but shorter, example of literary evasion (vv. 385–90) is discussed below (Appendix B, p. 81). The next rhetorical sequence, again a short one, comes after William's unhorsing by Gyrth and the refusal of a knight of Maine to aid him. William unhorses the knight with his bare hands and seizes his mount, and by this act and the appeal to heaven (vv. 495–500) to witness the slaughter of the English that follows, the ignominy of the *dux bellorum* afoot is erased. Interesting in this connection is the absence of any rhetoric at the next point where one would expect it, after vv. 507–12, in which William is not only unhorsed a second time, but clearly shaken, and has to reassure himself of fortune's favour. At this point, Guy substitutes for rhetoric Eustace II of Boulogne, his second hero, as Barlow has admirably called him, and the embarrassment is relieved by a description of the count's nobility and generosity.

The last example of rhetoric occurs near the end of the *Carmen*: London has submitted, and William bound the false hearts of the English with oaths; it is almost Christmas, the first day of one of those seasons during which, traditionally, the kings of the English were crowned. Suddenly, the poet turns to a description of the regalia, including a jewel-by-jewel account of the crown, which lasts thirty lines. He then, as suddenly, reverts to a description of the coronation procession, and the narrative continues. By Guy's own account, the last vestiges of English opposition have been removed; one is then left to wonder what danger or embarrassment

William could have encountered on the eve of his crowning. The version of the same sequence of events in the *GG* (pp. 216 f.) sheds some light on this problem. In William of Poitiers's account of the period between the submission of London and the coronation of William, the duke is suddenly a prey to qualms: the English have offered him the crown, but the kingdom is in turmoil; he would rather bring peace to England than further embroil the situation; besides, he wishes Mathilda to be crowned with him. Untouched by the lust to rule, but moved by conjugal devotion, he doubts whether so great a step should be taken in haste. He expresses these misgivings to those Normans in his entourage whom he knows to be wise and loyal; respectfully, but firmly, they oppose him, urging against his diffidence the unanimous will of his army.

At this point, Aimery of Thouars, a Frenchman, not a Norman,[1] urges upon the duke's subjects (as though they had not spoken) the speedy fulfilment of their dearest wish. And it is on hearing Aimery's argument (nothing new in itself) that William suddenly reconsiders: as king, he can better crush the rebels; he orders the building of a fortress in London. The peace of the kingdom seems to have been forgotten, as does the Duchess Mathilda.[2]

In appraising these two rather unsatisfactory accounts of the preliminaries to William's coronation, the following points seem to be significant: firstly, Eustace of Boulogne quarrelled with William at some time between the battle of Hastings and the period in 1067 when he invaded Kent (*GG*, pp. 264 ff.); next, the men of Kent rallied to Eustace, William of Poitiers says, because, if they had to endure foreign rule, they preferred it to be that of a neighbour whom they knew rather than that of William (*GG*, p. 266); thirdly, Aimery of Thouars, inexplicably present in a council of Normans, sways the duke simply by repeating what the Normans have already said to no (apparent) effect; and, finally, the author of the *Carmen*, an admirer of Eustace of Boulogne, but avowedly writing for William's favour, finds it necessary to lapse into rhetoric on reaching just that point in time at which Aimery was so persuasive with the duke.

---

[1] Aimery IV, viscount of Thouars, an old opponent of Geoffrey Martel of Anjou, and, apart from Eustace II of Boulogne, the only French noble of note who accompanied the Norman expedition. It is perhaps significant that the *Carmen* gives no hint of his presence.

[2] The council is omitted in OV iii. 182 (ii. 156), in a passage adapted from the *GG*.

Eustace of Boulogne had married, probably before the summer of 1036,[1] Godgifu, daughter of King Ethelred and Emma of Normandy. He may have had children by her; seemingly, he had to leave a son as a hostage with William before joining him as his ally in England—an odd provision, on the face of it.[2] He invaded Kent in 1067 with his *nepos*, usually taken as meaning his 'nephew', despite the fact that Lambert of Lens, his brother killed at Lille in 1054, apparently left no issue, and that Godfrey, bishop of Paris, also his brother, is not recorded as having any bastards. Eustace's sister, Gerberga, married to Frederick of Lorraine, had no sons; we know of no other sisters of Eustace (which is not to say that he had none), and the word *nepos* means 'grandson' as anciently and as often as 'nephew'.[3] Thirty-one years after his marriage with Godgifu, Eustace may well have had by a son or daughter of hers a grandson old enough to accompany him to Kent, and of the royal blood of England. The men of Kent, who should, twice over, have been Eustace's enemies, welcomed him as a neighbour and one whom they knew. One wonders what they knew of him, apart from the fracas at Dover in 1051 and the recent battle.

We therefore suggest the possibility that Eustace had considered himself as eligible a king as William, perhaps had even been given to expect a sharing of England of the kind set forth in Appendix A;[4] that William, excusing himself on the ground that he did not then have more than a small part of England subdued, put Eustace off. Such a situation would explain Eustace's rage, Guy's evasive rhetoric, and the need of William and his council to hear a *Frenchman* urge him to the crown.

England and the English in the Carmen

Considering the period at which he wrote, Guy of Amiens shows a remarkable interest in and knowledge of what was, after all, for him a foreign country. There is little or nothing in the *GND* or *GG* that approximates to his frequent informative asides about the English, much less his casual references to English institutions or customs that take them almost for granted. Guy had, of course, the best of opportunities to know a good deal of England. He was the protégé and contemporary of Fulk II, bishop of Amiens, Godgifu's son;[5] the scholar and patron of an abbey with strong English

---

[1] See note, genealogical table I. [2] *GG*, p. 264.
[3] As well as a variety of other relationships. Cf. *NG*, pp. 1210 f.
[4] See below, p. 59. [5] See above, p. xxxiii n. 3.

connections,[1] and well inclined, if no more, towards Eustace II of Boulogne, the second husband of Godgifu, himself the visitor on at least one ill-starred occasion to England, and perhaps on other quieter occasions as well. The information provided about the English by a mid-eleventh-century writer so connected is not only invaluable confirmation of much that might otherwise remain conjectural, but in some instances provides us with contemporary witness to an institution or event of which there is no record elsewhere so early.

Of the people of England, Guy says much to confirm what is already known or assumed of them at this time: they are stubborn (v. 147) and patriotic to the point of xenophobia (vv. 371–2), yet turbulent and difficult for even their own kings to control (v. 221). Their battle array is the classic Germanic one: although they may ride to the field, like the early Frankish kings (v. 377), they fight on foot (vv. 369–70) in close formation, the 'shieldwall' (vv. 367, 415). So densely are they marshalled that at Hastings, as at Zülpich, four centuries earlier,[2] the slain have no room to fall (vv. 417–20).

English institutions as they appear in the *Carmen* are of great interest. The king is not an autocrat, but admits himself that his nobles have rights in the kingdom (vv. 169, 211) and takes counsel with them as to the best course of action against William (vv. 189–200). Indeed his appeal is not merely to the *duces* and *comites* originally mentioned, but to both high and low (v. 203). Similarly, we find that the people not only have a voice in the designation or election of a king (vv. 292, 741), but could even force the election of one, however unsuitable, upon the magnates (vv. 654–60).

The terseness of Guy's narrative, once the rhetoric has been recognized and stripped away, precludes our learning much of England apart from London. Canterbury is a great city (v. 613); Dover has a fortified stronghold (v. 605); Winchester is the queen-dowager's jointure (v. 627). London is the greatest city of the land and the wealthiest (v. 638), and it is the Londoners, together with those seeking refuge after the battle, who assert their ancient right to choose a king in time of need (as they had done with Edmund

---

[1] See above, p. xxxiii. Abbot Gervin of Saint-Riquier visited Edward the Confessor's court and his abbey held lands in Norfolk. Cf. Dom J. Laporte, 'Rapports de l'Abbaye de Saint-Riquier avec l'Angleterre', *Revue Mabillon* xlix (1959), pp. 145–51, and Helen Cam, 'The English Lands of the Abbey of Saint-Riquier', *EHR* xxxi (1916), pp. 443–7.

[2] In 612 (Fredegar, *Chron.* iv. 38).

Ironside and Harold I), whereupon the cry goes forth, 'habet *Londonia regem*' (v. 653), and England rejoices. Guy knows the defences of the city (v. 639), and gives us, as well, confirmation that the royal hall at Westminster was either older than the abbey, or had been the more important building before Edward's re-founding of the latter (vv. 667–8).[1] Here, he adds, as the acts of former rulers attest, kings are wont to wear their crowns (vv. 671–2), a contemporary witness to pre-Conquest ceremonial crown-wearings.[2]

William and Harold in the Carmen

Just as Guy knew, directly or indirectly, much about England and the English, he had excellent opportunities to know the two protagonists of his poem. William was his neighbour and, *de jure* (after 1055), the suzerain of Ponthieu; he was allied to its comital house through the marriages of both his uncle and his sister (see genealogical table III), and the dukes of Normandy and counts of Ponthieu were also connected through marriages with the lords of Saint-Valery. It is not impossible that Guy had travelled in England; in any event, Harold made at least one trip to Flanders,[3] and his most fateful journey abroad was to begin in Ponthieu. Eustace will have known much of Harold, as will Godgifu and her son Bishop Fulk.

It is the more interesting, therefore, to examine the manner in which Guy presents both men to his readers—especially when the poem is recalled to be one aimed at winning the favour of the new king. Foreville has remarked that the William of the *Gesta Guillelmi* is at least as much a legendary hero of geste as a historical duke-king.[4] While the William of the *Carmen* performs the occasional military prodigy (e.g. v. 555), he is, for the most part, far from the literary fiction of a ruler invoked in the set eulogy at the beginning of the poem (vv. 26–39). Excesses of hope and despair assail him

[1] For an excellent estimation of the place of Westminster Palace among the buildings of its time see Urban T. Holmes Jr., 'The Houses of the Bayeux Tapestry', *Speculum* xxxiv (1959), pp. 179–83. We owe this reference to the kindness of Professor Frank Barlow and Mr. Stephen Price.

[2] This passage in the *Carmen* confirms the thesis of L. M. Larson, *The King's Household in England before the Norman Conquest* (Univ. of Wisconsin Bulletin no. 100, 1904), that William did not himself institute ceremonial crown-wearings on the three major feasts of the year, but merely continued an earlier custom.

[3] See P. Grierson, 'A Visit of Earl Harold to Flanders in 1056', *EHR* li (1936), pp. 90–7.   [4] *GG*, pp. xlivf.

(vv. 45, 59–61); sudden checks unnerve him (vv. 335, 508–10); he can be and is out-generalled (vv. 432 ff.); he needs and accepts help (vv. 521–2). The final triumph, his election as king, comes as a result of neither heroism nor a just cause, but through a cleverly timed and tempting offer to Ansgar (vv. 689–90) and by showing greater guile than the Londoners (vv. 724–6, 751–2). Guy is not even above using similes of the duke that are far from flattering (vv. 618, 723).

That he takes an active part in the battle (at least after the opening stages) and acquits himself well as a warrior (vv. 462, 476 ff., 513 ff.) is no doubt historical fact; and he perhaps shows to best advantage as a soldier and a commander when confronted with sudden and desperate dangers: when the English anticipate his move to seize the hill (see below, Appendix B, pp. 73–83) and in his stemming of the Norman rout (vv. 445–59). Guy, neither a Norman nor a lover of Normans, portrays a William who bears some resemblance to the William of the *ASC*, 1087; William of Poitiers carefully limns a lay figure that owes far too much to Einhard's Charlemagne.

William is, none the less, Guy's hero, and as such receives much fuller treatment than Harold. We comment below on the lack of detailed charges levelled against the latter by the author in his own person;[1] the king's 'adultery' (v. 261) and 'perjury' (vv. 239–40, 261) emerge only in speeches by the duke or his envoy. The only specific crime Guy himself mentions is fratricide (vv. 129–30, 137–8), but vv. 131–2 almost form the case for Harold's defence to this charge. For the rest, the terms of opprobrium used of him are general: he is, we are told, crafty and wicked; yet none of his actions as retailed by Guy is particularly crafty or wicked, unless the English surprise of William's army qualifies as the former—and Guy does not dwell on that event. Harold is an able general (v. 374) and his personal prowess at least as great as William's (vv. 533–4)—greater, if it be remembered that William himself called for aid to kill him (vv. 535–40). He speaks compellingly (vv. 177–88), and his army support him ardently (vv. 193–4); his death demoralizes them (vv. 551–4). Guy confirms the oft-made assumption that Harold was the elder,[2] as a difference of several years

---

[1] See below, Appendix A, p. 69.

[2] From the known date of his parents' marriage and the fact that he was the second son, and possibly the third child, 1022 has been postulated for Harold's

is implied by the king's taunt (v. 217) and William's riposte (v. 231).

The Battle of Hastings in the Carmen

See below, Appendices B, C, and D (pp. 73–120).

The Funeral of Harold in the Carmen

Nothing in the *Carmen* prepares the reader for the viking funeral which William gives his fallen rival. Yet in 1066 the Normans were less than two centuries from sea-raiding and not more than a hundred years from paganism.[1] It is impossible to determine to what degree the Christianity of the day was more than a mere veneer in men in whom stark realism and tormenting superstition were inextricably intermingled. William of Jumièges, a monk celebrating a duke who had become *rex orthodoxus*, passes over Harold's funeral in silence, but the basic facts of the *Carmen*'s story recur, with verbal echoes, in the *Gesta Guillelmi*,[2] whose author is at pains to veil the pagan connotations in a wealth of rhetoric. William of Poitiers would have refuted the tale, had it been possible, and his motive in revising it is as obvious as his embarrassment. We think that Guy's story may be accepted as telling evidence that 'Scandinavian qualities . . . clung to the settlers in France, and with them a profound ambivalence'. They acknowledged the church as a force to be reckoned with; at the same time, they remembered other ghostly powers venerated by their fathers, and the age-old traditions of the north.

It is in this context that the funeral which William gave to Harold is fascinating. The duke carries the mangled body to his sea-camp, shrouded in royal purple, seemingly to be given Christian burial (vv. 373–6). But when Harold's mother offers for her son's body more than his weight in gold, William refuses, raging (vv. 577–84). And yet there is no unceremonious bundling away of the dead rival; rather the pagan burial of a king under a mound

birth, a year that suits well with the date at which he received the earldom of East Anglia. William was probably born in 1028–9.

[1] D. C. Douglas, *William the Conqueror* (London, 1964), pp. 20 f.

[2] pp. 204–10. William of Poitiers adds that Harold's body was identifiable only by certain marks, that the bodies of his brothers were found near him, and that the man to whom the duke entrusted the burial (*Carmen*, v. 587) was William Malet. Gytha's offer is reduced to gold equal in weight to the body (in the *GR* ii. 306–7, William hands it over *sine pretio*), and the epitaph is interpreted as mockery. For later stories of Harold's burial see *NC* iii, Appendix MM.

on the sea-cliffs among lamenting warriors. An inscribed stone bids Harold guard shore and sea, and William, giving alms, assumes the style of king (vv. 585–96).[1]

The raising of howes over departed heroes on headlands from which they might guard the shore is a well-attested ancient practice. That the power of 'howe-dwellers' was still feared in 1066 was believed later: the howe of Ivar the Boneless allegedly terrified Harald Hardrada, and was demolished by King William.[2] What amazes in the *Carmen* is the re-enactment of old viking rites by a Christian prince, recorded without explanation or excuse. Further, the mound and the mourning described by Guy celebrate neither the duke's friend nor his kinsman,[3] but his fallen foe. The inscription, no prayer for the dead king's soul, but an injunction that he rest and keep his watch, savours of age-old magic, and the scene of mourning, led by the duke himself, thus seems to imply a bond between William and Harold older than Christianity—sworn brotherhood.[4] The most remarkable pagan note, however, lies in William's assumption of the kingly name beside the howe (vv. 595–6). This, rather than the duke's coronation in the abbey housing Edward's tomb, fits P. E. Schramm's suggestion of an appeal to 'that pre-Christian magic by which a king took his stand on the tumulus of his predecessor'.[5]

The giving of alms to 'the poor of Christ' is the only non-pagan element in this scene; yet it, too, resembles offerings made to the

[1] Cf. R. J. Adam, *A Conquest of England* (London, 1965), p. 97: 'Christianity might give a veneer of respectability to men like Olaf Tryggvasson, but no historian has ever assumed that the missionary kings of the north completely abandoned the values of the ancestors. The same truth is more likely to be forgotten in the case of William of Normandy. . . .'

[2] *Ragnars saga* (*Volsunga saga ok Ragnars saga loðbrokar*), ed. M. Olsen, Copenhagen, 1906–8, p. 169; *Hemingsþáttr Aslákssonar*, ed. G. Fellows Jensen (*Editiones Arnamagnaeanae*, series B, vol. 3, 1962), pp. cxxxix, 46, 55. For a twentieth-century parallel cf. P. V. Glob, *The Bog People* (London, 1969), pp. 76 f.

[3] Cf. Sven B. F. Jansson, *The Runes of Sweden* (transl. P. S. Foote) (London, 1962), pp. 20–32 (Pls. 7–13), and in particular the crude stone shown in Pl. 7; pp. 33–4 and 123 for an inscription intended to frighten away thieves; and pp. 62–9 for stones raised after battles. Most inscriptions were ordered to be made for kinsmen, but a few examples occur of stones raised to 'guild-brothers' (pp. 71–3).

[4] See below, Appendix A, pp. 59 (notes 2, 5) and 69–71. William and Harold might also have been thought of as connected by affinity, either because of a promise by the latter to marry a daughter of the duke (ibid., pp. 69, 72), or, more distantly, through their common affinities with both Edward the Confessor and Baldwin V of Flanders (whose half-sister Earl Tostig had married).

[5] P. E. Schramm, *A History of the English Coronation* (transl. by L. G. Wickham Legg), Oxford, 1937, pp. 4, 38.

dead themselves in burials of old. Bishop Guy shows us indeed 'a profound ambivalence' in William and his countrymen, at once Christians and pagans: to avert political danger and yet honour Harold, they can draw upon the superstitions of their viking ancestors.[1]

William's March after Hastings in the Carmen

According to Guy of Amiens (v. 597), William spent a fortnight at his base camp at Hastings after the battle,[2] and the *ASC* supplements this information by telling us that he waited to see if the English would now come in to submit to him. They did not, and, having meanwhile received reinforcements from overseas, he moved off, harrying the lands through which he passed.[3] William of Poitiers (*GG*, p. 210) says that he left Hastings after a stay of indeterminate length, and paused in his course to Dover to punish the people of Romney for their resistance to two of his ships which had put in there in error. The *Carmen*, on the other hand, says nothing of any fighting on the route to Dover, but rather that its people, terrified, met the duke on the way and offered the submission of the place (vv. 598–600). There is very little sign of any ravaging about Romney in Domesday Book,[4] so the *GG* may well be exaggerating any action there, and Guy of Amiens reasonably ignoring it.

William of Poitiers also recounts that some of William's followers fired the castle, even as it was capitulating, and that the duke, incensed and apologetic, paid the inhabitants an indemnity.[5] The *Carmen*, however, speaks of a peaceful entry (vv. 607–10), after

---

[1] For kings' howes cf. *Heimskr.*, 'The Ynglinga Saga', *passim*. Thomas Wright, shortly after the publication of the *Carmen*, called attention to the likenesses between Harold's burial and Beowulf's (*Biographia Britannica Literaria* ii. 15) and between Beowulf's and that of Themistocles (as described by Plato Comicus, quoted by Plutarch) (Wright, op. cit. i. 11):

> ὁ σὸς δὲ τύμβος ἐν καλῷ κεχωσμένος
> τοῖς ἐμπόροις πρόσρησις ἔσται πανταχοῦ,
> τούς τ' ἐκπλέοντας εἰσπλέοντας τ' ὄψεται,
> χὠπόταν ἄμιλλα τῶν νεῶν θεάσεται.

[2] The *Carmen* (v. 147) strongly implies that William had hoped for submission on his arrival in England. If, as we suggest below (Appendix B, p. 75), his strategy was to establish a bridgehead and attempt to demoralize Harold and his supporters by harrying and propaganda, he may well have issued some sort of proclamation.   [3] *ASC*, MS. D, 1066; FW, i. 228.

[4] Domesday Book i, fols. 5, 11, 12b, 13. Appreciable loss of value occurred only at Burmarsh (fol. 12b).   [5] *GG*, pp. 210–12.

which William quartered his men in the houses of the people there, whom he evicted. This must apply to the town, despite previous mention of the castle. Is there a similar confusion in the *GG*? The entry on Dover in the Domesday survey does not mention the castle, but states categorically that the *villa* was burnt.[1] It would seem at least possible that the duke here, as with Harold's funeral, reverted to viking type and fired the town on his departure (of which Guy tells us no details), and that William of Poitiers, as so often, has improved the story to his hero's credit.

The *Carmen* provides the earliest mention of Dover castle, *pendens a uertice montis*, already guardian of the realm (vv. 604–5), and the topographical sketch (vv. 602–3) is at once very vivid and most exact. Although on archaeological evidence it is as true to say of Dover as of any place that 'we cannot point to any certain pre-Conquest castle',[2] it is surely significant that Guy refers to the *castrum* of Dover no less than four times (vv. 601, 605, 607, 611), but uses the word of no other city or town in England, even London, impressive though its defences were (vv. 677–8). William of Poitiers distinguishes sharply, in retailing the terms of Harold's oath to William, between the *castrum Doveram*, which apparently already existed, and which Harold was to hand over to a Norman garrison, and the *alia castra*, which were to be erected by him when and where it pleased the duke (*GG*, p. 104). A later passage in the *GG* (p. 210) makes it clear that Dover castle was no mere earthwork.[3] Invisible though the remains of the pre-Conquest structure may be today, the *Carmen* provides contemporary witness that Dover, perhaps alone of English towns, possessed something that a man of Ponthieu could describe by the same word that he used of the massive fortifications familiar to him at Saint-Valery (v. 52).

According to Guy, the duke, once established in Dover, spent a month there, occupied solely with exacting and receiving the

---

[1] Domesday Book i. 1.

[2] Derek Renn, *Norman Castles in Britain* (London, 1968), p. 7.

[3] 'Situm est id castellum in rupe mari contigua, quae naturaliter acuta undique ad hoc ferramentis elaborate incisa, in speciem muri directissima altitudine, quantum sagittae jactus permetiri potest, consurgit, quo in latere unda marina alluitur.' See also p. 264, where the castle is called *firmissimus locus*, with a *portus marinus*; *GND*, p. 138 (*sub anno* 1067); Eadm., pp. 7 f.; and FW, i. 205 ff. Evidence as to the nature of the stronghold existing in 1066 is so far inconclusive, but it may be determined by the important excavations still in progress. It must have included the Iron Age earthworks, the Roman pharos, and the adjoining building, and was, perhaps, a formidable *burh*.

submission of Canterbury and other towns in the neighbourhood, and the surrender of the English (vv. 613–22). William of Poitiers, however, says that he spent eight days strengthening the defences of Dover; that his army was stricken with dysentery; and that he himself, having removed to 'the broken tower',[1] became very ill, although this did not prevent his moving on lest supplies for his army became short (*GG*, pp. 210–12). While the *GG*, unlike the *Carmen*, speaks of only eight days at Dover, and makes the surrender of Canterbury appear spontaneous (the envoys encountering the duke as he sets out for 'the broken tower'), delays of some kind clearly occurred, and the reasons given by our authorities are not concordant. The clue may lie in the surprising statement of Benoît de Saint-Maure, that the 'oit jorz' were spent, not in strengthening Dover's defences, but in besieging them, from a second castle that William had had set up at the foot of the cliffs (op. cit., vv. 39,922 ff.).[2] This story is of interest, for Benoît knew the *Gesta Guillelmi* and used it. According to him, the duke came from Hastings to join men sent ahead to build this castle in order to starve out the fortress above, which was considered impregnable and was thronged with men from all around. Is it possible that advance-parties were sent to Romney (above, p. xlv) and other ports?

The *Carmen* says that the duke finally left Dover to set up a camp (or camps) elsewhere (v. 624).[3] It then records that Duke William sent a mandate to Winchester, demanding a pledge and

---

[1] Perhaps the monument in the Roman fort at Richborough (Renn, op. cit., pp. 28 f.). From this fort William could dominate Sandwich and the mouth of the Wantsum.

[2] William used such tactics at Domfront (*GND*, p. 126; *GG*, p. 36), and at Arques (*GND*, p. 119; *GG*, p. 58) and elsewhere.

[3] A most interesting and ingenious analysis of the line of march, based on the decrease in value of properties between January 1066 ('tempus regis Edwardi') and William's accession, was formulated by F. H. Baring (*Domesday Tables for the counties of Surrey, Berkshire, Middlesex, Hertford, Buckingham, and Bedford, and for the New Forest*, London, 1909, Appendix A, pp. 207–16), and has been refined and developed by Lt.-Col. C. H. Lemmon, D.S.O. (*The Norman Conquest: its setting and impact*, London, 1966, pp. 116–22). Their conclusions fit well the general direction of movement indicated in both the *Carmen* and the *GG*, and are thus most valuable for the actual line of march. It must be borne in mind, however, that the south-eastern counties had also sustained the English fyrd throughout the summer of 1066, as well as attacks from Tostig (who had taken the Isle of Wight), and that the armies of Edwin and Morcar must have provisioned themselves about London. Therefore not all 'ravaging' need be laid to the passage of the Norman army.

tribute (vv. 625–6), such as he had received in other places. The city was the dower of Queen Edith, Edward's widow; in deference to the Lady, William would not seize it from her, asking merely an impost and a pledge (vv. 627–30). The magnates advised Edith to grant these and she yielded to their advice. Duke William, placated by her gifts and theirs, ordered that they should be left in peace, struck his tents, and moved on London (vv. 631–6). This episode is omitted by William of Poitiers (perhaps because he has alleged (*GG*, pp. 166–8) that the queen, Harold's sister, had been supporting the duke's cause with her prayers and counsels), but Domesday Book shows that Winchester was threatened.[1] Whether or not Edith's dower, the city was her residence and the site of the royal fisc, also the gateway to the west. William may have received the news of its submission at his camp near Wallingford (see below, p. lii).

The passage on Winchester in the *Carmen*, brief as it is, is important. Guy grasps the duke's diplomacy and shows something of his strategic plan.[2] No one else does this.[3] The *Carmen*, unlike the *GND* and the *GG*, also shows William's lively concern for his war-chest; at Winchester, as elsewhere, he demands tribute, and *dona* placate him (vv. 613–16; 625–6; 630).

Unlike Canute, the duke seems to have had no ships with which to beleaguer London.[4] Guy describes the city as of great size: rich, turbulent, crowded, and very strong. But yet the *Carmen* shows

---

[1] Cf. Baring, op. cit., p. 209, and Lemmon, op. cit., p. 120.

[2] William had, in effect, to deal with three capital cities: Canterbury, Winchester, and London (see Lemmon, op. cit., p. 115).

[3] The *GND* mentions only that the duke changed his line of march to ford the river Thames at Wallingford and made camp before attacking London, and the *GG* says nothing of his advance until he nears the city. MS. D of the *ASC* speaks merely of ravages on the march, and 'Florence' of Worcester names six counties said to have been harried (FW, i. 228).

[4] Compare the *EE*, p. 22, where it is implied that London could be taken only by attrition. Was her war-fleet blocking the Thames when William advanced? Her seamen are said to have had a share in the election of Edgar atheling (FW, loc. cit.). This apart, there is no hint as to the whereabouts of English or Norman ships at this time, but it has been suggested that William's vessels were needed to transport reinforcements from France to strategic ports (cf. Baring, op. cit., loc. cit., and Lemmon, op. cit., loc. cit.). He may, too, have feared intervention from Denmark (see below, p. xlix n. 3, and p. liii n. 5) and kept watch. For a late story that he had initially landed part of his force at Sandwich see the *Chronicle of Henry Knyghton*, ed. J. R. Lumby (London, 1889), i. 54 (*RS* xcii). This account at least shows the importance that Sandwich must have had for the duke, and squadrons would have been based there against any threat from Denmark.

that London was fatally weakened by divided counsels among the magnates, while the mob clamoured for a king (vv. 641–50). William of Poitiers changes this, his story being in need of a new villain, and the English nobles are united in the *GG* under the leadership of Archbishop Stigand (p. 214), in defiance of history. The author then recalls that he has forgotten to say where they are, and borrows from Guy's account of London, adding points of interest on her rich trade, her independence, and her warlike power. It is interesting, however, to find that he says nothing of her defences, for Guy states (vv. 639–40) that the city neither feared enemies nor dreaded stratagems. The river guarded her on the right, the wall on the left. Exceptional interest attaches to this early reference to London Wall.[1]

The siege of London in the Carmen

Augustin Thierry thought the passages on the siege of London the only part of the *Carmen* that added anything material to what was already known on the Conquest, and reproduced vv. 681–752 in the third edition of his history. Though his premiss was mistaken, he was right in thinking these passages of exceptional value, for here Guy of Amiens not only provides an unique and detailed picture of events, but also demonstrates knowledge of the internal politics and institutions of the city. Here, too, is the first of many accounts which depict Duke William's mastery of political intrigue; furthermore, Guy's narrative illuminates and calls out obscurities and evasions in other sources.

In the *Carmen* (vv. 641–2), survivors of Hastings fly to the city, 'hoping that in it they could live for a long time masterless'.[2] But the people, in terror and despair, force an election, believing the mere name of king can save them. The great men retain power for themselves,[3] yet a royal boy (Edgar atheling) is elected (vv. 643–

[1] Archaeological evidence makes it all but certain that even in Roman times the defensive wall of London did not continue along the river side of the city (R. Merrifield, *The Roman City of London*, London, 1965, p. 48; P. R. V. Marsden, 'The Riverside Defensive wall of Roman London', *Trans. of the London and Middlesex Arch. Soc.* xxi (1967), p. 156). The twelfth-century description by William FitzStephen of a great wall earlier fortifying the river, but eroded in his own time by the current (*Vita Sancti Thomae, Materials for the History of Thomas Becket* iii. 3 (London, 1877); *RS* lxvii), remains, therefore, misleading.

[2] Compare the *GG*, p. 214, where London is said to contain only citizens (i.e. it is not controlled by any earl), but possesses a large and famous military force.

[3] Ecclesiastical and lay magnates had houses in the city, and London's leaders included many Anglo-Danes, who would no doubt have preferred King Sweyn

52). This fatal division may explain the vague story in the *ASC*, MS. D, where Archbishop Aldred and the people of London urge Edgar's election and the great earls, Edwin and Morcar, promise aid, but all goes from bad to worse. MS. D gives an incoherent account of events after the battle, and seems to be a conflation of more than one text. The writer, who had some tie with Aldred, has been purposely obscure.[1] As to William's panegyrists, the *GND* is silent, mentioning Edgar subsequently; in the *GG*, Aldred (to be shown later as King William's saintly consecrator (p. 220)) is naturally absent. Stigand replaces him, supported by the earls and magnates. When the book was written, nemesis had overtaken this archbishop and both earls;[2] William of Poitiers therefore blames resistance upon them,[3] rather than upon Aldred of pious memory, and denies any strife (*GG*, p. 214). But if Stigand's influence exalted Edgar, no one else says so.[4] Guy of Amiens, on the other hand, though he names no one, suggests two, if not more factions, and vividly sketches the mob, to whom a king meant safety.

Guy continues by saying that England rejoiced at learning 'quod habet Londonia regem'.[5] Meanwhile, he who rightly claimed the whole realm burnt and ravaged. On having the news, he ordered the city to be invested, and his army at once beset it (vv. 653–64). William chose for his base the royal hall at Westminster, which pleased him, for there kings were wont to wear the crown (vv. 665–72).[6] Such a reason being incompatible with the portrait of the

of Denmark, Harold's cousin, who had a claim to England (see p. liii n. 5, and Appendix A).

[1] 'Florence' of Worcester (FW, i. 228), and William of Malmesbury (*GR*, ii. 307), both indebted to recensions of the *ASC*, bring specific charges against the earls, who appear to have failed Harold and then withdrawn their power from London. FW says they had been pledged to fight for Edgar; the *GR* says they withdrew before his election (having failed to get one of themselves elected), and went north—in the belief that William would not vex them. These accounts still leave much unrevealed.

[2] Stigand, deposed in 1070, was imprisoned for life in 1072. Edwin had been betrayed and killed in rebellion, and Morcar was William's captive.

[3] The *GG* says it was their supreme wish to have no king who was not English.

[4] Orderic Vitalis merely copies William of Poitiers.

[5] A most remarkable phrase, showing the excellence of Guy's information. For London's part in the election of Edgar's grandfather, Edmund Ironside, in 1016, see the *ASC*, MSS. C (D, E); and ibid., MSS. E (F), for the election of Harold I in 1035. London must also have partaken in the election of Harold Godwinson.

[6] This passage gives the first account of Westminster hall, as distinct from the abbey (see p. 42 below). The 'West' hall is here contrasted with the royal palace

duke in the *GG*, William of Poitiers (who is using the *Carmen*) has a most interesting circumlocution (loc. cit.). We read here that Duke William 'ubi frequentiorem audivit eorum (praepotentium) conventum, non longe a Lundonia consedit'.[1] King Edward's hall is clearly the place implied and (after a reference to the Thames) a short description of London gives a further verbal echo of the *Carmen*.[2] The close relation between these two authorities ends here, but since the circumlocution mentioned above possesses considerable importance, it may be well to analyse the significance of some earlier variants to be found in the *GG*. It will be remembered that the entire Winchester episode is passed over by the author, in whose work Duke William begins to march towards an unnamed objective from the 'broken tower' in Kent.[3] The word *Interea* then introduces Stigand and the earls and other *praepotentes*—united in support of Edgar atheling and threatening a new war. Thus his biographer makes the odds against William greater (compare vv. 641–52), and passages in the *Carmen* mentioning his ambition and his ruthless devastation (vv. 655, 657–72) are 'improved'.[4]

In the poem (vv. 673–8), William now begins to construct engines,[5] threatening London with annihilation. In the *GG*, five hundred Norman knights, sent in advance, repulse a sortie and quickly force the citizens to seek refuge within the walls; after this coup, they burn such buildings as are to be found *citra flumen*.[6] William marches to Wallingford,[7] crossing the river by ford and

---

in London. If Guy's league (v. 665) is identical with the modern French league, the distance between Westminster and the city is a close estimate, one and three-quarter miles. Westminster would certainly have been a prime objective for William; King Edward was buried in his minster, and Harold, crowned there at Epiphany, had celebrated Easter in Edward's hall. For William, these places would have incalculable value. See below for William of Poitiers's reaction to the *Carmen*'s story.

[1] 'Con*sedit*' echoes v. 679, 'Prouidus hanc *sed*em sibi rex elegit in edem.'

[2] *Carmen*, v. 637, 'Vrbs est *ampla nimis*'; *GG*, loc. cit., 'ambitu *nimis ampla*'.

[3] *GG*, pp. 212 f.

[4] *Carmen*, vv. 655 f., 'Interea, *regni totum qui querit habere* . . . Hostili gladio quę nec uastauerat igne . . .'; *GG*, ibid., 'Verum, *qui dominari debuit eis*, intrepide approperans . . .'

[5] See *Lanfranci Opera Omnia*, ed. J. A. Giles, 2 vols. (Oxford, 1844), vol. i. 57, Ep. 38, and FW, i. 227, for William's use of engines.

[6] i.e. on the right bank. The duke himself is on the left bank (see below).

[7] A strong *burh* on the right bank of the Thames, thirteen miles south of Oxford. William of Poitiers here intrudes earlier events, expanding the *GND*'s summary of the march after Hastings and altering it. See below, p. lii and n. 2.

by bridge, and there Stigand comes to make his submission (p. 216). Proceeding thence, the duke receives the surrender of London as soon as he comes in sight of the city, accepts hostages, and is subsequently offered the crown. One of the curious things in this narrative is that the duke withdraws to Wallingford—a march of forty-seven miles—though he has just established himself near the city, and after one engagement has so shattered the English morale that Stigand soon abandons his king and London surrenders. Duke William's movements in the *GND* (p. 136) appear much more intelligible. In this version, William diverts his march on the capital, fording the river at Wallingford and camping north of the Thames before moving on the city. His advance guard has a ferocious encounter with 'rebels' found *in platea urbis*[1] and inflicts heavy losses. London then capitulates. Unusually detailed about the river crossing, the *GND* is supported by Domesday Book.

If the chronology be correct, and if Stigand did submit at Wallingford, then he did so *before* London was threatened—in short, he did not play the role assigned to him in the *GG* (see p. li above). William of Poitiers, therefore, had an obvious motive for rearranging the duke's itinerary, and it is these changes which confuse his narrative.[2] Thus the *Carmen*, by its reference to Westminster, here acts as a catalyst, enabling us to interpret for the first time the heretofore obscure mention in the *GG* of the place 'not far from London', and so to evaluate the material given above. The way in which both his authorities were altered by William of Poitiers strongly suggests that Duke William did seize Edward's hall, and that Stigand had met him at Wallingford. Is it possible that Archbishop Stigand—who also possessed Winchester in plurality—came from that city, bringing the tribute mentioned in the *Carmen* (vv. 630–5)? It will be remembered that William of Poitiers omits the episode concerning Winchester, and his evidence that the archbishop of Canterbury was at this time in London stands alone.[3]

Domesday Book, which confirms Guy's story that Winchester

---

[1] *Platea urbis*, probably a *via Londiniensis*. See Niermeyer for *platea*, 'a highway'.

[2] The verbal echoes are exact, but the time and direction of the march are not those in the *GND*; William of Poitiers has juggled with his sources.

[3] The *Gesta Pont.*, 37, says that William 'venit Lundoniam' and met Stigand and others but the tense is not clear; if the meeting was in London, it was after the peace.

was at least threatened, and London beset from the north, suggests further that a force had earlier probed the bridge-head defences at Southwark, before rejoining the main body at Wallingford.[1] This *démarche*, the probable origin of the Norman stories of an affray,[2] does not explain London's surrender, for the bridge was not taken. The first explanation comes from Guy of Amiens (compare BB, vv. 530 ff.).

The *Carmen* says that when William's threats and preparations are terrifying the citizens (vv. 679–80), he sends secretly to Ansgar,[3] who, though disabled by wounds, has supreme authority in the city. Such a man, he suggests, is worthy of greater power. What if Ansgar give him the mere name of king, and himself rule England (vv. 681–90)? The sheer effrontery of this is breath-taking.[4] It is a gibe at the folly of electing Edgar (v. 650), a mockery of the cry, 'London has a king'—yet a realistic admission that William needs allies.[5] The prudent Ansgar draws his own conclusions and addresses the *natu maiores*. The situation is desperate[6] and the nation, panic-stricken, has not yet moved to aid the city. Before the enemy learns the worst, let them amuse him with negotiations—i.e. play for time. They agree. But Duke William blandly accepts their 'mandates',[7] sending the dazzled envoy back, laden with gold, to sing his praises and uphold his claim, and to declare resistance

---

[1] See Baring, op. cit. 209, and Lemmon, op. cit. 119.

[2] But were there two affrays? Only the *GG* speaks of the burning of buildings.

[3] See F. E. Harmer, *Anglo-Saxon Writs* (Manchester, 1952), pp. 560 f. *Ansgardus* is no doubt Esgar the staller (in DB, *Ansgarus* and *Asgarus*), grandson of Canute's standard-bearer. For his authority in London see Harmer, op. cit., p. 342, Instr. 75. He became William's prisoner (*Liber Eliensis*, ed. E. O. Blake (1962), p. 165). A staller (see Larson, *Canute the Great* (1962), p. 165) spoke for the king at public assemblies.

[4] 'Solum rex uocitetur, ait, set *commoda* regni / Vt iubet Ansgardus subdita cuncta regat.' This offer to an Anglo-Danish magnate would be astute; see above, p. lxix n. 3.

[5] See the *GG*, p. 234, and *Gesta Pont.*, loc. cit., for his flattery of Stigand. Not long after William's coronation, Sweyn of Denmark claimed England under threat of invasion. King William promised service and tribute, but bribed Sweyn's nobles; see *SRD*, iii. 252–4; the story comes from William's English agent to Sweyn Estrithsson.

[6] Ansgar depicts the city under assault; Guy says only that it was threatened.

[7] See the *GG*, p. 230 (and nn. 4 and 5 above), 'Multa Lundoniae postquam coronatus est, prudenter juste clementerque disposuit, quaedam ad ipsius civitatis *commoda* sive dignitatem, alia quae genti proficerent universae.' The *ASC*, MS. D, records at the same time the levying of a great geld. It looks as if Ansgar's 'mandates' and Sweyn's threats inspired concessions later embodied in London's charter and the 'Laws of King Edward', though at a price.

fatal. Neatly trapped, London can only repudiate Edgar and submit. With the atheling, a downcast procession sets out for Westminster (vv. 691–746). It was this extraordinary account, bearing all the marks of authenticity,[1] which impressed Thierry. Guy of Amiens ends the drama with a scene which gives William the fruits of his diplomacy, and shows it again in evidence (vv. 747–52). The duke receives the humiliated English with honours, kisses 'those remaining with the boy',[2] accepts offerings and invites trust—and then, 'iuramentis perfida corda ligat'. Here the treaty made at Berkhamsted (*ASC*, MS. D) may be related to its logical sequel—a formal ceremony in King Edward's hall.

The Coronation of William the Conqueror in the Carmen

Verses 787–835 of the *Carmen* comprise the only detailed contemporary account of the rite by which William the Conqueror was crowned king of the English on 25 December 1066.[3] This description is invaluable, not only as providing us with that rare phenomenon, a datable early *ordo*, but also as showing the modifications that could be and were made in such rituals as circumstances demanded. Most early *ordines* are, of course, syncretic to some degree, as ritual gradually becomes elaborated and a religious

---

[1] In the London scenes only, Guy speaks of *natu maiores, fratres, utile fraternum* (vv. 693, 695, 722); words suggesting *ealdormen* and a gild. Vv. 693–4, 741–2, also suggest the husting and the folkmoot. See, too, p. liii n. 3 above.

[2] Edgar himself, it seems, surrendered the kingdom (OV, iii. 182 (ii. 155)).

[3] Even a superficial analysis of medieval coronation rites lies, of course, without the scope of this edition; our intent is merely to demonstrate that Guy of Amiens's description is in no respect anachronistic or improbable. Indeed, had he wished to present a purely imaginary coronation, it might have been expected to reflect the procedure at the coronation, a few years before, of Philip I of France, at which Guy himself was present. For the background cf. L. G. Wickham Legg, *Three Coronation Orders*, Henry Bradshaw Society, v. xix (1900), pp. 54–64; L. G. Wickham Legg, *English Coronation Records* (London, 1901); P. E. Schramm, *A History of the English Coronation*, translated by L. G. Wickham Legg (Oxford, 1937), which contains a most valuable bibliography; P. L. Ward, 'The Coronation Ceremony in Mediaeval England', *Speculum* xiv (1939), pp. 160–78; H. G. Richardson, 'The Coronation in Mediaeval England: the Evolution of the Office and the Oath', *Traditio* xvi (1960), pp. 111–202; H. G. Richardson and G. O. Sayles, *The Governance of Mediaeval England from the Conquest to Magna Carta* (Edinburgh, 1963), pp. 136–52, 397–412; C. Vogel and R. Elze, *Le Pontifical romano-germanique du dixième siècle* i (*Studi e testi* 226) (Vatican City, 1963), pp. 246 ff.; J. Brückmann, 'The Ordines of the Third Recension of the Mediaeval English Coronation Order', in *Essays in Medieval History presented to Bertie Wilkinson*, ed. M. Powicke and T. Sandquist (University of Toronto Press, 1969). We warmly thank Dr. Brückmann for sending us a copy of his text before publication.

ceremony all but displaces the vestiges (in northern Europe, at least) of old Germanic king-making.[1] But the crowning of William I represented a sharp break with English tradition and in English culture; innovations were necessary, and the fluid state of the coronation ritual on the continent at this period enabled him to draw upon European practice.

Although the *Carmen* carefully omits to name the archbishop chosen both to anoint and to crown William, there seems no reason to doubt William of Poitiers's identification of the 'celeberrimus presul' with Aldred of York.[2] Aldred was by that time in good odour with Rome, and Stigand of Canterbury decidedly was not. A usurper needs all of the signs of legitimacy that he can muster; Guy of Amiens, however, makes it clear that Stigand, too, was present to assist.[3] Although the *GG* (p. 222), in remarking that William refused to allow Stigand to crown him and saying no more than that, leaves the reader with the impression that he played no part, William of Poitiers's other literary source, the *GND* (p. 136), speaks of William as anointed by the bishops of the kingdom; the plural may hint at Stigand's participation. Stigand was still a very powerful man, and William's rule by no means established, even in the south-east. The new king did not move against him until 1070[4] (and then had papal legates do his work), and in 1067 allowed him to consecrate Bishop Remigius. Had Stigand wished to share in the coronation ritual, it would have been both difficult and impolitic to exclude him.

In the *Carmen*, the coronation ceremony opens with a procession led by crucifers, with monks,[5] other clergy, and the bishops present following in the usual order. Last comes William, escorted by a crowd of nobles, and supported on either hand by an archbishop (vv. 797–804). While the procession is not mentioned in the earliest extant English *ordo*, this text is very sparing in rubrics. The second

---

[1] Cf. Vogel and Elze, op. cit., p. 246 n.; Ward, op. cit., pp. 167, 169; Schramm, op. cit., pp. 19 f.

[2] Vv. 791–3. Aldred, who had spent almost a year with Hermann, archbishop of Cologne, in 1054–5, just after the coronation of Henry IV, had had every opportunity to acquaint himself with the continental forms of the rite.

[3] Vv. 803–4. Two archbishops were traditional in England. See above, p. xxi n. 2.

[4] See the *GG*, p. 234, for an admission of William's motives in so delaying.

[5] The monastic chapter of Westminster Abbey alone later enjoyed the right of walking in the procession. If they are the *ordo cucullatus*, this would seem to be the earliest reference to their participation.

English *ordo*[1] briefly mentions a progress by king and clergy to the church where the ceremony is to be performed. The early tenth-century Romano-German rite describes a procession almost identical with that in the *Carmen*.[2] There is therefore no reason to assume that William introduced this procession, but an obvious source existed for his borrowing, if he indeed borrowed.

The *laudes*, however, which Guy says were sung at William's entry into the abbey (in place of the usual anthem), were certainly an innovation in the ceremony. William was crowned on the Nativity, and the *laudes* properly belonged not to the coronation, but, in Normandy, to that feast (see below, v. 805, note). The earliest English *ordo* is silent on the king's movements; in both the Romano-German *ordo* and the second English *ordo*, he next prostrates himself (together with the clergy in the former rite) before the altar. But in the *Carmen*, William seats himself upon a dais,[3] and is then presented to the assembled congregation successively by 'a certain Norman bishop' (identified in the *GG* (p. 220) as Geoffrey of Coutances) and the English archbishop who is to crown him (vv. 811–18).[4]

---

[1] As Ward has pointed out (op. cit., pp. 162 ff.), the nomenclature used of the English *ordines* leaves much to be desired. By 'first' English *ordo*, we mean that primitive short rite printed in Legg's *English Coronation Records*, pp. 3–9; by the 'second' English *ordo*, that existing in a number of versions between the late tenth and mid eleventh century, one of the later forms of which is printed by Legg in *Three Coronation Orders*, pp. 54–64, and in *English Coronation Records*, pp. 15–23. We reject the identification of this late form of the second *ordo* with that of William the Conqueror made by Schramm ('Die Krönung bei den West-franken und Angelsachsen von 878 bis um 1000', *Zeitschrift der Savigny-Stiftung* liv (1934), pp. 167 f.), which is founded on no more than that the king in question is not said to succeed 'paterna suggestione' or to be 'iuuenili flore laetantem'. These criteria could as well apply to Harold II, and even to Edward the Confessor, when the long period (of three Danish reigns) between his father's time and his is borne in mind, as well as his virtual disinheritance by Canute in favour of Hardicanute. [2] Vogel and Elze, op. cit., pp. 246 f.

[3] This is the earliest example of *pulpita* (or *pulpitum*) used of the dais at a coronation that we have been able to find.·

[4] The *GND* (p. 136) speaks of the Normans and English present, in the same order as the *Carmen*. The reason for which William of Poitiers (*GG*, p. 220) inverts the order given by his two literary sources, making Aldred present William to the congregation before Geoffrey of Coutances, lies apparently in his desire to emphasize the fervour of the English to have William as their king, which he has described at the beginning of his passage on the coronation. Schramm (*A History of the English Coronation*, p. 27) remarks that the presentation of the king to the people by two bishops (or archbishops) has no earlier English precedent, but was drawn from the French custom to satisfy William's special circumstances.

Both factions, Norman and English, then raise a shout for William and promise to serve him as his subjects (vv. 819–20). In the *Carmen*, therefore, the *recognitio* is not in the usual place, for in the Romano-German *ordo* it follows both the prostration and the oath of the king; in the second English *ordo*, it follows the prostration, and immediately precedes the oath; and in the first English *ordo*, it comes at the end of the rite, after the anointing and crowning, and is followed only by the *mandatum*.[1] Yet, in the special circumstances that applied, with not only English, but French and Bretons present (none of whom were already William's subjects), it is understandable that public consent to his crowning should have come at the outset of the ceremony; and, as the examples from the other *ordines* cited above show, the actual position of the *recognitio* was flexible.[2]

The account in the *Carmen* now reverts to the same order of events as in other *ordines*: the king is led to the altar; he and the clergy prostrate themselves while the *Kyrie* and litany are sung, after which the clergy rise.[3] The royal oath and the *recognitio* occur at this point in both the second English *ordo* and the Romano-German rite. The oath and *recognitio* of Philip I of France, on the other hand, took place much later in the ceremony, just before the reading of the epistle in the coronation mass.[4]

The coronation rite proper now commences (v. 832), as in almost all other early versions, and William's head is anointed with chrism.[5] The limitation of unction to the head of the king is in accord with the two earliest English *ordines*, but not the equally early

---

[1] Vogel and Elze, op. cit., pp. 249 f.; Legg, *Three Coronation Orders*, p. 164; Legg, *English Coronation Records*, p. 9.

[2] Cf. Schramm, op. cit., p. 151, who thinks that this ceremony at William's coronation might be called an 'election'. It would then naturally precede the coronation proper. The *recognitio* or 'election' at the opening of the second English *ordo*, before the oath, persists in the third *ordo* (Legg, *English Coronation Records*, p. 30) and in the modern service.

[3] Vogel and Elze, op. cit., pp. 247 f. In one family of manuscripts, the king apparently rises after the clergy, as in the *Carmen*.

[4] Bouquet, xi. 32.

[5] Schramm's differentiation between *chrisma* and *oleum sanctificatum* (op. cit., p. 3) will not hold. The terms are interchangeable to a great degree at this period, and no conclusions can be drawn from the use of one or the other. In any case, both the first and second English *ordines* and the Romano-German *ordo* specify *oleum sanctificatum*, not *chrisma*, as Schramm seems to imply. Cf. the articles on *chrisma* and cognate words in J. F. Niermeyer, *Mediae Latinitatis Lexicon Minus* (Leyden, 1954–), p. 177; and A. Blaise, *Dictionnaire latin–français des anciens chrétiens* (Strasbourg, 1954).

Romano-German *ordo*, in which the head, breast, shoulders, arms, and hands are anointed. Here, the text of the *Carmen* breaks off, and we have no description of William's crowning or investiture with sceptre and rod; yet, with but one important omission, the text of his coronation is complete, except for these last acts.

The royal oath was originally no more than a king's response to the promises of obedience and loyalty made by his subjects at the *recognitio*, and took the form of a *mandatum*, or charge to them to protect the church, put down evils, and show justice and mercy. The transformation of this charge into a pledge by the king himself that he will observe these three precepts comes only later, after political and cultural change has made it advisable that the sovereign, too, bind himself solemnly and publicly.[1]

William's coronation is not described in the *ASC*, but MS. D says Aldred made him promise and swear, before he would set the crown on his head, to rule the people as well as the best kings before him, if they would be loyal—clauses not included in the *ordines*.[2] By 1066, the tripartite oath, almost universal in Europe, was a normal and accepted part of the English coronation rite, too, and usually came early in the ceremony, immediately after the entry into the church and the prostration of the new king. Yet the implication of the *ASC* that William took the oath very late in the rite is supported by the *Carmen*, for Guy has not mentioned it up to the moment of William's anointing. And there are excellent reasons for thinking that the royal oath may have come at just that

---

[1] Cf. Schramm, op. cit., pp. 184–6.

[2] *ASC*, MS. D, 1066: 'Ða on midwintres dæg hine halgode to kynge Ealdred arceb. on Westmynstre · 7 he sealde him on hand mid Xp̄es béc · 7 eac swór · ærpan þe he wolde þa corona him on heafode settan · þ he wold þisne þeodscype swa wel haldan swa ænig kynge ætforan him betst dyde · gif hi him holde beon woldon.' It seems possible that the archbishop's mandate was due to an event which is not mentioned by Guy: according to the *GG* (p. 220), the Norman guards outside the abbey took alarm at the English shout of acclamation and began to fire houses. Orderic adds that there was panic in the church; the congregation rushed out, hearing an uproar, to quench the fire or to pillage; only the bishops and a few clergy and monks remained in trepidation before the altar and with difficulty completed the consecration of the quaking king (OV, iii. 184 (ii. 157)). These disturbances would certainly account for Aldred's addition to the oath and for William's willingness to swear. If the *Carmen* once recorded them, this might explain the sudden abbreviation of the coronation ritual in Guy of Amiens's poem. For the significant form of words exacted from William by Aldred cf. William of Malmesbury, *Gesta Pontificum* ii. 252: 'quod se (sc. Willelmum) modeste erga subjectos ageret, et aequo jure Anglos quo Francos tractaret.'

point: the mystic benefits conferred by anointing were greatly revered; it would therefore be most appropriate that William make his solemn pledge as the 'seven-fold gift of the Holy Spirit' descended upon him.[1] When the accounts of the *ASC* and Guy of Amiens are put together, it appears that William swore his oath as king immediately after unction, but before the crown itself was placed upon his head.

Guy of Amiens thus presents to his readers a coronation recognizably made up of elements drawn from both the Romano-German tradition of the Continent (which has affinities with earlier Frankish rites) and the English tradition, together with some common to both. The only novel addition is the Norman Christmas *laudes*, but these are not part of the coronation itself, though they later became so. While the royal oath and *recognitio* are out of their normal places and sequence, there were unique circumstances to justify both changes, and the first is not entirely without English precedent.

THE TRANSMISSION OF THE TEXT

The text of the *Carmen de Hastingae Proelio* is preserved in but one manuscript, Bibliothèque Royale de Belgique no. 10615–729, folios 227ᵛ–230ᵛ, written about the year 1100.[2] The first sixty-six lines of the poem were copied from this volume about thirty years later, and comprise the second column of folio 142ᵛ of another collection of texts, Bibliothèque Royale de Belgique no. 9799–809.[3] The earliest, and very brief, account of both books was given by J. Grimm and A. Schmeller in 1838;[4] G. H. Pertz, the discoverer of both manuscripts, printed a summary description of 10615–729 in 1839, thirteen years after they had come to light.[5] A detailed list

---

[1] The English had been subdued by force—and by chicane, according to Bishop Guy—and even later William's men ravaged (*ASC* MS. D). The most solemn moment possible for the oath must have seemed desirable.

[2] Professor Francis Wormald of London University, Mr. N. R. Ker of Oxford University, and Dr. R. Laufner, Direktor, Stadtbibliothek, Trier, have all independently dated the manuscript to *c.* 1100. Professor Wormald places the fragmentary copy at *c.* 1130, and Mr. Ker at that date or a little later. The opinions of these eminent palaeographers are confirmed by a comparison of the script of 10615–729 with that of two manuscripts from the same scriptorium, internally dated to 1125–6, the hands of which are similar to the fragmentary copy, and appreciably later than the script of its original.

[3] See below, p. lxi n. 1.

[4] *Lateinische Gedichte des X. und XI. Jahrhunderten* (Göttingen, 1838), pp. 276 ff.   [5] *Archiv*, pp. 1004–7.

of the contents of this volume, together with some remarks on its history, was published by Baron de Reiffenberg in 1841,[1] and again, with minor additions, in 1843.[2] The contents of both volumes are listed (inaccurately) in Marchal's *Inventaire*.[3] The origin, relationship, and later history of both these codices are also treated in various editions of other texts contained in them.

Each folio of 10615–729 is ruled for two columns of between seventy and seventy-two lines. The *Carmen* runs from line forty-nine of column two of folio 227ᵛ to line forty-three of column two of folio 230ᵛ. The parchment of the codicillus containing the *Carmen*[4] is fine and smooth, and the prickings regular, as though made by a wheel. Throughout the codicillus, as is the case with several others in the volume, the ink has faded to a pale reddish brown. The tiny late Carolingian minuscule script is illustrated in our frontispiece.

The codicillus in question begins at folio 224ʳ, with the caption, 'hunc modicum libellum Smaragdi . . .'; the text that follows it, however, is itself identified as 'cuiusdam Astiensis poete Nouus Auianus', being a series of fables that continues to line nineteen, column one of folio 227ᵛ, where it is interrupted (between the third hexameter and third pentameter of the fable *De Asino e Pelle Leonis Texto*) by the poem *Nulla salus aut pax tibi ueniat, gens tenebrosa*, followed by the 835 lines of the *Carmen*. After the *Carmen*, the remainder of column two of folio 230ᵛ contains the opening of Gellius' *Attic Nights*, xiv. 5. Folio 231ʳ begins with the third pentameter of *De Asino e Pelle Leonis Texto*, and is filled with the remaining text of the *Nouus Auianus*.[5]

The majority of the pieces in 9799–809 were copied from

---

[1] 'Notice d'un manuscrit de la Bibliothèque Royale', in *Bulletins de l'Académie Royale . . . de Bruxelles* viii (1841), pp. 247 ff.

[2] 'Manuscrit de Kues', in *Annuaire de la Bibliothèque Royale de Belgique* iv (1843), pp. 51 ff.

[3] F. J. F. Marchal, *Catalogue des manuscrits de la Bibliothèque Royale des Ducs de Bourgogne* i (*Inventaire*), Brussels, 1839, nos. 10615–729; 9799–809.

[4] The volume 10615–729 is made up of seventeen codicilli, written in several hands roughly contemporary with each other and with a strong resemblance. All are very small.

[5] An unbroken text of Astiensis survives in a Munich manuscript of the fourteenth century. See Édélestand du Méril, *Poésies inédites du Moyen Âge* (Paris, 1854), for a comparison of the texts. He shows that a leaf of the original from which the four works in our codicillus were copied must have either fallen out of place or been transposed in binding. The original order will have been: Astiensis, *Nulla salus aut pax*, *Carmen*, Gellius.

10615–729, and the fragment of the *Carmen* is no exception.[1] It occupies the entire second column of folio 142ᵛ. Folio 143, which has been pricked (irregularly), ends the gathering, which is in a coarser parchment than that of 10615–729. The hand is of the first half of the twelfth century, larger and more angular, and, it has been suggested to us, perhaps not the work of a trained copyist.

Both volumes belong to a group of manuscripts of common origin,[2] now known to have been written at St. Eucher-Matthias, Trier in the early to mid twelfth century.[3] All of this group of manuscripts came later into the possession of Cardinal Nicholas de Cusa, who bequeathed them in 1464 to the Hospital that he had founded at Kues. Their earliest remaining marks of ownership are those of the Hospital. Early in the seventeenth century they were removed, with other manuscripts, by the Bollandist redactors of the *Acta Sanctorum*, who transferred them to their then head-quarters at Antwerp. On the dissolution of the Society of Jesus in 1773, the majority of the Bollandist collection was removed to Brussels, where, after various vicissitudes, the manuscripts eventually became part of the Bibliothèque Royale de Belgique.

[1] 9799–809 consists of an eleventh-century copy of Isidore's *Origines*, a number of secular pieces in early twelfth-century hands, and a late twelfth-century text of Lactantius' *Contra gentes*. The Isidore, at least, was united with the rest of the volume only in the fifteenth century. The secular pieces are direct copies of those in 10615–729; they differ only in introducing some errors of their own. The copy of the first sixty-six lines of the *Carmen* contains no new mistakes, but faithfully reproduces those of its original, e.g. *morte* for *more* in v. 10. The correspondence of the texts in the two volumes seems to show that certain individual codicilli were copied in their entirety, intervening ones being omitted (this may be an indication that the codicilli were still separately bound at the time that the texts in 9799–809 were transcribed):

10671	9800	De annulo et baculo pontificis
10672	9801	Certamen regis cum papa
10673	9802	Gens Romanorum subdola
10715	9805	Ecbasis cuiusdam captiui
10716	9806	Enigmata Aldhelmi episcopi
10726	9807	Astiensis Nouus Auianus
10727	9808	Nulla salus aut pax
10728	(9808a)	Carmen de Hastingae proelio

9803 and 9804 are extracts from Martial not in 10615–729.

[2] See K. Manitius, 'Eine Gruppe von Handschriften des 12. Jahrhunderts aus dem Trier Kloster St. Eucharius-Matthias', in *Forschungen und Fortschritte* xxix (1955), pp. 317 ff.

[3] Conclusive evidence for their origin was first adduced by Horst Schlechte in *Erzbischof Bruno von Trier. Ein Beitrag zur Geschichte der geistigen Strömungen im Investiturstreit*, Inaugural Dissertation (Leipzig, 1934), pp. 74 f.

Although the text in 10615–729 is a copy of the *Carmen* made no more than thirty-five to forty years after its composition, it cannot have been copied from the autograph itself. An intermediate manuscript existed in which the poem was associated with the fables of Astiensis and the anti-papal poem, *Nulla salus aut pax*, for a leaf of the fables had got out of place in the original of our codicillus, and was copied after the end of the *Carmen*. This transposition allows one to conjecture the number of lines that each of the folios of the lost original contained. If the misplaced leaf of the fables was completely filled with writing,[1] each side of it will have held seventy lines, for the *recto* alone of folio 231 in 10615–729 holds 140 (the *verso* is blank).

Thus, the lost original will have contained the fables of Astiensis, *Nulla salus aut pax*, the *Carmen*, and perhaps more than one extract from Gellius. But even in this collection, the *Carmen* must have been already imperfect, for the scribe of our codicillus followed v. 835 of the poem with the opening line of *Attic Nights* xiv. 5. If the autograph consisted of a mere sheaf of vellum leaves, one or more of them may well have been lost or misplaced before it (or yet another intermediate copy) was transcribed into the lost original of our text.

There are several possibilities as to the provenance of this original. Saint-Eucher-Matthias and Saint-Jacques, Liège were in correspondence at the end of the eleventh century, and several of the texts copied into 10615–729 apparently came from Liège.[2] The *Carmen* may have been one of them. Another obvious possibility is Saint-Bavon, Ghent, from which Benedictines had been sent in the tenth century to refound Saint-Eucher-Matthias (burnt by the Normans). Saint-Bavon sent many manuscripts to Saint-Eucher-Matthias, and became for a time something of a mother house to it.[3] This possibility is enhanced by the fact that Thierry of Saint-Trond, several of whose works are represented in our volume, had fled to Saint-Bavon in 1088 and spent five years there.[4]

---

[1] An examination of manuscripts of this kind—miscellanies of secular literature—inclines us to think it unlikely that gaps were left in the original of our codicillus, any more than in the codicillus itself.

[2] Schlechte, op. cit., p. 75. J. Montebaur, *Studien zur Geschichte der Bibliothek der Abtei St. Eucharius-Matthias zu Trier* (Freiburg im Breisgau, 1931), p. 10.

[3] Montebaur, op. cit., pp. 10 f.

[4] J. Préaux, 'Thierry de Saint-Trond' (unpublished thesis, Université Libre de Bruxelles). We are most grateful to Professor Préaux for lending us the carbon

Saint-Bertin, at Saint-Omer, must also be considered as a source, if only because the *Encomium Emmae* and the *Vita Aedwardi* were apparently the works of monks of that house,[1] and a poem dealing with the acquisition of England by the new dynasty might well have been of interest to it. All three of these houses lie in what was then the county of Flanders—a county neighbouring Ponthieu, of whose comital house Guy of Amiens was a member; the county of Queen Mathilda, whose chaplain he was, however briefly.

The *Carmen* seems not to have had even a passing vogue. It is not pro-Norman, and the poet is often tactless, to say the least, in his references to William and his emphasis on the French role in the battle. Eustace of Boulogne, his second hero, was not reconciled with William until after William of Jumièges wrote, and that version of events established a Norman canon of the Conquest superseding the *Carmen*. We suggest that Guy may have deposited the poem, perhaps with other of his works, at the abbey of Saint-Riquier, of which he had been a distinguished scholar in his youth and to which he remained a generous patron as bishop of Amiens. The relations between Saint-Riquier and Saint-Jacques at Liège were close, and, as a great teaching abbey, Saint-Riquier had connections with all of the monasteries of Flanders. How Guy's poem might have come to be copied for one of them is not far to seek. In 1131, however, the library (and most of the abbey) was burnt by the count of Saint-Pol, and only Hariulf's chronicle and the 'Gospels of Charlemagne' were saved. If the autograph of the *Carmen* was among the manuscripts of Saint-Riquier, it has been lost since the early twelfth century.

On 3 November 1826, Georg Heinrich Pertz reached Brussels in the course of his search for materials for the *MGH*.[2] During a stay of three weeks, he unearthed both manuscripts of the *Carmen*, and, recognizing their importance, immediately wrote to Henry Petrie, who travelled to Brussels to copy them early in the next year.[3] Pertz's next stop was at Paris, where he met Augustin Thierry,[4] and apparently told him of his finds, for in the next (the

---

copy of the relevant portions of this thesis, and for the advice and encouragement that he has given us in conversation.

[1] *EE*, pp. xix f.; *VE*, pp. xliv–lix.   [2] *Archiv*, p. 2.
[3] Pertz, op. cit., loc. cit.; de Reiffenberg, *Bull. de l'Acad. Royale . . . de Bruxelles* viii (1841), p. 266; Petrie's expense sheet for March 1827–March 1828, in Minute Book of the Royal Commission on the Public Records, 1825–9, p. 278.
[4] G. H. Pertz, *Autobiography and Letters*, ed. L. Pertz (London, 1894?), p. 58.

third) edition of his *Norman Conquest*, Thierry printed vv. 681–752 of the poem, 'découvert dans la bibliothèque royale de Bruxelles par M. Pertz'.[1] Thierry had acquired a copy of the text from William Wickham, P.C., a member since 1806 of the Royal Commission on the Public Records, 1800–37.[2]

Besides Petrie's own transcription of the *Carmen*,[3] another had been made at Brussels for the Royal Commission,[4] but no trace survives at the Bibliothèque Royale of this copy, nor has the Public Record Office any knowledge of it, or of the facsimiles of the opening lines of both manuscripts that were reproduced at the head of the text in *Appendix C to a Report on Rymer's Foedera*.[5] The Royal Commission on the Public Records dissolved under something of a cloud; its documents were dispersed, and many are now lost.

The text of the *Appendix C* printing is, for the most part, that of Petrie, incorporating in the text itself the emendations suggested in the margins of the transcript and *MHB*. W. H. Black, the editor of *Appendix C*, differed but rarely from Petrie, and that only in emending (e.g. v. 544); the manuscript readings of both are identical, even to errors. We therefore think it likely that Black's text was entirely derived from that of *MHB*, which was in print by 1833,[6] and that the transcript sent to the Royal Commission by the Bibliothèque Royale is missing today from the Public Record Office because it was given by Wickham to Thierry. It is difficult to see where else Wickham could have got a copy. Further, it is noticeable that Michel's text of 1840 closely resembles that of Thierry's editions between 1830 and 1836. Is it possible that the transcript which Michel used—and which he found unsatisfactory[7]—was the one that Thierry had had from Wickham?

As the publication of Petrie's text in *MHB* was delayed until 1848, and *Appendix C* was, strictly speaking, never published, the first opportunity given scholars to examine the entire poem was in 1840, when Francisque Michel's edition appeared.[8] Michel says

---

[1] J. N. A. Thierry, *La Conquête de l'Angleterre par les Normands* (Paris, 1830), ii. 411 ff.

[2] Ibid. i. vi.

[3] Now apparently lost. That preserved at the Public Record Office is not in Petrie's hand, although he has made pencilled notes in it.

[4] De Reiffenberg, op. cit., loc. cit.   [5] Between p. 72 and p. 73.

[6] *Proceedings of the Commissioners on the Public Records, June 1832–August 1833*, p. 259. Cf. also Hardy, *Descriptive Catalogue* . . . i. 673.

[7] F. Michel, *CAN* iii. iv–v.   [8] Ibid. 1–38.

that, not satisfied with his transcript, he went himself to Brussels to collate it against the manuscript.[1] (He does not cite the fragment, and seems not to have known of its existence.) Either Michel found the tiny script hard to make out, or he scamped his task, for his manuscript readings are often wrong. His edition is further weakened by inconsistency in his attempt to retain the medieval spelling of the manuscript and by the deference that he paid to the extraordinary emendations suggested by Friedrich Duebner.[2] None the less, Michel's edition, while not in a class with Petrie's, is competent for its period and the haste with which it was prepared.

This cannot be said for the last edition of the poem to be prepared, that of J. A. Giles.[3] Giles had access to the then unpublished *MHB* text,[4] but, although he purported to have followed it,[5] his version is, in the main, that of Michel, even to reproducing Michel's errors of transcription and haphazard spellings, as well as some of Duebner's emendations. It is unfortunate that Giles's editions and translations of medieval texts are so often the easiest to come by. He was a slipshod scholar,[6] and his financial responsibilities forced him to publish far too much far too fast.

Since the posthumous appearance of *MHB*, the text of the *Carmen* has, by and large, received little attention. Brief quotations, either in Latin or in translation, occur in many histories of the Conquest, and these are, all too often, derived from Giles's edition. An exception to this rule was the translation of about half the poem (from William's sailing to the death of Harold) by Charles Dawson,[7] who used the *MHB* text as one of his sources in an elaborate set of parallel texts of the chief accounts of the battle of Hastings, an

---

[1] Ibid. iv f. Michel corresponded with the Commission Royale d'Histoire at Brussels (cf. their *Bulletins*, series i, *passim*), and visited Brussels at least once during this period (*Bulletins*, ser. i, vol. i (1837–40), p. 252).

[2] Friedrich Duebner (1802–67), an editor of classical texts in Paris, upon whom Michel relied heavily for textual criticism. [3] *Scriptores*, pp. 27–51.

[4] Cf. Hardy's preface to *MHB*, p. 49 n. 1 (referring to the chapter of *MHB* on classical descriptions of Britain): 'This portion of the work has been reprinted in two different publications by Dr. Giles, who had obtained the loan of a printed copy of Mr. Petrie's work from the Government, "for the common purposes of reference, on his pledging himself to show it to no one". Dr. Giles has nevertheless copied and without acknowledgement printed and published as his own the whole of Mr. Petrie's collection, even to the adoption of typographical errors.'

[5] Giles, *Scriptores*, p. xi.

[6] Cf. the comments of W. de Gray Birch, *Vita Haroldi* (London, 1885), pp. xiii f.

[7] *Hastings Castle* (London, 1909), ii. 565 ff.

admirable concept. His translation of these was uneven, but the work is worthy of attention, if only because he is the sole historian to have attempted it.[1]

THE LITERARY MODELS AND LANGUAGE OF THE *CARMEN*

The place of the *Carmen* in the literature of its time, which has received little attention,[2] unfortunately lies without the scope of this edition. We confine ourselves here to certain brief observations on the literary sources and the language and style of the poem. It has, of course, no sources in the literal sense of the word, except for what eyewitness accounts of the campaign Guy of Amiens received. Its direct literary models were not the epics of the classical period, which celebrated the deeds of mythical heroes or at best men of a past century, but the compositions of Carolingian poets written in praise of a living sovereign, from whom tangible favour might be hoped.

We have not thought it practicable to examine the *Carmen* closely for classical echoes. In northern Europe, the wholesale destruction of libraries and disruption of the monastic schools by the Norman incursions of the tenth century had reduced the state of learning almost to what it had been before the Carolingian renaissance.[3] When monastic libraries began to be reassembled or refounded, emphasis was placed primarily on liturgical, patristic, and grammatical works, and apart from quotations in such writers as

---

[1] As early descriptions and editions of the *Carmen* cite the manuscripts by varying numbers, some clarification of these seems in order:

	A	B
Shelfmarks of Jesuits at Antwerp	120*a*	105
Shelfmarks of Bibliothèque de Bourgogne (*a.* 1794–*c.* 1840)	8742–58	7925–?30
Numbers in the list of MSS. returned to Brussels from Paris in 1816 (looted in 1794)	629	330
Present shelfmarks	10615–729	9799–809

[2] E. R. Curtius, *Europäische Literatur und Lateinische Mittelalter* (Berne, 1954), pp. 171, 182, 431; L. J. Engels, op. cit., who gives the fullest available list of works placing the *Carmen* in its literary setting.

[3] e.g. Saint-Valery (which had to be refounded and rebuilt in the 970s); Saint-Riquier (whose library was hastily dispersed, some books never returning); and Saint-Eucher, Trier (which lost its entire collection).

Donatus and Priscian, such literature as was admitted was almost wholly late and Christian. Manitius's list of the works known to have been held by the libraries of the ninth to eleventh centuries[1] reveals a dearth of classical texts in northern France; more, many catalogues (such as that made at Saint-Riquier in 831) antedate the Norman raids. The true state was probably even worse than his list indicates.[2]

Even in its ninth-century heyday, Saint-Riquier possessed of the classical authors only Cicero, Virgil, Pliny the Elder, and Suetonius. Later writers were better represented, e.g. Cassiodorus, Boëthius, Arator, Fortunatus, Avianus, and the Trojan epics of Dictys Cretensis and Dares Phrygius. There was also a collection remarkably full for this period of the histories of Germanic peoples and their conquests: Jordanes, Gregory of Tours, Julian of Toledo, Paul the Deacon, and Bede. Priscian and Donatus were included; so must have been the *Flores poetarum* compiled late in the ninth century by the monk Micon, the most celebrated poet of the abbey.

We know that some at least of the books listed in 831 did not return to Saint-Riquier after their dispersal, e.g. Fortunatus, of whom they recovered but half. Both Abbot Enguerrand, under whom Guy studied, and his successor Gervin were austere men, and neither is likely to have added to the collection of pagan texts. Hence, apparent echoes of classical authors, such as that at v. 135 of the opening line of the *Pharsalia*, probably do not derive from a familiarity with the authors themselves.

On the other hand, Guy seems to have read and reread the Carolingian panegyrists Theodulfus of Orléans and Ermoldus Nigellus. Like them, he wrote to flatter a ruler to a purpose— in his case perhaps the reconciliation of William with Eustace of Boulogne—and he shows great familiarity with the work of Ermoldus, in particular.[3] The poem of Ermoldus on the deeds of

---

[1] M. Manitius, *Handschriften Antiker Autoren in mittelalterlichen Bibliotekskatalogen* (Leipzig, 1935). Manitius's list is far from complete, but it is representative, and to that extent valid evidence.

[2] The only classical authors found widely are Cicero, Virgil, and Terence (*Andria*). Ovid became increasingly popular in the course of the eleventh century. For apparent classical echoes in the *Carmen* see Engels, op. cit., notes 28–32.

[3] Ermoldus Nigellus, *De Gestis Ludovici Caesaris*, MGH PLAC, ii. 5. Ermoldus wrote *c.* 827, in an attempt to regain favour with the Emperor Louis. His work and the poems of Theodulfus, written a little earlier, are not listed in the Saint-Riquier catalogue of 831, and were evidently acquired later.

Louis the Pious contains an account of two great wars, in Spain and in Brittany, and the second of these forms a striking parallel to what Guy knew of the Norman Conquest: Murman of Brittany, we are told by Ermoldus, had acknowledged the emperor as his suzerain and sworn him homage, but had then set himself up as an independent monarch. Messengers were sent to parley with him, and finally a battle was fought in which he was defeated. It seems clear that this poem was running through Guy's mind as he wrote his own; a few examples of Guy's indebtedness to it may be of interest:

Carmen, v. 78	Protinus una fuit mens omnibus, ẹqua uoluntas
Ermoldus, ii. 135	Unus amor cunctis erat, omnibus una voluntas
Carmen, v. 90	Hinc resonando tubẹ uarios dant mille boatus
Ermoldus, iv. 435	Mox tuba Theutonis clare dat rite boatus
Carmen, v. 156	Rex redit a bello premia lẹta ferens
Ermoldus, i. 544	Bigo . . . aulam
	Primus adest Caroli, nuntia laeta ferens
Carmen, v. 168	Quamuis hec timeat, uelle tamen simulat
Ermoldus, iii. 104	Spem simulat vultu, contegit atque metum
Carmen vv. 97, 191	Diuersis feriunt uocibus astra poli . . .
	Nascitur extimplo clamor qui perculit astra
Ermoldus, i. 279	It fragor ad coelum, resonat clangoribus aether
Carmen, vv. 239–40	'Nescit que furtiua mihi periuria fecit,
	Nec penitus recolit quod meus ipse fuit?'
vv. 297–8	'Est igitur seruanda fides, iurata teneri,
	Nexibus atque sacris dextera stricta manus.'
Ermoldus, iii. 313–4	'Non memorat jurata fides, seu dextera Francis
	Saepe data, et Carolo servitia exhibita?'
Carmen, vv. 270–2	Contra quem misit . . .
	Reddere legatum pro uerbis uerba paratum
	Illi mitamus . . .
Ermoldus, i. 401	Reddidit e contra verbis contraria verba
Carmen, v. 541	Ast alii plures? Aliis sunt hi meliores.
Ermoldus, iv. 366	Ast alios plures turba levavit aquis . . .
Carmen, v. 622	Flexis poplitibus, oscula dant pedibus
Ermoldus, i. 138	Poplite flexato, lambitat ore pedes
Carmen, v. 733	Set Dominum testor, cui rerum seruit imago
Ermoldus, iv. 157	Culturamque Dei, cui servit cuncta potestas

Ermoldus Nigellus was an early exponent of a style of writing which Lair, the editor of Dudo of Saint-Quentin, described as 'l'école pittoresque',[1] and to which not only Dudo himself belonged (in Lair's estimation), but also Adalbero, bishop of Laon, to whom Dudo dedicated his chronicle in words similar to those Guy used of Lanfranc.[2] The 'Carmen ad Rotbertum Regem', Adalbero's most famous work in this genre, seems to have been known to Guy, for the rare words *quirites* (in the meaning 'knights') and *spirare* (in the meaning 'to live without care') occur in both poems.[3] Thus, in his literary heritage, Guy but exemplified the tendency of his time.

In the same way, there is little remarkable about his Latin, even to his somewhat precious liking for uncommon words[4] and aggregations of honorifics.[5] To what extent Latin was at this period (or during the whole of the Middle Ages) a language separate from classical Latin has been much debated, as has the relationship between the two.[6] Guy's Latin shows clearly, however, those traits usually thought of as 'medieval': a preference for periphrastic constructions, an irregular sequence of tenses,[7] and the breakdown of the distinctions between *suus* and *eius* and among *hic, ille, is, iste,* and *ipse.* While *ut* is occasionally used to introduce a subordinate clause, it is almost always one after a verb of command or speech (an exception occurs at v. 659); elsewhere, its place is

---

[1] Dudo, p. 24.

[2] 'quem genus ornat, sapientia decorat.'

[3] Cf. the notes to vv. 309 and 633.

[4] e.g., besides those cited above, *milicies, aggerie, Hectorides,* etc.

[5] e.g. vv. 26 ff. and 307 ff. Such aggregations are not unknown (though less copious) in classical Latin (e.g. Statius, *Theb.* 1. 22; 5. 125; 5. 610), and are popular in Carolingian panegyrics. Cf. Theodulfus of Orléans:

> O regina potens, o magni gloria regis,
> O populi, o cleri luxque decusque vigens . . .
> (*Carmen* xxxi. 1–2, *MGH PLAC* i. 552)

and Ermoldus, i. 139:

> O lux Francorum, rex et pater, arma decusque.

With v. 27, in particular, cf. Theodulfus of Orléans, *Carmen* xxxii. 1 (op. cit., p. 523):

> Rex benedicte, vale, valens, per tempora longa.

[6] For an excellent summary of the views, see Christine Mohrmann, 'Le dualisme de la latinité médiévale', in *Revue des études latines* xxix (1951), 330–48.

[7] His tenses are confused at vv. 41–7, 53–62, 70–3, 104–9, 135–8, 187, 191–2, 230, 233–4, 247–8, 285–6, 335–6, 341–2, 357–8, 363–8, 375–6, 377–8, 425, 435–6, 445, 449–50, 462, 475, 477–8, 501–2, 503–5, 522, 531–3, 533–6, 541, 553–4, 561–2, 563–6, 567–8, 573–4, 578, 587–90, 594–6, 598, 599–600, 625, 631–4, 646–8, 653, 655–60, 669–70, 681–4, 719, 725–6, 727–8, 747–50, 759–60, 822–4, 827–9, 833. In vv. 205–6, his mood changes inexplicably, too.

taken by *quod*. Relative and demonstrative pronouns often fall late in their clauses (see note to v. 256).

Guy's prosody, as well as his language, shows characteristics common to medieval Latin verse: systole, especially of the ablative final *o*; irregular lengthening of the final ablative *e*; avoidance of elision and but rare examples (vv. 434, 610) of hiatus. He practises caesura rhyme irregularly, but frequently, and, although he apparently tried to avoid using the leonines so popular in the tenth and eleventh centuries, he did not always succeed (cf. v. 436).[1]

His spelling of English names is remarkably accurate for a continental writer of this period. Guy had been the protégé of Fulk II, bishop of Amiens, the son of Godgifu of England, and was the friend, if no more, of Eustace II of Boulogne, once Godgifu's husband. Although the (*h*)*w* of Old English, initial or medial, troubled him, so that Winchester became *G*uincestra and Edwardus Et*g*uardus, other names are recognizably rendered, even to Gyrth (Gernt, perhaps originally Gerht).

The *Carmen* bears every sign of having been written in haste, as indeed it was, if, as we think, it was composed for the Easter celebrations after William's return in 1067. Here and there, a word necessary to the sense or grammar is omitted (e.g. v. 730), and twice the subject changes abruptly without a new noun or pronoun to indicate this (vv. 335, 476). It is, however, clear that Guy was practised in writing Latin verse, that he had considerable narrative skill, and that he knew well how to veil awkward events in fine rhetoric.[2]

Like the poem itself, the text as we have it is typical of its period. The forms and abbreviations of the manuscript are standard: *ę* for *æ* and *œ* (although rarely simple *e* is used); *ij* and *ijs* for final *ii* and *iis*; superscript *a*, *i*, and *o* for *ra*, *ri*, *ro* or *ua*, *ui*, and *uo*; the Tironian signs *7* and *?* for *et* and *con-*. The earlier editors were, however, misled by the use of the general mark of abbreviation (-) for final *-unt* (as well as for *-is*, *-it*, *ut*), which occurs in vv. 216, 381, 540, 616, 619, 621, 634, 672, and 746. They all failed to interpret the first two occurrences correctly. As in the *Epistulae* of Fulco of Beauvais, single consonants have occasionally been

---

[1] All of these characteristics are paralleled in the almost contemporary *Epistulae* of Fulco of Beauvais (written *c.* 1070–80). See M. L. Colker, 'Fulcoii Belvacensis Epistulae' in *Traditio* x (1954), pp. 205 f.

[2] See above, pp. xxxvi ff.

written for double ones (cf. *mititur*, v. 197 with *mittatur*, v. 272). There is no serious corruption of the text; errors are simple and obvious ones, often made (and corrected) by the scribe of our manuscript himself. A common fault is the omission of final *s* (e.g. *plani*, v. 321; *Mar*, v. 362; *gladio*, v. 416). *Tibi* is occasionally written for *sibi* (vv. 220, 494, 628). *r* and *t* resemble each other in this hand: *t* is written for *r* at vv. 99 and 214; *r* for *t* at v. 366 (*asperitate*); and a form intermediate between the two at v. 628 (*re*). There is rarely a confusion between *f* and long *s* (e.g. vv. 279, 827). In words such as *nihil/nichil*, the *c* is omitted, more often than not (vv. 382, 510, 530, but *ch* at vv. 148 and 440). We have therefore transcribed the abbreviation *m̊* as *mihi*, not *michi*. Apart from obvious errors, the manuscript spelling has been retained, with the addition of modern capitalization and punctuation.

The punctuation in the manuscript itself is a debased version of the classical form described by Donatus,[1] consisting chiefly of a raised dot at the end of each line. This is occasionally replaced by a semicolon, and these semicolons are often (but not invariably) followed by a larger initial letter than is usual at the beginning of the next line. Although such a sign was used at this period to show a lowering of voice pitch,[2] in the manuscript volume 10615–729 and its fellows the semicolons occur irregularly, and appear to have no particular significance. They do not mark 'paragraphs', and, although they are frequently found at the beginning or end of speeches, they occur elsewhere—nor are all speeches so marked. Very rarely, a raised dot occurs in the middle of a line (e.g. v. 817, after *peroratur*), but the sense of these lines militates against a pause having been intended.

---

[1] R. W. Southern has made an excellent summary of the medieval punctuation of this period in his *The Life of Saint Anselm by Eadmer* (London, 1963), pp. xxviii–xxxiii.

[2] Ibid., p. xxxiii.

ABBREVIATED REFERENCES

Appendix C   Royal Commission on the Public Records, 1800–37, *Appendix C to a Report on Rymer's 'Foedera'*, London, printed before 1837, but never published.

Archiv   *Archiv der Gesellschaft für ältere deutsche Geschichtskunde* vii, Berlin, 1839.

ASC   *The Anglo-Saxon Chronicle*, ed. B. Thorpe (*RS* xxiii), London, 1861.[1]

BB   Baudri of Bourgueil, *Carmen* cxcvi, ed. P. Abrahams, Paris, 1926.

Bouquet   *Recueil des historiens des Gaules et de la France*, ed. M. Bouquet *et al.*, Paris, 1738–1904.

Brunel   Brunel, Clovis, *Recueil des actes des comtes de Pontieu*, Paris, 1930.

BT   *The Bayeux Tapestry*, ed. Sir Frank Stenton *et al.*, New York and London, Phaidon Press, 1957 (2nd edn. 1965).

CAN   *Chroniques anglo-normandes*, ed. F. Michel, Rouen, 1836–40.

CIL   *Corpus Inscriptionum Latinarum*, Berlin, 1863– .

Dudo   Dudo of Saint-Quentin, *De moribus et actis primorum Normanniae ducum*, ed. J. Lair, Caen, 1865.

Eadm.   Eadmer, *Historia Novorum in Anglia*, ed. M. Rule (*RS* lxxxi), London, 1884.[2]

EE   *Encomium Emmae Reginae*, ed. A. Campbell, London, 1949 (Camden Third Series lxxii).

EHD   *English Historical Documents*, ed. D. C. Douglas *et al.*, London, 1953– (in progress).

EHR   *English Historical Review.*

Ermoldus   Ermoldus Nigellus, *De gestis Ludovici Caesaris*, in *MGH PLAC* ii.

Flores Hist.   The *Flores Historiarum* of 'Matthew of Westminster' i, ed. H. R. Luard (*RS* xcv), London, 1890.

---

[1] The only edition giving all the versions. Readers may prefer, as more accessible, *Two of the Saxon Chronicles Parallel*, ed. by C. Plummer on the basis of an edition by J. Earle (Oxford, i, 1892, ii, 1899, reprinted 1952). This edition gives a complete text of only two versions, A and E. The most recent translation is that edited by Professor Dorothy Whitelock with Professor David C. Douglas and Miss Susie I. Tucker: *The Anglo-Saxon Chronicle*, London, Eyre & Spottiswoode, 1961.

[2] The text has been translated recently by Geoffrey Bosanquet, *Eadmer's History of Recent Events in England*, London, Cresset Press, 1964.

FW — 'Florence' of Worcester, *Chronicon ex chronicis*, ed. B. Thorpe, London, 1848–9.

GG — William of Poitiers, *Gesta Guillelmi*, ed. R. Foreville (*Histoire de Guillaume le Conquérant. Les classiques de l'histoire de France au Moyen Âge* xxiii), Paris, 1952.

Giles, *Scriptores* — J. A. Giles, *Scriptores rerum gestarum Willelmi Conquestoris* (Caxton Soc. publ. no. 3), London, 1845.

GND — William of Jumièges, *Gesta Normannorum ducum*, ed. J. Marx, Rouen, 1914.

GR — William of Malmesbury, *De gestis regum Anglorum*, ed. W. Stubbs (*RS* xc), London, 1887.

Hariulf — Hariulf, *Chronicon Centulense*, ed. F. Lot (*Chronique de l'Abbaye de Saint-Riquier*), Paris, 1894.

Heimskr. — Snorri Sturluson, *Heimskringla*, London, 1964 (Everyman no. 847), transl. S. Laing, ed. P. Foote.

JEH — *Journal of Ecclesiastical History*.

Latham — R. E. Latham, *Revised Medieval Latin Word-List*, London, 1964.

Lewis and Short — *A Latin Dictionary*, ed. C. T. Lewis and C. Short, Oxford, 1966.

MGH — *Monumenta Germaniae Historica*:
AA — *Auctores Antiquissimi*
PLAC — *Poetae Latini Aevi Carolini*
SS — *Scriptores*
SSRG — *Scriptores Rerum Germanicarum*
SSRM — *Scriptores Rerum Merovingicarum*.

MHB — *Monumenta Historica Britannica*, ed. H. Petrie and W. Sharpe, London, 1848 (in print in 1833).

Muratori — *Scriptores Rerum Italicarum*, ed. A. Muratori.

NC — Freeman, E. A., *The Norman Conquest*, Oxford, 1867–86.

NG — *Novum Glossarium Mediae Latinitatis . . . usque ad annum MCC*, ed. Franz Blatt, Copenhagen, 1958– (in progress).

OV — Orderic Vitalis, *Historia ecclesiastica*, ii, ed. M. Chibnall (*The Ecclesiastical History*), Oxford, 1969 (references also given to A. Le Prévost and L. Delisle's edition, 5 vols., Paris, 1838–55).

P.L. — Migne, J. P., *Patrologiae cursus completus. Series Latina*, Paris, 1844–64.

RR — Wace, *Roman de Rou*, ed. H. Andresen, Heilbronn, 1877.

RS — *Chronicles and Memorials of Great Britain and Ireland during the Middle Ages*, London, 1858–96 (the *Rolls Series*).

SRD — *Scriptores Rerum Danicarum*, ed. J. Langebek, Copenhagen, 1772–1878.

VE — *Vita Aedwardi Regis*, ed. F. Barlow, Nelson's Medieval Texts, London, 1962.

ABBREVIATIONS USED IN THE TEXTUAL NOTES

A   MS. Bibliothèque Royale de Belgique 10615–729, fols. 227ᵛ–230ᵛ.

B   MS. Bibliothèque Royale de Belgique 9799–809, fol. 142ᵛ.

P. Petrie, Henry, *De Bello Hastingensi Carmen, Auctore W.* In his *Monumenta Historica Britannica*, pp. 856–72. Printed before 1833, but published only posthumously, by Thomas Duffus Hardy (London, 1848). *Editio princeps.*

C. [Black, William Henry]. *De Bello Normannico seu de Conquisitione Angliae per Guillelmum Ducem Normanniae, Carmen Elegiacum.* A more finished version of Petrie's text. Printed before 1837 in *Appendix C to a Report on Rymer's 'Foedera'*, pp. 73–86, by Charles Purton Cooper, Secretary to the Royal Commission on the Public Records, 1800–37. Distributed, with the other Appendices, to certain libraries of the United Kingdom in 1869, but never published.

M. Michel, Francisque Xavier. *Widonis Carmen de Hastingae Proelio*, in his *Chroniques Anglo-Normandes*, t. i, pp. 1–38 (Rouen, 1840).

G. Giles, John Allen. *Widonis Carmen de Hastingae Proelio*, in his *Scriptores Rerum Gestarum Willelmi Conquestoris*, pp. 27–51 (London, 1845).

T. Thierry, J. N. A. *Histoire de la Conquête de l'Angleterre par les Normands*, 3ᵉ édition (Paris, 1830), ii. 411 ff. Lines 681 to 752 of the poem, wrongly numbered, are printed under the heading 'Extrait d'un poëme latin découvert dans la Bibliothèque royale de Bruxelles par M. Pertz, archiviste de S.M.B. au royaume de Hanovre'. Except for lines 751–2, this text remains unchanged in three subsequent editions of Thierry's book.

T2. Ibid. Seventh (1846) and later editions, in which Thierry altered his text considerably.

THE CARMEN
DE HASTINGAE PROELIO

CARMEN
DE HASTINGAE PROELIO

PROOEMIUM

Quem probitas celebrat, sapientia munit et ornat,
Erigit et decorat, L⟨anfrancum⟩ W⟨ido⟩[1] salutat.
Cum studiis clarus uidearis lucifer ortus
Et tenebras pellis radiis dum lumina spargis,
Per mare nec fragilis set sis tutissima nauis.   5
Te precor ad portum carmen deducere nostrum;
Inuidię uentis[a] agitari nec paciaris,
Nec Boreę flatum timeat, set litus amęnum
Remige te carpat, ne lęsum rupe labescat.
Sis iudex illi iustus, de more magistri[b]   10
Quod minus est addens et quod super, obsecro,[c] radens.
Nullus, credo, sibi sub te tutore nocebit;
Sic tuus incipiat fieri meus iste libellus,
Vt careat uiciis et laudibus amplificetur.
Euitare uolens dispendia desidiose   15
Mentis et ingenii, placeant cum carmina multis,[2]
Carminibus studui Normannica bella reponi.
Elegi potius leuibus cantare camęnis
Ingenium mentis uanis quam subdere curis.
Cum sit et egregium describere gesta potentum,   20
Finibus occiduis quę gessit regia proles
Willelmus, titulis commisi posteritatis;
Nam sibi sublatum[3] regnum uirtute redemit
Et uictor patrios extendit trans mare fines:
Ergo decet memorare suum per secula factum.   25

[a] m̅tis, A, B; ventis *edd.*   [b] iust⁹ de morte A, B; justus, de *morte (n.*
'more?') *P.*; justus, de morte *C.*; justa de morte Magistri *M., G.*   [c] obsecᵃ
A; obsecro B. A's *writing is quite unlike its usual 'a' superscript and is probably
a misformed 'o' superscript (for 'ro')*

---

[1] On 'L. W.', see pp. xxv f. above.
[2] Guy of Amiens would have had every opportunity to hear the Saint-Riquier
version ('ceo dit la geste a Saint Richier') of the song celebrating the victory of

THE SONG OF
THE BATTLE OF HASTINGS

PROEM

G(uy) salutes *L*(anfranc),[1] whom virtue honours, whom wisdom
strengthens and adorns, exalts and graces.

Since, illustrious in studies, you seem the Morning Star arisen,
and banish darkness as you shed light with your beams, so on the
deep may you be no fragile vessel but most seaworthy. Bring our
song to haven, I implore you; neither suffer it to be tossed by the
winds of envy nor may it fear the blast of the north wind, but with
you as oarsman gain a pleasant shore, not founder broken on a
rock. Be to this poem an impartial critic; adding in the manner of
a master what is lacking and, I entreat, erasing what is excessive.
No one, I believe, will harm himself under your tutelage, so let
this my little work begin to become yours, that it may be free from
errors and enhanced by merits.

Idly wishing to avoid undue taxing of intellect and talent, I have
applied myself—since songs please the multitude[2]—to putting
the Norman campaign into verse. I have preferred to sing in light
measures rather than to constrain the bent of my mind to profitless
toil and, as it is admirable to describe the deeds of mighty men,
I have put together for the records of posterity what William, scion
of a royal line, accomplished at the furthest confines of the west;
for he recovered by valour a kingdom taken from[3] him and, a
conqueror, extended his ancestral realms beyond the sea. Therefore it is right to preserve the memory of his achievement throughout the ages.

Louis III over the Normans at Saucourt in 881, a song still popular in the time
of Hariulf (*Chronicon Centulense* iii. 20, p. 141). Although its language was no
longer the old Frankish of the ninth century and its historical matter, reworked
out of all recognition, it remained, none the less, a lively witness to the popularity
of verse. Cf. R. Heiligbrodt, 'Fragment de Gormund et Isembard' in E. Böhmer's
Romanische Studien iii (Strasbourg, 1878), pp. 501–96.

[3] The context demands that *sublatum* be understood as the p.p.p. of *tollo*,
not *suffero*.

CARMEN

Iusticię cultor, patrię pax, hostibus hostis,
Tutor et ęcclesię, rex benedicte, uale![1]
A modo torpentes decet euigilare Camenas
Et calamos alacres reddere laude tua.
Mutasti comitis regali nomine nomen   30
Quod tibi nobilitas contulit et probitas;
Iulius alter,[2] enim, cuius renouando triumphum
Effrenem gentem cogis amare iugum.
Innumerus terrę populus, nec perfida nautis
Ęquora, nec litus saxa nociua ferens,   35
Incumbens hẏemis nec te deterruit horror,
Quin ab auis peteres regna relicta tibi.
Posteritate fauet tibi ius, legis quoque summa;
Ergo tibi terror omnis ademptus erat.
Tempore set longo te trans freta ducere classes   40
Tempestas prohibet, imber et assiduus,
Dum prestolaris uentorum prosperitatem
Et mare turbatum cogit abire retro,
Eurus et equoreas crispabat flatibus undas.
Tunc tibi planctus erat spesque negata uię;   45
Tuque, uelis nolis,[a] tandem tua litora linquens,
Nauigium[3] uertis litus ad alterius.
Portus ab antiquis Vimaci[4] fertur haberi;
Quę uallat portum Somana nomen aquę.
Docta nimis bello, gens est per cuncta fidele   50
Fluctiuagis prebens sepius hospicium.

---

[a] nolis *superscript* A

---

[1] Such aggregations of honorifics are not unknown in classical Latin (e.g.
Statius, *Theb.* 1. 22; 5. 125; 5. 610), and are popular with Frankish eulogists. Cf.
above, p. lxix n. 5, for parallels, and also BB, v. 394, where William says this of
himself:

> Hostibus hostis ero; pax, mea terra, tibi!

[2] William is again compared to Caesar at vv. 350–3, where Caesar is again
identified as *Iulius*. Guy's Carolingian models used *Caesar* as an imperial title
after the later Roman manner, and he would have hesitated to confer it on a
mere duke. William of Poitiers, classically trained, does not hesitate even to
portray William as Caesar's better.

[3] *Nauigium*, 'fleet'. Cf. *NG*, p. 1121, *navigium*, 2.

[4] Guy is the only early writer to identify Saint-Valery as lying in Vimeu, that
part of Ponthieu between the Somme and the Bresle. Vimeu, which disappeared
as a separate county in the twelfth century, was at this time ruled by Bernard II,

THE SONG

Hail, blessed king, supporter of justice, peace of the homeland, a foe to foemen, and protector of the church![1] From this time it is right to arouse the slothful Muses and let pens be swift to write your praise. You have changed the name of count for the royal style which birth and merit have conferred upon you; another Caesar,[2] indeed, in renewing whose triumphs you force a headstrong race to love the yoke.

Not the countless inhabitants of the country, nor a sea treacherous to voyagers, nor a shore fraught with punishing rocks, nor yet the threatening approach of winter, deterred you from seeking the realms left to you by your forefathers. Justice and the whole of law supported you before posterity; therefore, for you all fear was gone.

But for a long time foul weather and ceaseless rain prevented you from leading the fleet across the Channel, while you awaited the favour of the winds; and the troubled sea forced you to put back, and gusts of the east wind curled the ocean waves. Then you lamented, and the hope of passage was denied; and, at last, leaving your own shores willy-nilly, you directed the fleet[3] to the coast of a neighbour.

The port of Vimeu[4] is said to have been known by the ancients; the river which encompasses the port is called the Somme. Most

lord of Saint-Valery, related to both the comital house of Ponthieu and the ducal house of Normandy. The accuracy of the description of Saint-Valery given in vv. 48–52 shows close knowledge of Vimeu: the Romans used a port located near by, at least from the fifth century, and Roman remains have been found (H. Dusevel and P.-A. Scribe, *Description historique et pittoresque du Département de la Somme* i (Amiens/Paris, 1836), pp. 46–8). We have already remarked on the description of the estuary (above, p. xxv). The *castrum . . . sancti Walarici*, founded under King Dagobert, stands on the cliffs above, and was at the time that Guy wrote protected by fortifications set up in the last century (see Benedict VII, Bull of 1 April 981, in *P.L.* cxxxvii, col. 338; he praises Hugh Capet for strengthening and re-endowing the abbey).

In vv. 50–1, Guy is apparently defending Vimeu against the charge, unspoken here, that its people were wreckers. Vimeu, like Ponthieu and Normandy (see C. H. Haskins, *Norman Institutions* (London, 1960), p. 39), held the right of *lagan*, holding or asking ransom for ships, chattels, and persons driven on to its shores, a right granted Vimeu in the first instance by Charlemagne. Undoubtedly, in any maritime province with this privilege, wrecking went on from time to time. There is no reason to think that Vimeu was particularly prone to it, despite the allegations in the *GG*, p. 102.

Desuper est castrum quoddam Sancti Walarici;
Hic tibi longa fuit difficilisque mora,
Nam ter¹ quinque dies complesti finibus illis,
Exspectans summi iudicis auxilium.   55
Ęcclesiam sancti deuota mente frequentans,
Illi pura² dabas, ingeminando preces.
Inspicis et templi gallus qua uertitur aura:
Auster si spirat, lętus abinde redis;
Si subito Boreas Austrum diuertit et arcet,   60
Effusis lacrimis fletibus ora rigas.
Desolatus eras; frigus faciebat et imber
Et polus obtectus nubibus et pluuiis.
Set pater omnipotens, in quo tibi spem posuisti,
Tempora qui fecit, temperat, atque regit—   65
Qui palmo cęlum, terram, mare ponderat ęque;ᵃ
Cui proprium constat omnibus esse locis
Presentem; precibus dedit et calcabile Petro
Equor sub pedibus, compaciendo sibi—
Velle tuum tandem pius ut Deus est miseratus,   70
Pro uotoque tibi suppeditauit opus:
Expulit a cęlo nubes et ab equore uentos,
Frigora dissoluit, purgat et imbre polum.
Incaluit tellus, nimio perfusa calore,
Et Phebus solito clarior emicuit.   75
Festa dies Michaëlis erat celebranda³ per orbem,
Cum pro uelle tibi cuncta Deus tribuit.
Protinus una fuit mens omnibus, ęqua uoluntas,
Iam bene pacato credere se pelago.
Quamquam diuersi tamen adsunt letificati;   80
Nec mora; quisque suum currit ad officium.
Sublimant alii malos; aliique laborant
Erectis malis addere uela super.
Plurima cogit equos equitum pars scandere naues;
Altera festinat arma locare sua.   85
Haut secus inuadit classis loca turba pedestris
Turba columbarum quam sua tecta petit.

ᵃ *The fragment B ends with this line*

---

¹ *Ter quinque dies*, i.e. a fortnight. The same phrase occurs below at v. 597,
where the edd. have misread it. Cf. the note there.

skilled in war, the people often show all manner of true hospitality to seafarers. Above this harbour there stands a certain stronghold of Saint-Valery.

Here you had a long and difficult delay, for you spent fully fifteen days[1] in those parts, awaiting the help of the Supreme Judge. Frequenting the church of the saint with devout purpose, you offered him free alms,[2] redoubling your supplications. You looked to see by what wind the weathercock of the church was turned. If the south wind blew, at once you returned thence joyful; if suddenly the north wind diverted and held off the south, lamenting, you bedewed your face with welling tears. You were in despair; it was cold and wet, and the sky hidden by clouds and rain.

But the Almighty Father, in whom you placed your hope, who makes the seasons, tempers and controls them, who weighs equally in his hand heaven, land, and sea, whose nature it is to be present in all places—he who granted Peter for his prayers, having compassion on him, a still sea for his feet to tread—the Gracious God at last pitied your intention, and gave you all the means for your sworn endeavour. He drove the clouds from the sky and the winds from the sea, dispelled the cold and rid the heavens of rain. The earth grew warm, pervaded by great heat, and the sun shone forth with unwonted brilliance. The feast of Michael was about to be celebrated[3] throughout the world when God granted everything according to your desire.

Immediately all had one aim, a single purpose: to trust themselves to the sea, quite calmed at last. Although scattered, they arrived rejoicing and without delay each man ran to his duty. Some stepped the masts, with these in place others laboured to hoist the sails; the most part forced the knights' horses aboard the ships, the rest hurried to stow their arms. A host of foot-soldiers descended on the harbours where the fleet lay, much as a flock of doves homes to its dove-cotes.

---

[2] For *pura* see Latham, and the verb *puro* 'to remove encumbrances from (property donated to an abbey)' in *Annales Monastici*, ed. H. R. Luard, iii (London, 1866), pp. 256, 257, 314, 326.

[3] The date given by Guy for William's sailing means no more than toward the end of September; *erat celebranda* indicates any day shortly before the feast of St. Michael (29 September).

O quantus subito fragor illinc ortus habetur,
    Cum nautę ramos, arma petunt equites!
Hinc resonando tubę uarios dant mille boatus,   90
    Fistula cum calamis et fidibus cỳthara,
Timpana taurinis implent mugitibus auras,
    Alternant modulos cỳmbala clara suos.[1]
Terra tremit; cęlumque pauet; miratur et equor.
    Quadrupedes fugiunt, piscis auisque simul.   95
Quippe decem decies, decies et milia quinque
    Diuersis feriunt uocibus astra poli.
Set tu templa petis sancti supra memorati,
    Muneribusque datis, curris adire[a] ratem.
Clangendoque tuba, reliquis ut littora linquant   100
    Precipis, et pelagi tucius alta petant;
Hactenus adfixę soluuntur littore pupes,
    Equor et intratur agmine composito.[2]
Iam breuiata dies, iam sol deuexus abibat,
    Cum tua preripuit preuia nauis iter.   105
Nox ubi cęca polum tenebrosis occupat umbris,
    Et negat obsequium Cinthia tecta tibi,
Imples non aliter facibus rutilantibus undas
    Sỳdera quam cęlum, sole ruente, replent.
Quot fuerant naues, totidem tu lumina spargis;   110

                    *   *   *   *   *[3]

Impositę malis permulta luce laternę[4]
    Tramite directo per mare uela regunt.
Set ueritus ne dampna tuis nox inferat atra,
    Ventus et aduerso flamine turbet aquas,   115
Sistere curua iubes compellat ut anchora puppes;
    In medio pelagi litus adesse facis.
Ponere uela mones, exspectans mane futurum,
    Vt lassata nimis gens habeat requiem.
At postquam terris rutilans Aurora refulsit
    Et Phebus radios sparsit in orbe suos,   120
Precipis ire uiam, committere carbasa uentis;
    Precipis ut soluat anchora fixa rates.

_____

[a] adire *edd.*; adite A

_____

[1] Cf. with the foregoing lines Venantius Fortunatus II, 9, 57 ff. (*MGH AA*
iv. 39).

O what uproar suddenly arose from that place, as seamen sought their oars and knights their weapons! Thence, sounding and re-sounding, a thousand trumpets blared different calls, together with pipes and reed-pipes, harps and citherns; drums filled the air with the bellowings of bulls, the clear-ringing cymbals alternated their measures.[1] The earth shook, heaven quivered, and the stunned sea lay wonder-stricken. The beasts fled, and the birds and fish as well, for indeed a hundred and fifty thousand conflicting voices struck the firmament.

But you sought the church of Saint-Valery; then with offerings made, you hastened to your ship. And by the sounding of a trumpet you ordered the rest to leave the coast and put out in safety to the deeps of the ocean. The vessels, till then made fast to the shore, cast off and stood out to sea in ordered formation.[2] Already the day was waning, already the setting sun was low, when your ship, racing ahead, set the course.

But when gloomy night overcast the heavens with shades of darkness and the hidden moon denied you her service, you filled the waves with the ruddy glow of torches, even as stars replenish the sky when the sun has gone. Distributing as many lights as there were ships . . .[3] By their strong beams lanterns[4] set on the masts guided the sails on a straight course over the sea. But fearful lest the dark night cause your men losses, lest the wind blowing contrary should roughen the water, you ordered the ships to heave to, held by the fluked anchors; you made a harbour appear in the midst of the open sea. And you passed word to strike sail and await the coming day, so that your wearied people might find rest.

But after rosy dawn brightened the lands and the sun cast his beams over the world, you gave command to set course and make sail, ordering that the vessels should weigh anchor. When you

---

[2] Guy uses the terms *agmen* and *acies* with strict classical accuracy, the former of a body in motion, the latter of a battle-line. Here and at v. 774, the movement is a formally ordered one.

[3] Here a pentameter is missing in the MS.

[4] Cf. *GG*, p. 162 (in which only William's ship has a lantern to give the signal for sailing at dawn), and *BT*, Pl. 43.

Tertia telluri supereminet hora diei[1]
Cum mare postponens litora tuta tenes.
E cęlo fulgens, extenso crine, cometes   125
Anglis fatatum nunciat excidium.[2]
Debita terra tibi, pauidis nudata colonis,
Lęta, sinu placido, teque tuosque capit.
Rex Heraldus enim sceleratus ad ultima terrę
Fratris ad exicium perfida tela parat;   130
Non modicam regni partem nam frater adeptus,
Tecta dabat flammis et gladiis populum.
Marte sub opposito currens Heraldus in hostes,
Non timuit fratris tradere membra neci.[3]
Alter in alterutrum plus quam ciuile peregit   135
Bellum,[4] set uictor (proh dolor!) ipse fuit.
Inuidus ille Caïn fratris caput amputat ense,[5]
Et caput et corpus sic sepeliuit humo.
Hęc tibi preuidit qui debita regna subegit:
Criminis infesti quatinus ultor eas.[6]   140
Littora custodis, metuens amitere[7] naues,
Męnibus et munis, castraque ponis ibi.
Diruta quę fuerant dudum castella reformas;
Ponis custodes ut tueantur ea.
Non multo spacio, tua gens, set pace potita,   145
Inuadit terram; uastat et igne cremat.
Nec mirum, regem quia te plebs stulta negabat;
Ergo perit iuste, uadit et ad nichilum.
Ex Anglis unus, latitans sub rupe marina,
Cernit ut effusas innumeras acies,   150
Et quod agri fulgent pleni radiantibus armis;
Vulcano flammis depopulante domos
Perfidię, gentem ferro bachante perire,
Quasque dabant lacrimas cede patrum pueri.

---

[1] For *superemineo* with dative direct object cf. *Chronicon Monasterii de Bello* (London, 1846), p. 38, and A. Souter, *Glossary of Later Latin* . . . (Oxford, 1949). 'The third hour', i.e. about nine o'clock in the morning, refers to the time of the fleet's entry into the bay (v. 128), not that of the disembarking, as Beeler thought (J. Beeler, *Warfare in England, 1066–1189*, Cornell University Press, 1966, p. 12). Although the precise size of William's fleet is unknown, it must have been considerable, and he would have wished to begin his landings at the minute the tide turned, that is between 11.00 and 12.00 (ibid. n. 6).

[2] The comet, mentioned here for dramatic effect, actually appeared on 24 April (cf. *ASC*, MSS. C, D, 1066; *Chronicon Breve Ecclesiae Sancti Dionysii*

reached safe landing-places, leaving the sea astern, the third hour of day was rising over the earth[1]—and blazing from heaven the streaming hair of a comet proclaimed to the English foreordained destruction![2]

Robbed of her terrified inhabitants, the land destined for you joyfully received you and yours in a calm bay; for Harold, the wicked king, was preparing treacherous weapons for a brother's destruction at the farthest end of the land, because this brother— having gained no small part of the kingdom—was putting houses to the torch and people to the sword. Rushing upon the enemy in arms,[3] Harold did not fear to do his brother to death. Each waged on the other a worse than civil war,[4] but he, alas, was victor. That envious Cain hewed off his brother's head,[5] and thus he buried head and body in the earth. He who subdued the destined realms foresaw this mission for you: that you should go as the avenger of a violent crime.[6]

Fearing to lose[7] the ships, you surrounded them with earthworks and guarded the shores. You restored the dismantled forts which had stood there formerly and set custodians to hold them. Having gained control, though over no great space, your people attacked the region, laid it waste, and burnt it with fire. Small wonder, for the foolish folk denied that you were king! Therefore they perished justly and went to destruction.

One of the English, lying hidden close to a sea-rock, perceived how the countless ranks spread far and wide and saw that the fields glittered, full of glancing arms. He saw the people, their homes ravaged by flames for their perfidy, perish by the raging sword, and

ad cyclos paschales, Bouquet xi. 377E). Both the Bayeux Tapestry (Pl. 35) and the *GG* (p. 208) make it clear that it was seen not long after Harold's coronation, but long before the battle.

[3] The battle of Stamford Bridge, in which the attempted invasion of England by Harald Hardrada, king of Norway, and Tostig Godwinson was crushed and both leaders killed, took place on 25 September 1066.

[4] Cf. Lucan, *Pharsalia* i. 1.

[5] This line has been taken literally, but there is no more reason to assume that Harold personally beheaded Tostig than to assume that he personally interred him (v. 138).

[6] It is perhaps not without significance that William is spoken of as the avenger of Tostig, and that there is no allusion here or elsewhere in the *Carmen* to Alfred atheling. Cf. Appendix A, pp. 59 ff.

[7] For *amittere*, 'to lose', cf. *Rôles gascons*, ed. F. Michel, i. 272: 'terram . . . quam timet amittere'.

Scandere currit equum, festinat dicere regi.   155
    Rex redit a bello premia lęta ferens;
Nuncius occurrit; quę fert hoc ordine pandit:
    'Rex, tibi pro certo nuncia dira fero.
Dux Normannorum, cum Gallis atque Britannis,
    Inuasit terram; uastat et igne cremat.   160
Milia si queris, tibi dicere nemo ualebit:

f. 228ᵛ   Quotᵃ mare fert pisces, tot sibi sunt equites;
Et ueluti stellas cęli numerare nequires,
    Eius sic acies nec numerareᵇ uales.
Captiuos ducit pueros, captasque puellas,   165
    Insuper et uiduas, et simul omne pecus.'
Rusticus hęc retulit. Rex contra sibilat[1] illi;
    Quamuis hec timeat, uelle tamen simulat.
Aduocat ipse duces, comites, terręque potentes;
    Verbis, ut fertur, talibus alloquitur: 170
'Milicię pars summa meę, magnatibus orta,
    Solus non bello uincere cui pudor est,[2]
Nothica quos misit per te superauimus hostes,
    Et per te nostrum strauimus equiuocum.[3]

*   *   *   *   *   *

*   *   *   *   *

Nutriuit proprio matris quemᶜ lacte papilla.[4]   175
    Tu mihi presidium, murus, et auxilium,
Audisti nostrum quod gens Normannica regnum
    Intrauit; predans, pauperat, exspoliat.
Hoc Willelmus ⟨agit⟩,ᵈ qui te sibi subdere querit.
    Nomen habet magnum; cor tamen est pauidum;   180
Est uafer et cupidus nimiumque superciliosus;
    Nec nouit pacem nec retinere fidem.
Si possitᵉ leuiter, molitur tollere nostra,
    Set Deus omnipotens non erit hoc paciens.

ᵃ Quod A   ᵇ numerale A; numerare *edd.*   ᶜ matrum quam A. *The
end of* matrum *is overwritten and* 'û' *is very like* 'i' *followed by long* 's' *in this
hand*   ᵈ ⟨agit⟩ P., *followed by* C., G. om. A   ᵉ poss; A; posset P., C.;
possit M., G.

---

[1] *Sibilat illi*, lit.: 'he whistled for him'; cf. Vulgate, Zech. 10: 8, Isa. 7: 18,
where the meaning approximates 'summon'. Harold motioned the peasant to
follow him when he gathered his captains. The verb might, however, be *sibylo/
sibilo*, 'speak in a sibylline, i.e. misleading manner' (cf. John of Salisbury, *Poli-
crat.* ii. 25), in which case the meaning would be that Harold feigned to welcome

what tears the children shed for their fathers' slaughter. He ran to mount a horse and sped to tell the king.

The king was returning from battle, laden with rich spoils. The messenger rushed to meet him and poured out the tale he bore in this way: 'O king, truly I bring you fearful news! The duke of the Normans, with Frenchmen and Bretons, has invaded the land; he is ravaging and burning. If you ask how many thousands he has, no one will be able to tell you. He has as many knights as there are fish in the sea, and you could no more number his ranks than the stars of heaven. He is seizing boys and girls, and the widows also; and at the same time all the beasts.'

Thus the country fellow reported. The king called him to his side;[1] although he feared this news, he feigned to desire it. He himself summoned to him the captains, the lords and great men of the land, and is said to have addressed them in such words as these: 'Leaders of my army, sprung from great forebears, to whom the only shame is not to conquer in war:[2] Through you we have overthrown the enemies that Norway sent, and through you we have laid low our namesake[3] . . . (and) him whom (our) mother's breast nourished with its own milk.[4] My guard, my help, and my defence, you have heard that the Normans have entered our kingdom, plundering, robbing, and despoiling! William does this, because he seeks to subject you to himself. He has a great name, but a queasy stomach! He is cunning and avaricious and arrogant beyond measure; he knows neither peace nor how to keep faith. He is striving to seize what is ours, if he can do it easily. But this Almighty God will not suffer! How great will be the grief, how

what he in fact dreaded. We have preferred to understand the more common verb.   [2] Cf. Lucan, *Pharsalia* i. 145.

[3] The *equiuocum* is Harald Hardrada. For examples of this word cf. *VE*, p. 58 n. 3; Ermoldus Nigellus i. 37; and Abbo (*Le Siège de Paris par les Normands*, ed. H. Waquet, Paris, 1942, p. 68, v. 33).

[4] Verse 175 apparently refers to Tostig, in which case a copula is wanting, as the *equiuocum* of v. 174 can only be Hardrada. We suggest that a couplet is missing here, like the pentameter after v. 110, which would have further described the *equiuocum*, provided a copula, furnished an antecedent for *quem* in v. 175, and completed the rhetorical sequence of verbs with some such word as *prostrauimus*.

Quantus erit luctus, quantus dolor et pudor ingens,   185
Regni quanta lues, quam tenebrosa dies,
Si quod querit habet, si regni sceptra tenebit!
Hoc omnes fugiant uiuere qui cupiunt.'
His ita prolatis, querit responsa suorum;
Scrutantur taciti dicere quid ualeant.   190
Nascitur extimplo clamor qui perculit astra,
Et uox communis omnibus una fuit:
'Bella magis cupimus quam sub iuga colla reponi
Alterius regis, uel magis inde mori.'
Exultans fatuus rex grates reddidit illis;   195
Insuper hoc unum consilium retulit:
'Primum legatos decet ut mitamus ad illum,
Illi qui dicant si placet ut redeat.
Pacificum si uult nobiscum fędus inire,
Vestro consilio, non ego reiciam.   200
Sin aliter, non sponte sua mea littora linquet.
Desinat hoc quod agit, trans freta regna petat.'
Equo consultu maiorum necne minorum
Prouidus eloquio monachus eligitur
Exploret qui castra ducis, qui credita caute   205
Verba sibi referat. Regis ab imperio,
Accelerauit iter, pedibus transuectus equinis,[1]
Sub tunica nigra uerba querenda gerens.
Dux erat in castris;[2] intrans, hęc monachus inquit:
'Est opus ut nostrę sic ualeas patrię.   210
Rex et primates regni quoque iura tenentes
Precipiunt dicto quod cicius redeas.
Mirantur super his de te quę fama reportat,
Quod sine re[a] regnum ducis ad excidium.
Captiuos reddas et quicquid ui rapuisti.   215
Indulget si uis cętera dampna tibi:
Ętati parcit; morum parcit leuitati;[b]
Olim quę fuerat parcit amicicię.[3]
Si contradicis, uel si sua reddere tardas,
Bella sibi[c] mandat; ergo decet caueas.   220

---

[a] te A, edd.; re nos. For the frequent confusion of 'r' and 't' in this hand see above, p. lxxi; on our emendation, below, n. 3   [b] lenitati A   [c] tibi A. See below, n. 3

---

[1] Monks were normally forbidden to ride horses.

great the anguish and how mighty the shame, what ruin for the kingdom, how dark a day, if William gain what he seeks—if he shall wield the sceptre of the realm! May all shun this who wish to live!'

Having spoken, Harold sought answer from his men. Silent, they searched for words; straightway a shout arose that struck the stars, and there was but one voice among them all: 'We would have war sooner than bow our necks to the yoke of another king; nay, more, rather die!'

Exulting, the foolish king returned them thanks, and in addition put forward this one suggestion: 'It is fitting that we first send him envoys, to tell him to withdraw, so please him. If he wishes to enter into a peace-pact with us, by your counsel I shall not be the one to refuse. If otherwise, however, he will not leave my shores at his own choice. Let him cease what he is about, let him look for kingdoms beyond the sea!'

By common consent of the great men and also the lowly, a monk prudent in speech was chosen, to spy out the duke's camp and carefully report the words entrusted to him. On the king's orders, he hastened his journey by riding a horse.[1]

The duke was in camp;[2] entering, the monk said this: 'As matters are now, it is necessary that you leave our land! The king and the nobles (who also hold rights in the kingdom) command you to withdraw immediately. They wonder at what rumour reports of you; that you are bringing the country to destruction wantonly. Give up the prisoners and whatever you have seized by force! The king forgives other injuries if you wish; he makes allowance for your years, for the inconstancy of your nature, for the alliance that once existed.[3] But if you refuse, or if you delay in returning what is his, he directs the war in person—therefore you had best take care! He himself can hardly hold back his soldiers and the people,

---

[2] Cf. *GG.* pp. 172 ff.

[3] In his reply to this speech, William takes up each of Harold's points: at v. 231, he says that he is no longer a child, and is not acting *leuiter*; at v. 233, he claims that it is Harold who has broken their *fędus amicicię*. The *inmerito* of v. 237 may echo an original *sine re* for the meaningless *sine te* of v. 214. Similarly, William's warning in v. 230 that Harold cannot hide from him at a distance suggests that the MS. *tibi* of v. 220 may be an error for *sibi* (an error that occurs elsewhere in the MS.; cf. above, p. lxxi). The idiom in v. 220 would then be *bellum alicui mandare*, 'to give one the chief command in a war', meaning that Harold himself will lead the English against the Normans. William's reply in v. 230 is but a contemptuous reminder that Harold can do no other.

Miliciam uix ipse suam populumque cohercet;
Gens est quę nullum nouit habere modum.
Nam, Dominum testor, bis sex sibi milia centum
Sunt pugnatorum, prelia qui siciunt.'
Talibus obiectis, mutata leonis imago.   225
Pondus uirtutum, miles et intrepidus,
Dux, flocipendens quicquid sibi uana cuculla
Attulerat, fatuas approbat esse minas.
'Verba tui regis', dixit, 'non sunt sapientis.
Nil latitare¹ procul poterit; hoc sapiat.   230
Excessi puerum, leuiter nec regna petiui,
Defunctis patribus, debita iure mihi.
Fędus amicicię nostrę dissoluit inique,
Dum tenet iniuste quę mea iure forent.
Quod monet, ut redeam, furor est, demencia summa;   235
Tempus enim prohibet, et uia non facilis.
Inmerito quamuis committere bella minetur,
In Domino fidens, gens mea non refugit.
Nescit queᵃ furtiua mihi periuria² fecit,
Nec penitus recolit quod meus ipse fuit?   240
Si periura manus nondum, dampnata, resultat,
Diuino tamen est iam rea iudicio.
Si querit pacem, si uult delicta fateri,
Indulgens culpę parcere promtus ero.
Terram quam pridem tenuit pater,³ hanc sibi reddam,   245
Vt meus ante fuit, si meus esse uelit.'ᵇ
Monachus accelerat reditum. Dux preparat arma;
Heraldi mentem nouerat atque dolum.
Admonet, inflammat, confortans corda suorum:
'Francia quos genuit, nobilitate cluens,   250
Belligeri sine felle⁴ uiri, famosa iuuentus,
Quos Deus elegit uel quibus ipse fauet,⁵

ᵃ *Original* quod *corrected to* que A   ᵇ *The argument of this line would be
more logical if the two clauses were reversed, and this is metrically possible*

---

¹ *Latitare* may here bear its juridical meaning, 'evade the justice of the court'.
Cf. vv. 301 (*colla retorquens*); 303 (*Iudice . . . Domino . . . pars iusta*); 542 (*actio
uera probat*); 543 (*bellica iura tenentes*) for similar plays on the legal meanings
of words or phrases.
² For the implications of the phrase *furtiua . . . periuria* see below, Appendix
A, pp. 69 ff.

it is a race that brooks no restraint. Now as the Lord is my witness, he has twelve hundred thousand fighting-men who thirst for battle!'

With such charges levelled against him the appearance of the lion was changed and the duke—the epitome of heroic virtues and an intrepid knight—judging whatever the foolish monk had told him to be worthless, proved the threats empty. 'The words of your king', he said, 'are not those of a wise man; he could not possibly hide at a distance![1] Let him savour this: I have passed boyhood, nor have I wantonly attacked the realms due to me, the former rulers being dead. The pact of our alliance he wickedly annuls while he unjustly holds what lawfully would have been mine. His counsel that I should return is insanity, the height of madness; the season, indeed, and the difficult voyage forbid it. Though he threaten to wage war undeservedly, my people, trusting in the Lord, will not fly! Does he not know what secret oaths he falsely swore to me,[2] nor recall in his heart that he was once my man? If his perjured hand does not recoil condemned, none the less it is defendant now before the Divine Tribunal. If he seek peace, if he be willing to confess his transgressions, I shall be swift to pardon, condoning his crimes. The fief his father once held,[3] this I shall restore to him, if he is willing to be my vassal now as he was formerly.'

The monk hastened his journey back; the duke prepared for battle, he knew Harold's intent and also his craft. Strengthening the hearts of his men, he admonished and inspired them: 'O you whom France famed for nobility has bred, chivalrous[4] warriors, renowned young men whom God himself chooses and whom he favours,[5] whose lasting and unconquered name for valour resounds

---

[3] i.e. the better part of southern England. Godwin held Kent and Wessex and received a third of the London wharf revenues.

[4] For *sine felle*, 'without (personal) rancour or malice', cf. Martial, *Epigr.* x. 48. 21–2:

> Accedent sine felle ioci nec mane timenda
> Libertas, et nil quod tacuisse uelis

and St. Ambrose, *De excessu fratris Satyri* i. 41: 'quam grata contentio tua! Quam sine felle ipsa indignatio! Quam servulis ipsis coercitio non amara . . .'.

[5] The sentiment of vv. 251–2 appears to echo Ermoldus iii. 153–4:

> Gens est Francorum nulli virtute secunda,
> Vincit amore Dei, exsuperatque fide

and ibid. ii. 44:

> Hunc petit ecclesia, Christus et ipse favet.

As Dr. J. M. Wallace-Hadrill has kindly pointed out to us, the foreshadowing here of the later *gesta Dei per Francos* 'is almost the *leitmotiv* of Carolingian rule', and goes back at least as far as the prologue to the revised *Lex Salica* of the eighth to ninth century.

C

Fama uolat quorum per climata quatuor orbis
Inuictusque manens milicię titulus:
Gensque Britannorum, quorum decus extat in armis,   255
Tellus ni fugiat, est fuga nulla quibus:[1]
Viribus illustres Cenomanni, gloria quorum
Bello monstratur per probitatis opem:
Apulus et Calaber, Siculus, quibus iacula feruunt;[a 2]
Normanni faciles actibus egregiis: 260
Falsus et infamis periurus rex et adulter
Molitur nobis tendit et insidias.
Eius enim mos est non ui set uincere fraude,
Spondendoque fidem porrigit ore necem.
Ergo cauere decet ne decipiamur ab illo,   265
Ni simus risus, ludus et in populo.
Mandamus uobis quapropter castra tueri,
Irruat in castris ne malus ille latro.
Set cras, si dignum uobis uideatur et ęquum,
Contra quem misit uana referre mihi   270
Reddere legatum pro uerbis uerba paratum
Illi mitamus, qui minimum timeat.
Monachus est nobis quo non moderancior alter,
Et nulli cedens rethoris officio,
Signifer insignis, ni regula sacra negaret;   275
Si uobis placeat, hic mea dicta ferat.'
Dixit, et est actum; compleuit et actio dictum.
Monachus accitus, nec mora, carpit iter.
Interea, sedes[b] fuscatę fraudis et heres,
ᴵ Nocte sub obscura, furis in arte uigens   280
Rex acies armare iubet, ducis atque latenter
Mandat ut inuadant agmina si ualeant.
Estimat inuigiles prosternere fraudibus hostes;
Fallere dum querit, fallitur atque ruit:
Dux quia, directo legato, peruigil extat;   285
Eius et ingenio conscius artis erat.
Diuertens legatus iter per deuia terrę,
Nescius accessit rex ubi furta facit.
'Pro merito, de parte ducis, rex', inquit, 'aueto,
Quem non ex ęquo cogis inire malum.   290

---

[a] ferú A; fervet *P., G.*; ferve[n]t *C.*; ferum *M. For* ⌣ *as abbreviation for* -unt,
frequent in A, *cf. above, p.* lxx   [b] fedes A

through the four quarters of the world: And you, race of the Bretons, whose honour shines forth in arms, for whom—unless the earth itself should flee away—there is no flight:[1] You men of Maine, illustrious for strength, whose glory in war is shown by mighty prowess: Apulian and Calabrian, Sicilian, whose darts fly in swarms:[2] Normans, ripe for incomparable achievements! The false, infamous, and perjured king and adulterer is devising and laying snares for us. Indeed, it is his wont to conquer by cunning, not by strength, and pledging faith with his lips he offers destruction. Therefore we should take care not to be deceived by him, lest we become a laughing-stock, a show before the people! We command you for this reason to guard the camp, so that that wicked thief may not break in. But tomorrow, if it seem meet and right to you, let us send Harold—in return for him whom he sent to bear windy lies to me!—an envoy ready to give word for word; one who shall little fear him. There is a monk of ours, by no means less outspoken than the other and yielding to none in the art of oratory; bold enough to be a noted standard-bearer, did not the Holy Rule forbid. If it please you, let this man bear my words.'

He spoke and it was done, the plan was put in action. The monk was summoned and without delay he took the road.

Meanwhile the king—the abode and heir of dark deception, active in the craft of a thief—ordered his lines to arm under cover of darkness and further commanded that if they could do it they should surprise the duke's forces on the march. He counted on overthrowing the watchful enemy by stratagems, but while he sought to deceive, he was himself deceived and rushed to destruction; because the duke, having sent the envoy, showed himself most vigilant and was alive to his opponent's cunning.

The messenger, turning aside through the wilds of the country, approached the place where the king, unaware, was devising his schemes. 'Fitting salutations, O king,' he said, 'on the part of the duke, whom you are unjustly compelling to enter on an evil course!

---

[1] For the late position of *quibus* cf. *cui* (v. 172), *huic* (v. 306), *Hos* (v. 538), and *Quam* (v. 754).

[2] The scansion of *iacula* in this line is abnormal; elsewhere (vv. 382, 410, 506) the first syllable is short. Although the usual meaning of *ferueo/feruo* is 'glow with heat', we think it unlikely that the southern Normans used burning arrows in open battle (as distinct from sieges), and have preferred the alternative meaning, 'swarm, fill the air'.

Hoc quia perplures testantur, et asserit idem,
    Assensu populi, consilio procerum,
Etguardus[1] quod rex ut ei succederet heres
    Annuit et fecit, teque fauente sibi.
Anulus est illi testis concessus et ensis,[2]   295
    Quę per te nosti missa fuisse sibi.
Est igitur seruanda fides, iurata teneri,
    Nexibus atque sacris dextera stricta manus.
Ergo decet uideas ne te periuria lędant,
    Et iurata tene, saluus ut esse queas.'   300
Heraldus,[a] uultu distorto, colla[3] retorquens,
f. 229ʳ   Legato dixit, 'Vade retro, stolide!
Iudice cras Domino regni, pars[4] iusta patebit:
    Diuidet ex equo sacra manus Domini.'
Ille retro gressum uertens per deuia rursum,   305
    A quo missus erat huic maledicta refert.
Imperiale decus, dux, pax et gloria regni,[5]
    Preuius incedens ante suas acies,
Aggregat et strictim compellit abire quirites,[6]
    Et faciles hasta conglomerare facit.   310
Legati facies natiuo cassa rubore,
    Pallor et ostendit proxima bella fore.
Dux ait, 'Est ubi rex?' 'Non longe', monachus inquit.
    Dixit in aure sibi, 'Signa uidere potes.
Plurima uerba fero quę censeo non referenda;   315
    Illa tamen dicam quę reticere nocet:
Ex inprouiso sperat te fallere posse;
    Per mare, per terram, prelia magna parat.
In mare quingentas fertur misisse carinas,
    Vt nostri reditus prepediatur iter.   320

ᵃ Herardus A, Heraldus *edd.*

---

[1] *Etguardus.* For the spelling in the *Carmen* of English names see above, p. lxx.

[2] *Anulus . . . ensis.* Significant as gifts because they were among the five regal insignia with which a king at this period was invested at his coronation. The remaining three, crown, sceptre, and rod, are mentioned together at vv. 783–4.

[3] *Colla* for *collum.* Cf. Ermoldus iii. 423:

    Colla jugo Christi en monitans mea vestra subegit
    Suasio . . .

and Gregory of Tours, *Historia* ii. 31: 'Mitis depone colla, Sicamber'. Cf. also the note to v. 230.

[4] We understand *pars* as 'side', 'party to a dispute', a meaning that seems to

This he does because many bear witness and he himself asserts that King Edward,[1] with the assent of the people and by counsel of the nobles, promised and decreed that William should succeed him as his heir; and you were supporting him. In token, a ring and a sword[2] were granted him, which you know to have been sent to him through you. Therefore it is right that faith be kept, the oaths upheld, and your right hand is bound by sacred knots. Accordingly, it behoves you to see that perjuries may not harm you and to honour your oaths that you may rest secure.'

Harold, his face distorted, throwing back his head,[3] said to the envoy: 'Give place, fool! Tomorrow, with the Lord as arbiter of the kingdom, the rightful claimant[4] will appear. The holy hand of the Lord will deal justly!' The messenger, retracing his path through the wilds, bore back abusive words for him who had sent him. The duke—royal virtue, peace, and glory of the kingdom![5]— going ahead, advancing before his lines, called in the knights[6] and summarily compelled them to fall back, and with a lance he made them readily assemble in close order; the envoy's face was robbed of its natural ruddy hue and his pallor showed the battle to be imminent.

The duke said: 'Where is the king?' 'Not far off,' answered the monk. He said to him in his ear: 'You can see the standards! I bear many words which I hold unfit to be repeated, yet I will report what it would be harmful to conceal. He hopes to be able to take you by surprise; by sea and by land he is planning great battles. He

suit the context best. The earlier editors, however, took it as 'lot', 'inheritance', governing *regni* (as their punctuation shows):

Judice cras Domino, regni pars justa patebit.

Pars in this less common meaning occurs in the Vulgate (Ps. 15: 5; Isa. 61: 7; Ecclus. 17: 25) and later.   [5] See the note to vv. 26–7.

[6] The medieval meaning of *quirites*, 'knights', stems from its derivation by Isidore from the Sabine word for spear (*Origines*, ix. 2. 84), and 'spearmen' is apparently the meaning in the earliest example that we have found of this usage (before 1017):

Millia mille viri procedunt, ante quirites

('ces mille et milliers de guerriers, partis en campagne, lanciers en avant', Adalbero of Laon, *Carmen ad Rotbertum Regem*, v. 145, ed. G. A. Hückel, Paris, 1901).

Gilo Parisiensis (ob. 1142) uses *quirites* twice in contrast with *pedites*:

Jamque fatigatis nostris, opibusque minutis,
In praedam pedites Christi misere quirites.
(*Historia Hierosolymitana* ii. 36.)

Atque necant pedites tria millia; turma quiritum
Evasit latitans per colles . . .   (Ibid. ii. 255.)

Quirites regii, 'the king's knights', is a phrase used twice by Suger (*Vita Ludovici Regis*, ed. H. Waquet, Paris, 1929, pp. 144 and 158).

Quo graditur siluas planis[a] deducit adesse,
Et per quę transit flumina sicca facit.
Fors numerum metues? Numerus[1] set, uiribus expers
Pluribus,[b] a minimo sepe repulsus abit.
Est sibi milicies[2] unctis depexa capillis,   325
Feminei iuuenes, Martis in arte pigri.
Et quot sunt, ouibus totidem sunt equiparandi,
Vel[c] uulpes pauidi fulguris ad sonitum.[3]
Nobilium memor esto patrum, dux magne, tuorum,
Et quod fecit auus quodque pater, facias: 330
Normannos proauus superauit, auusque Britannos,
Anglorum genitor sub iuga colla dedit.[4]
Et tu, quid facies, nisi quod, maiora parando,
Succedas illis per probitatis opem?'
Paulo conticuit; faciens et se remoratum,   335
Armatas acies ordinat imperio.
Premisit pedites commitere bella sagittis
Et balistantes[5] inserit in medio;
Quatinus infigant uolitancia uultibus arma
(Vulneribus datis, ora retro faciant).   340
Ordine post pedites sperat stabilire quirites,
Occursu belli set sibi non licuit:
Haut procul hostiles cuneos nam cernit adesse,
Et plenum telis irradiare nemus.
Mars deus o belli, gladiis qui sceptra coherces,   345
Corpora cui iuuenum sanguinolenta placent,
Et cruor effusus permulta cede uirorum,
Quis tibi tunc animus, quanta cupido[d] mali,
Cum medius seuas acies miscere[e] iubebas!
Quo pocius nullum te iuuat excidium   350

---

[a] plani A; planis *edd.*   [b] plurib⁹ A; plurimus *edd.*   [c] Vt A,
edd. (*M. suggested* Aut); *see below, note* 3   [d] cupiendo A; cupido *edd.*
[e] miserere A, *M., G.*; miscere *P., C.*

---

[1] We understand *numerus* here as 'a great number', a sense supported by vv.
321–2. Cf. v. 528. There is therefore no need to emend *pluribus*, v. 324.

[2] *Milicies* is rare; in the one classical example that we have found (*CIL* iii.
6687) it appears to be only a variant form of *militia* (cf. *amicitia/amicities*,
avaritia/avarities). Here, however, and in *EE*, p. 20, it apparently has a specialized sense, 'omnes enim erant nobiles, omnes plenae aetatis robore ualentes,
omnes cuiuis pugnae satis habiles . . . Talis itaque milicies . . . intrat pelagus.'
Milicies here cannot mean all Canute's forces, nor in the *Carmen* is the combed
and anointed *milicies* likely to have included the fyrd—*rustica gens*, as they are

is said to have sent five hundred ships to sea to hinder our voyage back. Where he goes he leads forests (of spears) into the open country, and he makes the rivers through which he passes run dry! Perhaps you fear the number? But the greater number[1] lacking greater strength often retires worsted by very few. He has champions with combed anointed hair,[2] effeminate young men, sluggish in the art of war; whatever their number, they may be likened to as many sheep, or to foxes terrified by a thunderbolt.[3] Remember your ancestors, great duke, and may you achieve what your grandfather and your father achieved! Your forefather subdued the Normans, your grandfather the Bretons, your sire laid the neck of the English under the yoke.[4] And what will you do, planning greater things, if not follow them through abundance of valour?'

He kept silence for a little and then, causing himself to delay there, he drew up the armed ranks by a command. He dispatched the foot in advance to open the battle with arrows, and set crossbowmen[5] in the midst so that their speeding shafts might pierce the faces of the English (these wounds given, they might fall back). He hoped to establish the knights in the rear of the foot but the onset of the battle did not allow this; for he perceived companies of the English appearing not far off and could see the forest glitter, full of spears.

O Mars god of war, who curbest kingdoms by the sword, to whom the gory corpses of striplings are acceptable and the shedding of men's blood in manifold slaughter, what then was thy intent, how great thy thirst for evil, when in their midst thou wert ordering the fierce ranks to join battle? No destruction gave thee

later called. It seems rather that we have in these two passages an attempt to distinguish a king's picked private troops, the Housecarls, who were required to have just those qualities enumerated in the *EE*, and who groomed themselves carefully—especially their hair—before battle. It is possible that the rarity of this word (and its seeming limitation in the eleventh century to the bodyguard of a Scandinavian or semi-Scandinavian king) was due to the elimination by this time, except in the north, of the sort of sworn brotherhood of warriors (*comitatus, antrustions, gardingi*) kept by early Germanic kings. Elsewhere we have found *milicies* only in Gower's Latin works. In two instances it is used of the king's knights (*Vox clamantis* i. 1265; 'Verses on Henry IV', in T. Wright, *Political Poems and Songs* ii. 1. 15); in the one other example it means the second estate: 'Clerus, Milicies, et Agricultores' (*Vox clamantis* iii, cap. 1).

[3] *P., C.*, and *G.* evidently took the MS. *Vt* as 'like', 'as'. Sheep are not, however, much like foxes, and *M.* suggested *Aut*. We prefer *Vel*, written *Vł* in the MS., a simpler corruption.

[4] On the foregoing passage see Appendix A, pp. 60 f.

[5] *Balistantes*. See Appendix C.

Ex quo Pompeium superauit Iulius armis,
Et Romana sibi mę̨nia subripuit,
Compulit atque metu uili transire per amnem—
Nulla reor cedes tam tibi grata fuit.

Nec iuuenile decus nec te reuerenda senectus,   355
Nec peditum uilis et miseranda manus,
Flectere nec ualuit te nobilitudo parentum,
Quin ageres quicquid mens tua torua cupit.

Cę̨catos miseros radiantia trudis in arma,
Et ueluti ludum cogis adire necem.   360

Quid moror in uerbis cum iam furor extat in armis?
Exple uelle tuum, Mars,[a] age mortis opus!

Ex inprouiso diffudit silua cohortes,
Et nemoris latebris agmina prosiliunt.[1]

Mons siluę̨ uicinus erat, uicinaque uallis,   365
Et non cultus ager asperitate sui.

Anglis ut mos est, densatim progredientes,
Hę̨c loca preripiunt Martis ad officium.

(Nescia gens belli solamina spernit equorum,
Viribus et fidens, heret humo pedibus;   370
Et decus esse mori summum diiudicat armis
Sub iuga ne tellus transeat alterius.)

Ascendit montem rex bellaturus in hostem,
Nobilibusque uiris munit[b] utrumque latus.

In summo montis uexillum uertice fixit,   375
Affigique iubet cę̨tera signa sibi.

Omnes descendunt et equos post terga relinquunt;
Affixique solo, bella ciere[c] tubis.

Dux, humilis Dominumque timens, moderantius agmen
Ducit, et audacter ardua montis adit.   380

Prelia precurrunt[d] pedites miscere[e] sagittis;
(Quadratis iaculis[2] scuta nihil faciunt).

Festinant parmas galeati iungere parmis;
Erectis astis hostis uterque furit.

[a] mar A; Mar P.; Mars alii   [b] mun⁹ A; P., C.; munit M., G.
[c] sciere A; ciere edd.   [d] p̄curr̄ A; praecurrit P., C.; percurrit M., G. For
⌢ as abbreviation of -unt, frequent in A, see above, p. lxx   [e] miscere A,
misread by M. as mistere and emended to miscete. G. follows M.'s error

[1] On the English tactical surprise, the seizing of Battle Hill, see Appendix B
(pp. 73–83).

more delight since Julius overcame Pompey in arms, stole the Roman citadel for himself, and forced his enemy in base fear to cross the sea—never, I think, was bloodshed more grateful to thee. Neither the grace of youth nor the venerability of age, neither the mean and pitiable multitude of common soldiers nor nobility of birth, could turn thee from doing what thy grim spirit desired. Thou didst force the blinded wretches into glittering armour and madest them come to death as to a game! Why toy with words when already Madness appears in arms? Perform thy will, Mars, do the work of Death!

Suddenly the forest poured forth troops of men, and from the hiding-places of the woods a host dashed forward.[1] There was a hill near the forest and a neighbouring valley and the ground was untilled because of its roughness. Coming on in massed order—the English custom—they seized possession of this place for the battle. (A race ignorant of war, the English scorn the solace of horses and trusting in their strength they stand fast on foot; and they count it the highest honour to die in arms that their native soil may not pass under another yoke.)

Preparing to meet the enemy, the king mounted the hill and strengthened both his wings with noble men. On the highest point of the summit he planted his banner, and ordered his other standards to be set up. All the men dismounted and left their horses in the rear, and taking their stand on foot they let the trumpets sound for battle.

The humble and God-fearing duke led a more measured advance and courageously approached the steeps of the hill. The foot-soldiers ran ahead to engage the enemy with arrows (against crossbow-bolts[2] shields are of no avail!). The helmeted warriors hastened to close ranks; on both sides the foemen raged with brandished spears. As a wild boar standing wearied by the hounds

---

[2] The four-sided bolts fired from crossbows; see Appendix C. The diminutive derivative *quadrellum* gives the Old French *quarrel*:

> 'Plus qu'arcbaleste ne poet traire un quarrel'
> (*Chanson de Roland* (ed. J. Bédier), v. 2265).

Although the words *quadrata iacula* are used only of crossbow-bolts, the bolts themselves are often referred to by various more general words for 'arrow' or 'dart', both in classical Latin (cf. Vegetius, *De Re Militari*, ii. 15 end; iii. 21; iii. 24 end) and in medieval (e.g. the passage of Baudri de Bourgueil quoted at the end of Appendix C). A good example of this variety occurs in the several accounts of the death of Richard I. In most, the shaft that struck him is called *sagitta*, but it also appears as *quoddam quarellum* (and shot from an *arcubalista*) in John of Oxenedes (*RS* xiii. 102); *quadratum telum* (again from an *arcubalista*) in Gervase of Canterbury (*RS* lxxiii. 91); *iaculum balistae* in the Bermondsey annalist (*Annales Monastici* iii. 448–9); and *spiculum* in the Margam annalist (ibid. i. 26).

Vt canibus lassatus aper stans dente tuetur   385
Oreque spumoso reicit arma pati,
Non hostem metuit nec tela minancia mortem,
Sic plebs Angligena dimicat inpauida.
Interea, dubio pendent dum prelia Marte,
Eminet et telis mortis amara lues,   390
Histrio, cor audax nimium quem nobilitabat,
Agmina precedens innumerosa ducis,
Hortatur Gallos uerbis et territat Anglos:
Alte proiciens ludit et ense suo.
Anglorum quidam, cum de tot milibus unum   395
Ludentem gladio cernit abire procul,
Milicię cordis tactus feruore decenti,
Viuere postponens, prosilit ire mori.
Incisor-ferri[1] mimus cognomine dictus,
Vt fuerat captus, pungit equum stimulis.   400
Angligenę scutum telo transfudit acuto;
Corpore prostrato distulit ense caput.
Lumina conuertens sociis hęc gaudia profert,
Belli principium monstrat et esse suum.
Omnes letantur, Dominum pariter uenerantur;[2]   405
Exultant ictus quod prior extat eis,
Et tremor et feruor per corda uirilia currunt,
Festinantque simul iungere scuta uiri.
Inuadunt primi peditum cetus pharetrati,
Eminus et iaculis corpora trahiciunt.   410
Et balistantes clipeos, ad grandinis instar,
Dissoluunt, quaciunt ictibus innumeris.[3]
Set leuam Galli, dextram peciere Britanni;[4]
Dux cum Normannis dimicat in medio.
Anglorum stat fixa solo densissima turba,   415
Tela dat et telis et gladios[a] gladiis.
Spiritibus nequeunt frustrata cadauera sterni,
Nec cedunt uiuis corpora militibus.
Omne cadauer enim, uita licet euacuatum,
Stat uelut illesum, possidet atque locum.   420
Nec penetrare ualent spissum nemus Angligenarum,
Ni tribuat uires uiribus ingenium.
Artibus instructi, Franci, bellare periti,

[a] gladio A; gladios *edd.*

defends himself with his tusks and with foaming jaws scorns to submit to weapons, fearing neither his opponent nor the spears that threaten death, so the great throng of the English contended dauntlessly. Meantime, while the battle hung in ominous suspense and the dread scourge of death in war was pending, a player, whom his most valiant soul greatly ennobled, rode out before the countless army of the duke. He heartened the men of France and terrified the English, and, tossing his sword high, he sported with it. A certain Englishman, when he saw a lone man out of so many thousands move off at a distance, juggling with his sword, was fired with the ardour proper to a soldier's heart—heedless of life, he sprang forward to meet his death. The mummer, surnamed Taillefer,[1] as soon as he had been reached, pricked his horse with the spurs; he pierced the Englishman's shield with his keen lance and hewed the head from the prostrate body with his sword. Turning his eyes on his comrades, he displayed this trophy and showed that the beginning of the battle favoured them. All rejoiced and at the same time called upon the Lord.[2] They exulted that the first blow was theirs, both a tremor and a thrill ran through brave hearts and at once the men hastened to close shields.

First the bands of archers attacked and from a distance transfixed bodies with their shafts and the crossbow-men destroyed the shields as if by a hail-storm, shattered them by countless blows.[3] Now the French attacked the left, the Bretons the right;[4] the duke with the Normans fought in the centre. The English stood firm on their ground in the closest order. They met missile with missile, sword-stroke with sword-stroke; bodies could not be laid down, nor did the dead give place to living soldiers, for each corpse though lifeless stood as if unharmed and held its post; nor would the attackers have been able to penetrate the dense forest of Englishmen had not guile reinforced their strength.

---

[1] Taillefer. The *Carmen* is the only eleventh-century source to name him. For an appraisal of his role in the battle see below, Appendix B, pp. 81 f.

[2] Apparently a reference to the Norman battle-cry, 'Dex aïe'.

[3] The matter of vv. 411–12 expands that of v. 382. See below, Appendix C (p. 113).

[4] Cf. vv. 429–30. 'Right' and 'left' are given in both passages from the point of view of the subject in each case: French and Bretons here, the *Rustica . . . gens* there.

Ac si deuicti fraude fugam simulant.
Rustica letatur gens,[1] et superasse putabat;   425
Post tergum nudis insequitur gladiis.
(Amotis sanis, labuntur dilacerati,
Siluaque spissa prius rarior efficitur.)
Conspicit[2] ut campum[a] cornu tenuare sinistrum,
Intrandi dextrum quod uia larga patet: 430
Perdere dispersos uariatis cladibus hostes
Laxatis frenis certat[b] utrumque[3] prius.
Quique fugam simulant instantibus ora retorquent;[c]
Constrictos cogunt uertere dorsa neci.[d]
Pars ibi magna perit—pars et densata resistit—   435
Milia namque decem sunt ibi passa necem.
Vt pereunt mites bachante leone bidentes,
Sic compulsa mori gens maledicta ruit.
Plurima quę superest pars bello[4] acrior instat,
Et sibi sublatos pro nichilo reputat.   440
Anglorum populus, numero superante, repellit
Hostes, uique retro compulit ora dari.

f. 229ᵛ   Et fuga ficta prius fit tunc uirtute coacta.
Normanni fugiunt; dorsa tegunt clipei.
Dux, ubi perspexit quod gens sua uicta recedit,   445
Occurrens illi signa ferendo, manu
Increpat et cedit; retinet, constringit et hasta.[5]
Iratus, galea nudat et ipse caput.
Vultum Normannis dat; uerba precantia Gallis
Dixit, 'Quo fugitis? Quo iuuat ire mori?   450

ᵃ câpû A, *written as in vv.* 503, 569; campum *P., C.*; captum *M., G.*
ᵇ cretat A; certat *edd.*   ᶜ retorqᵃnt A; retorquant *P., C.*; retorquent *M., G.*
ᵈ *V.* 434 *omitted in original text; added in margin by different, but contemporary hand*

---

¹ *Rustica . . . gens* is probably to be taken literally. See Appendix B1 for a
detailed analysis of the tactical situation as described by Guy. Although Harold
has been said to have strengthened his wings with noble men (v. 374), most of
these forces will have been shire levies. The French were on William's right
(v. 413); the Bretons, on his left, are known to have been in difficulties.
² The subject of *Conspicit* is the *Rustica . . . gens* of v. 425. For the inversion
of the temporal conjunction *ut*, cf. v. 747. *Cornu tenuare sinistrum* we understand
to mean that the terrain of battle broke up the Breton force into small and
separate groups. Cf. Ovid, *Remedia amoris* 445:
             Grandia per multos tenuantur flumina rivos
and *Ars amatoria* i. 761:
             leves Proteus modo se tenuabit in undas.

The French, versed in stratagems, skilled in warfare, pretended to fly as if defeated. The English peasantry[1] rejoiced and believed they had won; they pursued in the rear with naked swords. (The unwounded gone, the maimed sank down and the once dense wood was thinned!) When they saw[2] that the ground was weakening the duke's left wing, that a wide road lay open for penetrating the right, charging headlong, each[3] wing of the English vied to be first to slaughter the scattered enemy in various ways. But those who feigned flight wheeled on the pursuers and forced them, held in check, to flee from death. A great part fell there (but the part in close order stood fast), for indeed ten thousand suffered destruction in that place. As meek sheep fall before the ravening lion, so the accursed rabble went down, fated to die. But the very powerful force that survived in the battle[4] attacked more furiously and counted their losses nothing. The English people, prevailing by their number, repulsed the enemy and by their might compelled him to turn—and then the flight which had first been a ruse became enforced by valour. The Normans fled, their shields covered their backs!

When the duke saw his people retreat vanquished, he rushed to confront the rout. He rebuked and felled them with his hand, and with his spear he checked and marshalled them.[5] Raging, he himself bared his head of the helmet.[6] To the Normans he showed a furious countenance—to the French he spoke words of entreaty: 'Where are you flying? Where does it avail you to go to die? O France,

[3] The unexpressed antecedent of *utrumque* is the English *cornu* opposed to each of the duke's *cornua*. It cannot be the French and Bretons who are vying with each other to wipe out the enemy, nor can the contest be between the opposing armies as a whole, for the Bretons are in trouble and the French do not wheel round on their pursuers until v. 433.

[4] One of the two examples of hiatus in the poem. Cf. v. 610 and see above, p. lxx.

[5] *Signa ferendo* (v. 446), the 'movement'—actually a near-rout—of William's troops that he hastened to stem. Cf. Caesar, *De bello Gallico* vi. 37. 4: 'Totis trepidatur castris, atque alius ex alio causam tumultus quaerit; neque quo signa ferantur neque quam in partem quisque conveniat provident.' Although Lewis and Short give no examples of the use of *increpare* with a noun of physical instrument, it is not infrequent: cf. Tibullus i. 1. 30, 'stimulo tardos increpuisse boves'; Statius, *Theb.* iii. 431, 'increpat hasta'; Ovid, *Metam.* xiv. 820–1, 'equos . . . ictu verberis increpuit'. Thus *manu* of v. 446 parallels *hasta* of v. 447, each modifying two verbs. William's use of his lance for signals has already been mentioned (v. 310).   [6] Cf. *GG*, p. 190; *BT*, Pl. 68.

Quę fueras uictrix, pateris cur uicta uideri
Regnis terrarum Gallia nobilior?
Non homines set oues fugitis, frustraque timetis;
Illud quod facitis dedecus est nimium.
Est mare post tergum; maris est iter ad remeandum   455
Pergraue,[a] quod uobis tempus et aura negat.
Ad patriam reditus grauis est, grauis et uia longa;
Hic uobis nullum restat et effugium—
Vincere certetis, solum si uiuere uultis.'[1]
    Dixit, et extimplo serpit ad ora pudor;   460
Terga retro faciunt;[2] uultus uertuntur in hostes.
    Dux, ut erat princeps, primus et ille ferit;
Post illum reliqui feriunt. Ad corda reuersi,[3]
    Vires assumunt reiciendo metum.
Vt stipulę flammis pereunt spirantibus auris,   465
    Sic a Francigenis, Anglica turba, ruis.
Ante ducis faciem tremefactum labitur agmen,
    Mollis cera fluit ignis ut a facie.
Abstracto gladio, galeas et scuta recidit;
    Illius et sonipes corpora multa facit.   470
Heraldi frater, non territus ore leonis,
    Nomine Gernt, regis traduce progenitus,
Librando telum celeri uolitante lacerto
    Eminus emisso cuspide, corpus equi
Vulnerat, atque ducem peditem bellare coegit.   475
    Set, pedes effectus, dimicat et melius:
Nam uelox iuuenem sequitur ueluti leo frendens.
    Membratim perimens, hęc sibi uerba dedit:
'Accipe promeritam nostri de parte coronam;[4]
    Si periit sonipes, hanc tibi reddo pedes.'   480
Dixit et ad bellum conuertit protinus actum,
    Obstat et oppositis uiribus Herculeis.
Hos truncos facit, hos mutilos; hos deuorat ense;
    Perplures animas mitit et ad tenebras.

---

[a] Pgraue A, graue *added in same hand above an original* mare *deleted by the scribe*

---

[1] Vv. 450–9 bear comparison with *EE*, p. 20, where Canute, in much the same predicament, says almost the same things: 'Namque memorabat ille abesse diffugium, in terra scilicet hostes, et a litore longe remotas pupes, ideoque, si non uincerent, quod pariter occumbere deberent.'

nobler than all the kingdoms of the earth,—you, who had been the victor—how can you bear to be seen vanquished? You fly from sheep, not men, and fear without cause; what you are doing is most shameful! The sea lies behind: the sea-voyage back is formidable, wind and weather against you. It is hard to return home, hard and long the voyage; here no way of escape remains for you! You will fight to conquer, if you want only to live!'[1] He spoke, and at once their faces grew red with shame. They wheeled,[2] they turned to face the enemy. The duke, as leader, was the first to strike; after him the rest laid on. Coming to their senses,[3] they regained strength by scorning fear. As stubble consumes in flames before the breath of the wind, so, O English horde, you went to destruction before the French. At the appearance of the duke the trembling host fell back, as soft wax melts away in face of fire. With drawn sword he hewed to pieces helms and shields, and even his war-horse slew many.

Harold's brother, Gyrth by name, born of a royal line, was undaunted by the face of the lion; poising a javelin, he hurled it from afar with a strong arm. The flying weapon wounded the body of the horse and forced the duke to fight on foot; but reduced to a foot-soldier, he fought yet better, for he rushed upon the young man like a snarling lion. Hewing him limb from limb, he shouted to him: 'Take the crown you have earned from us![4] If my horse is dead, thus I requite you—as a common soldier!'

He spoke, and wheeled round to the mêlée which had instantly sprung up around him; with the strength of Hercules he withstood his opponents. Some he maimed, some he mutilated, some the sword devoured, very many souls he sent to darkness. When he

---

[2] *Terga retro faciunt* is a play on the expressions *terga uertere*, 'to flee', and *ora retro facere*, 'to turn away, fall back'. Here the French turn about to *face* the enemy.

[3] *M.*, followed by *G.*, took v. 463 as a single sentence; the punctuation of *P.* (followed by *C.*) shows that he understood *ad corda reuersi* as the idiom 'having come to their senses'. Cf. 'Imperator, versus in arcum pravum, non est adhuc ad cor reversus' (*Flores Hist.* ii. 103); 'Ego permodum ad cor revertens absolutionis beneficium petii humiliter ac devote' (*Pat. Rolls Hen. III* (1903), p. 210).

[4] William apparently thought that he had killed Harold himself.

Per medias strages equitem dum prospicit ire   485
Ex Cenomannorum^a progenitum genere,
Infecto gladio cerebro uel sanguinis unda
Innuit, ut ueniat et sibi subueniat.
Ille timens cedem negat illi ferre salutem,
Nam pauitat^b mortem ceu lepus ante canem.   490
Dux, memor ut miles, subito se uertit ad illum;¹
Per nasum galeę concitus accipiens,
Vultum telluri, plantas ad sýdera uoluit;
Sic sibi^c concessum scandere currit equum.
O cęli rector, nostri pius ac miserator,   495
Nutu diuino qui regis omne quod est,
Quas patitur clades Anglorum turma superstes!
Occidit hic pietas, regnat et impietas;
Vita perit; mors seua furit; bachatur et ensis;
Nullus ibi parcit, Mars ubi sceptra regit.   500
Postquam factus eques dux est, mox acrius hostes
Vulnerat, aggreditur, fulminat, insequitur.
Vincere dum certat, dum campum cede cruentat,
Filius Hellocis,² uir celer et facilis,
Insidiando, ducem tractabat fine grauari;   505
Set, misso iaculo, traditur ictus equo.
Corruit in terram; pedes est dux, plenus et ira.
Quomodo se teneat cogitat, aut quid agat,
Nam binis miratur equis priuatus haberi.
Heret in hoc paulo, set nihil esse putat;   510
Censet enim, uirtute sibi fortuna fauebit,
Subueniet uotis et sine fraude suis.
Ergo sui mors iurat equi, si dextra manebit,
Non sine uindicta transiet. Absque mora,
Auctorem sceleris, multos inter latitantem   515
Longe perspiciens, perdere currit eum.
Inpulsu dextrę duro mucronis et ictu
Ilia precidens, uiscera fudit humi.
At comes Eustachius,³ generosis patribus^d ortus,
Septus bellantum multiplici cuneo,   520

---

^a cenonmanno&A   ^b pauitem A, *probably influenced by* salutem, mortem, canem *in preceding lines*; *edd.* pavitat   ^c t̶ A; sibi *edd.*   ^d partib⁹ A; patribus *edd. See above, p.* lxxi

¹ *P.* and *C.* punctuate, 'Dux memor, ut miles, subito se vertit ad illum'; *M.*, followed by *G.*, 'Dux memor, ut miles subito se vertit ad illum'. It is surely

saw a knight of Maine riding through the slaughter, he signed to him with a sword dyed with brains and gore to come to his aid. But he, dreading to be cut down, refused to save him—terrified of death as a hare before a hound! The duke, like a resourceful warrior, suddenly turned upon him;[1] seizing him furiously by the nasal of the helmet, he tumbled him head over heels to the ground, and rushed to mount the horse thus left to him.

O Ruler of Heaven, thou who art tender and pitiful towards us and by divine will rulest all things, what destruction the surviving band of English suffered! Then pity died and cruelty triumphed, life perished, savage death raged, and the sword ran wild! Where Mars holds sway, no man shows mercy!

When the duke was horsed, he then assailed the enemy more strongly; he attacked, he struck like lightning, he pursued. As he strove to win, as he dyed the field with the blood of the slain, the son of Helloc,[2] a swift and able man, lay in wait, meaning to kill him. But when the javelin was cast, the horse received the blow. It fell to the ground, and the duke was on foot and filled with rage! He wondered how he could defend himself or what to do, for he was stunned to have been robbed of two horses in a single encounter. For a moment this left him confounded, then he made light of it; he judged that with courage Fortune would smile on him and further his vows without deceit. Therefore he swore that if his right hand had not lost its cunning, the death of his horse should not go unavenged! Seeing the author of the crime lurking at a distance in the press, he rushed forthwith to destroy him. Cutting through his groin with a thrust of his right hand and a merciless sword-stroke, he spilt his entrails on the ground. And then Count Eustace,[3] sprung from noble ancestors, surrounded by a great band of warriors, hastened to be held first to the duke's aid and

William who turns toward the other. The knight of Maine has already been characterized as a coward, and is unlikely to have changed his mind and approached a duke beset by English and in a very bad temper.

[2] Helloc's son is otherwise unknown, although a similar incident is recounted by Wace (*RR*, vv. 8809-14). The name is not English and may be an attempt at Havelock. But cf. also 'Haruc' mentioned in *The Chronicle of Æthelweard*, ed. A. Campbell (Nelson's Medieval Texts, 1962), pp. lix, 52.

[3] Eustace II, count of Boulogne. See above, pp. xxiii f., and below, genealogical table IV. The *Carmen* is the only source not to particularize him as 'of Boulogne'.

Ad ducis auxilium festinat primus haberi;
Efficiturque pedes dux ut abiret eques.
Miles erat quidam comitis, nutritus ab illo,
Fecerat ut domino, fecit et ille sibi.
Talibus auspiciis, comes et dux associati   525
Quo magis arma micant, bella simul repetunt.ᵃ
Amborum gladiis campus rarescit ab Anglis,
Defluit et numerus, nutat et atteritur.
Corruit apposita ceu silua minuta securi,
Sic nemus Angligenum ducitur ad nihilum.   530
Iam ferme campum uictrix effecta regebat,
Iam spolium belli Gallia leta petit,¹
Cum dux prospexit regem super ardua montis
Acriter instantes dilacerare suos.
Aduocat Eustachium; linquens ibi prelia Francis,   535
Oppressis ualidum contulit auxilium.
Alter ut Hectorides, Pontiui nobilis heres
Hos comitatur Hugo, promtus in officio;
Quartus Gilfardus, patris a cognomine dictus:²
Regis ad exicium quatuor arma ferunt.³   540
Ast alii plures? Aliis sunt hi meliores.
Si quis in hoc dubitat, actio uera probat:
Per nimias cedes nam, bellica iura tenentes⁴
Heraldus cogit pergere carnis iter.
Per clipeum primus dissoluens cuspide pectus,   545
Effuso madidatᵇ sanguinis imbre solum;

ᵃ repetim⁹ A; repetunt *edd.*   ᵇ macidat A, *P.*; madidat *al. edd.* Perhaps
maculat ?

---

¹ That plundering had begun before the death of Harold is borne out by the
Bayeux Tapestry (*BT*, Pl. 71, lower margin).
² The four knights who killed Harold are identified by Guy as William,
Eustace of Boulogne, Hugh of Ponthieu, and a 'Gilfard', probably Giffard. See
below, Appendix D, pp. 116 ff.
³ That it took several men to kill Harold is supported by FW (1066) and
Wace (*RR*, vv. 8859–60). The omission of any description of Harold's death by
William of Jumièges and William of Poitiers (who has just said that William
would not have feared to meet Harold in single combat) is understandable.
⁴ Both *P.* and *C.* have a comma after *tenentes*, indicating that it was read as
modifying *cedes*: 'By overwhelming slaughter, holding in itself the decision of
battle, Harold was forced to go the way of (all) flesh.' This interpretation, however, required that the text be emended. *P.* would have replaced *Heraldus* with
Heraldum (the note is missing, but *Heraldus* is the word starred for comment);
cogit⟨ur⟩, the emendation in *C.*, is unmetrical.   [Continued on facing page]

became a foot-soldier so that he might depart mounted. There was a certain knight whom the count had reared; what Eustace had done for his commander, that man did for him.

Under such auspices, the count and the duke, joining forces, renewed the battle together wherever the clashing arms glittered most brightly. By the swords of both the field was cleared of English, and a number deserted, tottering and exhausted. As a waning wood falls to the stroke of the axe, so the forest of Englishmen was brought to nothing.

Now the victor, joyful France almost ruled the field; already she was seeking the spoils of war[1] when the duke sighted the king far off on the steeps of the hill, fiercely hewing to pieces the Normans who were besetting him. He called Eustace to him; leaving the conflict in that place to the French, he brought strong aid to those hard pressed. Like a second son of Hector, Hugh, the noble heir of Ponthieu, escorted these two, prompt in service; fourth was Giffard, known by his father's surname:[2] these four bore arms for the destruction of the king.[3] Yet there were many others? These were better than the rest! If anyone doubts this, the true course of the action proves it, for by measureless slaughter Harold was forcing the masters of the field[4] to go the way of (all) flesh. The first, cleaving his breast through the shield with his point, drenched the earth with a gushing torrent of blood; the

There are two strong reasons for leaving the text as it stands, in addition to the undesirability of unnecessary emendation. Firstly, it is Harold who is said to have been hewing down the Normans, not the reverse (vv. 533–4), and it was the very success of the four in achieving what these others could not that made them in v. 451 *aliis . . . meliores*. Secondly, *bellica iura* is neither an idiomatic phrase nor even a common combination of words; where it occurs, it means not 'the verdict of battle', but 'the way of war'. Cf.:

> Nec querimur caesos: haec bellica jura vicesque
> Armorum . . .
>
> (Statius, *Theb.* xii. 552.)

> Mox adolescentis vestitus flore juventae,
> Armorum studium tractabat, patre jubente,
> Sed nec in hoc segnem senserunt bellica jura:
> Id quoque posteris cognovit publica cura.

(Tenth-century poem in praise of King Athelstan, quoted in *GR* i. 145–6.)

Bellica iura must not, therefore, be confused with the singular form *bellico iure* or *iure belli*, 'by right of conquest', in which the operative word is *iure*, as in *iure hereditario, iure naturali, iure sanguinis*, etc. We have here nothing more than the common medieval idiom *iura tenentes, bellica* merely indicating what kind of rights were possessed: 'Harold was forcing those possessing the rights of war (i.e. the rightful victors) to go the way of (all) flesh.' This view is supported by the statement in vv. 531–4 that the duke had all but won, save for Harold's stubborn resistance. *Actio uera probat* in this passage also bears a quasi-legal meaning; see above, the note to v. 230.

Tegmine sub galeę caput amputat ense secundus;
Et telo uentris tertius exta rigat;
Abscidit coxam quartus; procul egit ademptam:[1]
Taliter occisum terra cadauer habet.   550
Fama uolans 'Heraldus obit!' per prelia sparsit;
Mitigat extimplo corda superba timor.
Bella negant Angli. Veniam poscunt superati.
Viuere diffisi, terga dedere neci.
Dux ibi per numerum duo milia misit ad orcum,   555
Exceptis aliis milibus innumeris.
Vesper erat; iam cardo diem uoluebat ad umbras,
Victorem fecit cum Deus esse ducem.
Solum deuictis nox et fuga profuit Anglis
Densi per latebras et tegimen nemoris.   560
Inter defunctos noctem pausando peregit
Victor, et exspectat lucifer ut redeat.
Peruigil Hectorides sequitur cedendo fugaces;
Mars sibi tela gerit; mors sociata furit.
Duxit ad usque diem uario certamine noctem;   565
Nec somno premitur; somnia nec patitur.
Illuxit postquam Phebi clarissima lampas
Et mundum furuis expiat a tenebris,
Lustrauit campum, tollens et cęsa suorum
Corpora, dux terrę condidit in gremio.   570
Vermibus atque lupis, auibus canibusque uoranda
Deserit Anglorum corpora strata solo.
Heraldi corpus collegit dilaceratum,
Collectum texit sindone purpurea;[2]
Detulit et secum, repetens sua castra marina,   575
Expleat ut solitas funeris exequias.
Heraldi mater, nimio constricta dolore,
Misit ad usque ducem, postulat et precibus,
Orbate miserę natis tribus, et uiduatę,
Pro tribus, unius[a] reddat ut ossa sibi,   580
Si placet aut corpus puro preponderet auro.
Set dux iratus prorsus utrumque negat,

Iurans quod pocius presentis littora portus
Illi committet aggere sub lapidum.

---

[a] unis A; unius *edd.*

second smote off his head below the protection of the helmet and the third pierced the inwards of his belly with his lance; the fourth hewed off his thigh and bore away the severed limb:[1] the ground held the body thus destroyed.

The flying rumour 'Harold is dead!' spread through the fray and forthwith proud hearts were tamed by fear. The English refused battle. Vanquished, they besought mercy; despairing of life, they fled from death. Two thousand in number the duke sent to Hades then, not counting the other thousands beyond telling. It was evening; already the wheeling heavens were turning day to twilight when God made the duke the victor. Only darkness and flight through the thickets and coverts of the deep forest availed the defeated English. The conqueror, resting meanwhile, passed the night among the dead and waited till day should return. Ever vigilant, the son of Hector pursued the fleeing with slaughter; Mars served as his squire, death raged, his comrade. Till it was fully day he spent the night in varying conflict, not overcome by sleep, nor suffering himself to dream.

After the glorious light of the sun began to shine and cleanse the world of brooding darkness, the duke surveyed the field, and taking up the bodies of his fallen, he buried them in the bosom of the earth. The corpses of the English, strewn upon the ground, he left to be devoured by worms and wolves, by birds and dogs. Harold's dismembered body he gathered together, and wrapped what he had gathered in fine purple linen;[2] and returning to his camp by the sea, he bore it with him, that he might carry out the customary funeral rites.

The mother of Harold, in the toils of overwhelming grief, sent even to the duke himself, asking with entreaties that he would restore to her, unhappy woman, a widow and bereft of three sons, the bones of one in place of the three; or, if it pleased him, she would outweigh the body in pure gold. But the duke, infuriated, utterly rejected both petitions, swearing that he would sooner entrust the shores of that very port to him—under a heap of stones!

---

[1] Cf. the description of this incident in *GR* ii. 303, and see below, Appendix D, pp. 119 f. *Coxa* may be a euphemism; cf. 'Essai d'interprétation du thème iconographique de la paternité dans l'art byzantin', by S. A. Papadopoulos, in *Cahiers archéologiques: Fin de l'Antiquité et Moyen Âge* xviii (Paris, 1969), pp. 120–36.

[2] *Sindon* is used at this period of linen, rather than of cotton, and frequently of both altar-cloths and shrouds. Cf. Petrus Comestor, *Hist. Schol.*, *Exodus* 63. Alan of Lille also speaks of *sindon purpura* (*Planc. Nat.*, *P.L.* ccx. 432c).

Ergo uelut fuerat testatus, rupis in alto   585
 Precepit claudi uertice corpus humi.
Extimplo quidam, partim Normannus et Anglus,
 Compater Heraldi,[1] iussa libenter agit.
Corpus enim regis cito sustulit et sepeliuit;
 Imponens lapidem, scripsit et in titulo: 590
'Per mandata ducis rex hic Heralde quiescis,
 Vt custos maneas littoris et pelagi.'
Dux, cum gente sua, plangens super ossa sepulta,
 Pauperibus Christi munera distribuit.
Nomine postposito ducis, et sic rege locato,   595
 Hinc regale sibi nomen adeptus abit.
Hastinge portus castris ter[a] quinque diebus[2]
 Mansit, et ad Doueram uertit abinde uiam.
Nec medium complerat[b] iter cum territus, illi
 Occurrit populus, partus in obsequio,[3]   600
Obtulit et claues castri,[c] portasque reclusas
 Testatur,[4] simulans uelle subesse sibi.
(Est ibi mons altus, strictum mare, litus opacum.
 Hinc hostes cicius Anglica regna petunt.
Set castrum Douerę, pendens a uertice montis,   605
 Hostes reiciens, litora tuta facit.)
Clauibus acceptis, rex intrans męnia castri
 Precepit Angligenis euacuare domos.
Hos introduxit per quos sibi regna subegit,
 Vnumquemque misit suum ad[5] hospicium.   610
Ilico peruasit terror uicinia castri,
 Vrbes et burgos, oppida queque replens.
Nobilior reliquis urbs Cantorberia[d] dicta,
 Missis legatis, prima tributa tulit.

---

[a] t̄ A; tunc *P.*, *C.*; tum *M.*, *G.*   [b] cōpat A; complerat *edd.*   [c] cast́s
A; castris *P.*, *G.*; castri *C.*, *M.*   [d] Cantorbeia A

---

[1] i.e. William Malet (cf. *GG*, p. 204 n. 4). The manner in which Malet was
part English has not been definitely established. If it could be shown that he had
descent from the family of Leofric of Mercia, he would have been a cousin of
Harold's queen, and thus connected with him by affinity. *Compater*, at this
period, can mean 'godfather', 'connection by spiritual affinity', and 'comrade,
intimate friend'; it is not attested in the sense of 'fellow godfather' until the
thirteenth century, and there is no other evidence to support the assertion often
met with that Harold and Malet had stood sponsors together. *M.* and *G.* read
Compatit, in error, for *compatior* is normally deponent and takes its object in the

Therefore, even as he had sworn, he commanded the body to be
buried in the earth on the high summit of a cliff; and forthwith
a certain man, part Norman, part English, Harold's comrade,[1]
willingly did his behest; for he swiftly took up the king's body and
buried it, setting over it a stone, and he wrote as epitaph:
> 'By the duke's commands, O Harold, you rest here a king,
> That you may still be guardian of the shore and sea.'

The duke, lamenting amidst his people over the buried bones,
distributed alms to the poor of Christ. And with the name of duke
laid aside, and the king being thus interred, he departed from that
place, having himself assumed the royal title.

* * * * * *

II.

For a fortnight[2] William remained in the camp at the port of
Hastings and from there he directed his march towards Dover; nor
had he completed half the distance when the people, terrified, came
to meet him in submission.[3] They both offered the keys of the
stronghold[4] and declared the gates open, pretending they wished
to be subject to him. (In that place there is a lofty height, a narrow
sea, an overshadowed strand. From here enemies most readily
attack the English realms, but the castle of Dover, looming from
the height, beats off assailants and protects the shores.)

The keys received, the king, entering the stronghold, ordered
the English people to leave their homes. He brought in those by
whose help he had subdued the lands to himself, and each one he
sent to his own[5] lodging. Instantly terror swept through the towns
and boroughs near the stronghold, filling every inhabited place.
Envoys having been dispatched, the city of Canterbury, more

dative (cf. above, v. 69: 'compaciendo sibi'). For comment on Harold's funeral
see above, pp. xliii ff.
    [2] The same phrase as in v. 54 (q.v.). *Ter*, whether as a separate word or as part
of one, is always written *t̂* in A. *Tum*, read here and in v. 54 by *M.* and *G.*, is
abbreviated *tū* (v. 695, twice); *tunc*, read here by *P.* and *C.*, is written *t̂c* (vv. 45,
348, 443). Therefore chronologies of this part of the campaign based on the texts of
the editors rather than on the manuscript, such as that of D. C. Douglas (*William
the Conqueror*, London, 1964, pp. 398, 451), are nine days out in their reckoning.
    [3] *Partus in obsequio*. This unusual phrase seems to be the passive equivalent
of *obsequium pario*. Cf. Terence, *And.* i. 1. 41:
> obsequium amicos, veritas odium parit.
We owe this reference to Professor Jean Préaux.
    [4] *C.*'s and *M.*'s emendations are justified. Dover is elsewhere (vv. 605, 607,
611) always called *castrum*, and Guy distinguishes carefully between *castrum*,
'stronghold, fortified place', and *castra*, '(temporary) camp'.
    [5] See the note to v. 439.

Post, aliȩ plures nimium sua iura tenentes[a]   615
Regi sponte sua munera grata ferunt.[1]
Et ueluti muscȩ stimulo famis exagitatȩ
Vlcera densatim plena cruore petunt,
Vndique sic Angli regi currunt famulari.
Pergit muneribus nec uacuata manus;   620
Omnes dona ferunt et sub iuga colla reponunt;
Flexis poplitibus, oscula dant pedibus.
Per spacium mensis cum gente perendinat illic;[2]
Post, alio uadit castra locare sibi.
Guincestram misit; mandat primatibus urbis,   625
Vt faciunt alii, ferre tributa sibi.
(Hanc regina tenet regis de dote prioris
Hetguardi, qua re dedecus esse putat
Sic sibi[b] concessam si uadit tollere sedem.
Solum uectigal postulat atque fidem.)   630
Vna primates reginȩ consuluerunt,
Illaque, concedens, ferre petita iubet.
Taliter et regis precepto spirat[3] uterque,
Nam domine pariter et sua dona ferunt.
Rex sic pacatus tentoria fixa resoluit;   635
Quo populosa nitet Londona uertit iter.
(Vrbs est ampla nimis, peruersis plena colonis,
Et regni reliquis dicior est opibus.
A leua muris, a dextris[4] flumine tuta,
Hostes nec metuit nec pauet arte capi.)   640
Hanc bello superata petit gens improba, sperans
Viuere per longum libera tempus in hac.
Set quia pernimius terror uallauerat omnes,
Vndique planctus erat meror et impaciens,
Vna postremum rectores atque potentes   645
Tali consilio consuluere sibi:
Scilicet ut puerum natum de traduce regis[5]
In regem sacrent, ne sine rege forent.

[a] timtes A; timentes edd.   [b] t̊ A; sibi P., C., M.

---

[1] A's reading presents difficulties: *timeo* with accusative object cannot mean
'fear for', and yet *sua* in v. 616 must have the same antecedent as *sua* in v. 617,
that is, *aliȩ plures*. The only translation possible, 'fearing their own laws', is
meaningless.
We therefore suggest that the original reading may have been 'nimium sua

renowned than the rest, was the first to pay tribute. Afterwards many other places—in possession of their own rights—[1] presented acceptable gifts to the king voluntarily; and just as flies, spurred on by hunger, throng in swarms to sores full of blood, so from all sides the English hastened to attend the king. Nor did any come with a hand empty of offerings, all bore gifts and set their necks under his yoke; going upon their knees, they kissed his feet.

For the space of a month he tarried there[2] with his people; afterwards he went to set up a camp for himself elsewhere. He sent to Winchester and ordered the chief men of the city to pay tribute to him as others were doing. (This place the queen held in dower from Edward the former king, for which reason he considered it would be dishonourable if he went to take away the seat thus granted her; he asked only an impost and a pledge.) The chief men took counsel together for the queen and she, yielding, ordered them to take what was demanded. And in this way she and they lived in peace[3] by the king's order, for they bore the lady's gifts together with their own.

Thus placated, the king struck his pitched tents. He directed his march to where populous London gleamed. (It is a great city, overflowing with froward inhabitants and richer in treasure than the rest of the kingdom. Protected on the left side by walls, on the right side[4] by the river, it neither fears enemies nor dreads being taken by storm.) The obdurate people conquered in battle sought this place, believing that in it they could dwell for a long time masterless. But because far too great terror surrounded them—everywhere there was lamentation and ungovernable grief—at length the rulers and the magnates made provision for themselves by a plan of this kind; namely, that they consecrate as king a boy of the old royal line,[5] in order that they might not be kingless; for

iura tenentes' (cf. vv. 211, 543), 'possessing, to a great degree, their own rights', i.e. 'almost wholly self-governing'. Such an emendation would suit the context: Canterbury has submitted only after urging by William's envoys. The other towns, however, come in without coercion, and not because the surrender of their metropolis binds them (they are *sui iuris*), but of their own free will.

[2] See above, pp. xlvi f.

[3] As William is said to have thought it shameful even to confiscate Edith's dower (vv. 628–9), *spirat* can hardly mean 'breathe', 'live', implying that he might have killed her had she not paid. For the meaning 'live without responsibility, carefree', cf. Adalbero of Laon, *Carmen ad Rotbertum Regem* (ed. G. A. Hückel, Paris, 1901), v. 211, describing the two classes that inhabit heaven:

Pars quedam regnat, quedam pars altera spirat.

[4] *Dextris* instead of *dextra*, perhaps because of the preceding *muris*; cf. v. 490. For the lack of a wall on the river-side of London, see above, p. xlix n. 1 and the note to v. 677 below.

[5] Edgar the atheling, son of Edward the Exile and grandson of Edmund Ironside.

Autumat insipiens uulgus se posse tueri
Regali solo nomine, non opere.[1]   650
In statuam regis puer est electus ab illis,
Cuius presidium contulit exicium.
Sparsit fama uolans quod habet Londonia regem,
Gaudet et Anglorum qui superest populus.
Interea, regni totum qui querit habere,   655
Et, uotis compos, cui fauet omnipotens,
Hostili gladio quę nec uastauerat igne,
Vt non ingenio uindicat imperio.[2]
Comperit ut factum fatuis quod non erat ęquum;
Prescriptę muros urbis adire iubet.   660
Paruit extimplo celeri uelocius aura
Agmen belligerum castra locare sibi.
Densatis castris a leua męnia cinxit,
Et bellis hostes esse dedit uigiles.
Dimidię leugę spacio distabat ab urbe   665
Regia regalis, aula decora nimis,
Fertur ab antiquis quę Guest[3] uocitata colonis;
Post, Petri nomen auxit ab ęcclesia.
Prouidus hanc sedem sibi rex elegit ad edem,
Quę sibi complacuit iure nec inmerito: 670
Nam ueluti patrum testantur gesta priorum,
Ex solito reges hic diadema ferunt.[4]
Edificat moles, ueruecis cornua ferro
Fabricat et talpas, urbis ad excidium.
Intonat inde minas, pęnas et bella minatur,   675
Iurans quod, licitum si sibi sit spacium,
Męnia dissoluet, turres equabit harenis,
Elatam turrem[a] destruet aggerie.[5]

---

[a] turre A; turrem *edd.*

[1] Cf., on the later Merovingians: 'qui nomen tantum regis, sed nullam potesta-
tem regiam habuerunt' (Eginhardi *Annales, P.L.* cv, col. 373), and on the later
Carolingians: 'Lotharius rex Franciae praelatus est solo nomine, Hugo vero non
nomine sed actu et opere' (*Lettres de Gerbert* (Pope Sylvester II), ed. J. Havet
(Paris, 1889), p. 46).
[2] We understand the elliptical vv. 657–8 as follows:
'⟨Dux uastat⟩ hostili gladio ⟨ea⟩ quę nec⟨dum⟩ uastauerat igne, ⟨quia⟩ uindicat
non ingenio ⟨sed⟩ imperio.' The artifice of Edgar's election is contrasted with
the hard fact of William's military power.
[3] *Guest.* The palace of Westminster. Cf. *RR* vv. 5541–2; *Historia Ramesiensis,*
ed. W. Dunn Macray, London 1886 (*RS* lxxxiii), p. 178.

the foolish populace believed it could protect itself merely by the royal name devoid of power.[1] The boy was elected by them to be the shadow of a king, a defence fraught with ruin. The flying rumour that London had a king spread abroad, and what remained of the English nation rejoiced.

Meanwhile, he who sought to possess the whole realm, and to whom the Almighty, partaker of his vows, showed favour, laid waste by the hostile sword what he had not ravaged by fire; for *he* made his claim by right of authority, not by a ruse.[2] He received word that what was not just had been done by these fools, and he ordered the walls of that city to be invested. At once, swifter than the wind, the valiant army appeared to set up its camps. He surrounded the walls on the left side with encampments, set close together, and kept the enemy alert for battle.

The royal palace stands apart from the city at a distance of half a league, a most stately hall which is said to have been called West[3] by the inhabitants of old; afterwards its name was lengthened from that of Peter's minster. The prudent king chose for his abode this seat, which was very acceptable to him—rightly and not without cause—for here, as the acts of former rulers attest, kings are accustomed to wear the crown.[4]

He built siege-engines and made moles and the iron horns of battering-rams for the destruction of the city; then he thundered forth menaces and threatened war and vengeance, swearing that, given time, he would destroy the walls, raze the bastions to the ground, and bring down the proud tower in rubble.[5]

---

[4] How the phrase 'patrum . . . gesta priorum' is to be taken is not certain. Harold II may have had a crown-wearing when he came from York to Westminster at Easter 1066 (*ASC*, MSS. C, D, 1066). Osbert of Clare speaks of Edward the Confessor as arrayed in his crown and sceptre holding feast at Easter, 'apud Westmonasterium, in regali palatio' (*VE*, pp. 66 f.). The connection between Saint-Riquier and England became close only in Edward's reign, and Guy was probably still a youth when Edward succeeded. He may be simply assuming an antiquity for the palace. On the other hand, if the palace Canute is said to have built at Thorney be identical with his 'aula', in which Godwin held first place among the nobles (*VE*, p. 7), the royal hall at Westminster would have been, in Guy's time, the seat, actual or potential, of five earlier kings.

[5] *Mœnia dissoluet* and *turres equabit harenis* mean much the same thing—to make the walls of London as though they had never been, to make them level with the river-shore, which, as we have already been told (v. 639), was unfortified. The third phrase in the rhetorical sequence of William's threat presents a problem, as it is impossible in our present state of knowledge of pre-Conquest London to identify the *elata turris*. It may have been a particularly imposing gate-tower, but could equally well have been any large or lofty building. *Aggerie* is a variant of *aggeratim*, 'in heaps', and the implication that the *elata turris*, alone of London's structures, could not be utterly obliterated, suggests a massive fortification.

Talibus auditis, ciues pauor atterit urbis,
Occupat, exagitat, torquet et excruciat. 680
Intus erat quidam contractus debilitate
Renum sicque pedum segnis, ab officio
Vulnera pro patria quia non^a numerosa recepit.
Lectica uehitur, mobilitate carens;
Omnibus ille tamen^b primatibus imperat urbis, 685
Eius et auxilio publica res agitur.
Huic per legatum clam rex pociora reuelat,
Secretim^c poscens quatinus his faueat:
Solum rex uocitetur, ait, set commoda regni[1]
Vt iubet Ansgardus[2] subdita cuncta regat. 690
Ille quidem cautus caute legata recepit,
Cordis et occulto condidit in thalamo.
Natu maiores, omni leuitate repulsa,
Aggregat, et uerbis talibus alloquitur:
'Egregii fratres, tum ui, tum sepius arte— 695
Est ubi nunc sensus uester? Et actus ubi?[3]
Cernitis oppressos ualido certamine muros
Et circumseptos cladibus innumeris.
Molis et erectę transcendit machina turres,
Ictibus et lapidum^d męnia scissa ruunt. 700
Casibus a multis, ex omni parte ruina
Eminet, et nostra corda timore labant;
Atque manus populi, nimio percussa pauore,
Vrbis ad auxilium segniter arma mouet.
Nosque foris uastat gladius, pauor angit et intus, 705
Et nullum nobis presidium superest.
Ergo, precor, uobis si spes est ulla salutis,
Quatinus addatis uiribus ingenium;
Est quia precipuum, si uis succumbat in actum,
Quod uirtute nequit, fiat ut ingenio. 710

---

^a cęn A; quùm non *T.*; quoniam *M., G., T2*   ^b taṁ *superscript over deleted* carens A   ^c Secreti A; '*An* secretim?' *M.*   ^d palidû A; validis *T.*; lapidum *alii*

[1] Here *commoda regni* might mean 'the goods of the kingdom', but this is a meaning difficult to assign at v. 784 (q.v.). In both instances, the meaning seems close to 'commonweal'. Cf. 'pro tocius regni comodo quantum in vobis est auxilium porrigatis' (*Historia Aurea*, ed. V. H. Galbraith, *EHR* xliii (1948), p. 211), the meaning confirmed by the French version of this letter (A. H. Thomas, *Calendar of Plea and Memoranda Rolls (1323–64)*, pp. 41–2). Similar

When they heard such things, dread wore down the citizens of London, dread possessed them, tormented them, racked and tortured them. In the city there was a certain man crippled by a weakness of the loins and therefore slow upon his feet, because he had received some few wounds in the service of his country. He was borne on a litter, lacking the ability to move, yet he commanded all the chief men of the city and the affairs of the community were conducted by his aid. To this man, by an envoy, the king secretly revealed a better choice, privately seeking to learn how far he favoured this. Let him only be *called* king, he said, but merely in order that he may administer all the interests of the kingdom[1] subject to him as Ansgar[2] directed. However, that cautious man received this communication warily and laid it away in the secret chamber of his heart. He assembled the elders, all trifling rejected, and addressed them, it is said, in such words as these: 'Worshipful brethren: First by force, then more often by expedient, (we have opposed the enemy); towards which is your inclination now, for which is your verdict?[3] You perceive the walls beset in a great contest and hemmed in by a countless host bent on destruction. The siege-engine on the huge mound that has been raised overtops the towers and the ramparts fall, riven by the blows of stones. With many falls in all parts collapse is imminent, and our hearts quail with fear. Moreover the mass of the nation, panic-stricken, is slow to take up arms in aid of the city. And so from without the sword destroys us and dread gnaws within, and no help remains for us. Therefore, if you have any hope of deliverance, I entreat you to add craft to strength; for if force fail in opposing an action, it is best that what cannot be done by valour be achieved by guile. It is for us, therefore, to act discreetly in this

expressions occur in the letters of Stephen of Tournai ('nostre reipublice commodis', *Ep.* xxviii, ed. J. Delisle, Paris, 1893, p. 42), and the *Carolinus* of Gilo Parisiensis ('comoda publica', *Carol.* v. 215, in Bouquet, xvii. 293).

² Ansgardus. Probably Esegar the Staller, grandson of Tofig the Proud. See above p. liii nn.

³ Like vv. 657–8, an elliptical sentence. We understand the sense to be: '(We have attempted to stop William) once by force (at Hastings) and more often (since) by diplomacy. Towards which is your inclination now? What course of action do you favour?' *Tum . . . tum* in v. 695 expresses at once both internal contrast and joint contrast of past time with the *nunc* of v. 696. With v. 696 cf. Cicero, *De oratore* i. 51, 222: 'qui est iste tuus sensus, quae cogitatio?'

Est igitur nobis super hoc prudenter agendum,
Et pariter sanum querere consilium.
Censeo quapropter, si uobis constat honestum,
Hostes dum lateant omnia quę patimur,
Actutum^a docilis noster legatus ut hosti   715
Mittatur, uerbis fallere qui satagat:
Seruicium simulet^b nec non et fędera pacis,
Et dextras dextrę subdere,[1] si iubeat.'
Omnibus hoc placuit; dicto uelocius implent.
Mititur ad regem uir racione capax[2]   720
Ordine qui retulit, decorans sermone faceto,
Vtile fraternum, non secus ac proprium.

f. 230^v

Set quia uix patula teneatur compede uulpes,
Fallitur a rege fallere quem uoluit;
Namque palam laudat rex, atque latenter ineptat   725
Quicquid ab Ansgardo nuncius attulerat.
Obcecat donis stolidum, uerbisque fefellit,
Premia promitens innumerosa sibi.
Ille, retro rutilo gradiens honeratus ab auro,
A quibus est missus talia dicta refert:[3]   730
'Rex uobis pacem dicit profertque salutem;
Vestris mandatis paret et absque dolis.
Set Dominum testor, cui rerum seruit imago,[4]
Post Dauid regem nescit habere parem!
Pulchrior est sole,[5] sapientior et Salomone;   735
Promptior est Magno largior et Carolo.[6]
Contulit Eguardus quod rex donum sibi regni
Monstrat et adfirmat, uosque probasse refert.
Hoc igitur superest, ultra si uiuere uultis,
Debita cum manibus reddere iura sibi.'   740

---

^a Acutũ A; Accitùs *T.*; Actutum *M.*, *G.*, *T2.*   ^b simul 7 A

[1] This phrase can be taken literally, as describing the act of homage, 'to set (our) right hands beneath (his) right hand', but is more likely to be a play on *subdere*, 'to counterfeit' and *dare dextram*, 'to swear homage', and to mean, 'counterfeit (our) homage'. Ansgar is playing for time.

[2] For *ratione capax*, 'one skilled in presenting a case', cf. Ermoldus iii. 72:

> Witcharium vocat, qui forte advenerat illuc,
> Vir bonus, atque sagax, et ratione capax.

Cf. also Stephen of Rouen, *Draco Normannicus* iii. 2. 95 (ed. H. Omont, Rouen, 1894, p. 123):

> Ut ratione capax vim perspicit ipsa loquentis,
> Dat monachis caris corporis casa sui.

business and at the same time to seek a prudent plan. For this reason I counsel—if it seem good to you—that while all we suffer is still unknown to the enemy an apt messenger of ours be sent to him immediately; one who may seek to deceive him with words, feign submission and even peace-pacts, and, if he so order, counterfeit our homage!'[1]

This was acceptable to them all; they put the plan into action forthwith. A persuasive[2] man was sent to the king. He reported in due order, embellished with fine speech, what was to his brethren's advantage no less than to his own. But because the fox can hardly be held by open snares, he was deceived by the king whom he sought to deceive; for the king, indeed, openly commended whatever message the herald brought from Ansgar, but in secret derided it. He blinded the fool with gifts and deceived him with words, promising him innumerable rewards. Returning weighed down with red gold, this man reported as follows to those who had sent him[3]: 'The king proclaims peace and offers you safety; he complies with your demands unfeignedly. But I take to witness the Lord —Master of Truth[4]—He cannot have had such a king since David! He is more glorious than the sun[5] and wiser than Solomon; more valiant and more bountiful than Charlemagne![6] He shows and maintains that King Edward granted him the gift of the kingdom, and reports that you approved it. This one course remains, therefore, if you wish to survive; to render him homage, with the rights due to him.'

Capax can take the ablative from late classical times; cf. Fortunatus, *Vita S. Martini* iv. 540 (*MGH AA* iv. 365):

> nec se mente capax, sensu spatiante vacillans.

[3] Cf. v. 306. Here, *his* has been omitted.

[4] Cf. Hebrews 10: 1 for *rerum imago* in the sense, 'reality', 'truth', appropriate in an oath asserting truthfulness. There may be, as well, a play on *imago*; the lines following consist of a number of comparisons.

[5] *Sole* must have a long final 'e'. Cf. Godfrey of St. Victor, *Fons Philos.* i. 50. 451:

> Ut gustavi tertii fluminis saporem
> Terrae globum sexies luna grossiorem
> Sole tamen octies didici minorem.

Similar irregular lengthening of final 'e' occurs in the poems of Fulco of Beauvais (cf. M. L. Colker, *Traditio* x (1954), p. 206), as does the comparison of William to both David and Solomon (ibid., p. 245, *Epist.* xi).

[6] *M.* punctuated this line so as to read *Magno* and *Carolo* as two persons—Pompey and Charlemagne. However, Pompey, a Roman general, would be

[Note continued on p. 49]

Annuit hoc uulgus, iustum probat esse senatus,
Et puerum regem cętus uterque negat.
Vultibus in terram^a deflexis, regis ad aulam
Cum puero pergunt agmine composito.
Reddere per claues urbem, sedare furorem   745
Oblato querunt munere cum manibus.
Nouit ut aduentum, factus rex obuius illis
Cum puero reliquis. Oscula grata dedit,
Culpas indulsit gratanter, dona recepit,
Et sic susceptos tractat honorifice.   750
Per fidi^b speciem[1] proprium commendat honorem,
Et iuramentis perfida corda ligat.
Christi natalis, nostrę spes una salutis,
Quam mundus celebrat, proxima lux aderat;
In qua promeritam disponit ferre coronam,   755
Et ducis abiecto nomine, rex fieri.
Auro uel gemmis iubet ut sibi nobile stemma
Illud quod deceat, fiat ab artifice.
Misit Arabs aurum, gemmas a flumine Nilus;
Grecia prudentem dirigit arte fabrum   760
Qui Salomoniacum, uix deterior Salomone,
Mirificum fecit et diadema decens.[2]
Principio, frontis medium carbunculus ornat;
Post hinc iacinctus lucifer insequitur;
Tercius aurifico resplendet in orbe topazon;   765
Saphirus quartum ditat honore gradum;
Sardonicus quintus regales obsidet aures;
Cui calcedonius ordine sextus adit;^c
Septimus est iaspis, procul a quo pellitur hostis;
Sardius octauus igniuomus rutilat.   770
Figitur in nona sella lux crisolitana;^d
Tuque, berille, locum clarificas decimum;
Vndecimum uiridis numerum smaragdus^e adimplet;
Huic quoque crisoprasus^f fert duodenus^g opem.[3]
Verticis in summo stat margarita suprema,   775
Quę sibi subpositos^h luce replet lapides,

^a terra A, *edd., but* deflectere in *requires the accusative*   ^b P̶ fid̂ i A; Perfidià
T.; Per fidei *P., C., T2.*; Perfidiae *M., G.*   ^c abit A, *P., C.*; adit *M. G.*
^d c̊sontana A   ^e smarag̊ A   ^f crisoprassus A   ^g duden⁹ A   ^h subposito A

The people approved this, the Witan allowed that it was just, and both assemblies denied that the boy was king. With downcast bearing they proceeded in an orderly concourse to the king's hall, together with the child. They planned to surrender the city by means of the keys, and to appease wrath by a gift offered with homage.

When he knew of their coming, the king made himself gracious towards those remaining with the boy. He gave them grateful kisses, cheerfully forgave crimes and accepted presents, and showed honour to those thus taken into his favour. Appearing to be one in whom they could trust,[1] he enhanced his own repute and bound their treacherous hearts fast with oaths!

The day which the world celebrates as the Nativity of Christ, sole hope of our salvation, was at hand; on which feast William determined to wear the crown that he had won and, with the name of duke renounced, be made a king. He commanded that a noble crown of gold and jewels, such as would be seemly, be fashioned for him by a master-craftsman. Arabia provided gold, Nilus gems from the river; Greece inspired a smith skilled in the art as he who[2]—scarcely inferior to Solomon—created Solomon's wondrous and befitting diadem.

Foremost a ruby adorned the centre of the brow; next after this a radiant jacinth followed; third in the circlet of wrought gold a topaz glittered; the fourth place a sapphire enriched with beauty; fifth was sardonyx, set at the king's ears, to which chalcedony came next, the sixth in order. Seventh was jasper, which from afar repels the foe; the eighth, a fire-breathing sard, glowed red. In the ninth seat a lucent chrysolite was throned, and you, beryl, illumined the tenth place. A green emerald completed the eleventh number, to which colour also chrysoprase, the twelfth, gave strength.[3] At the

completely out of place in a list made up otherwise of rulers with a mystique in the eyes of the Middle Ages. In addition, Guy elsewhere calls Pompey 'Pompeius,' not 'Magnus', and has last mentioned him with some contempt (vv. 351–3).

[1] The construction is 'per speciem alicuius', 'in the guise of something'. M.'s emendation is unnecessary, and destroys the play on words between this phrase and the *perfida* of the next line. P. misread the minute script. The redundant stroke on the 'd' of *fidi* occurs also on the 'l' of *colonis* (v. 637), *leua* (v. 777), and *Anglorum* (v. 654). The second word is simply the genitive of *fidus*, 'one in whom one can trust', and the sense of the line that of v. 724, 'Fallitur a rege fallere quem uoluit'.

[2] As in v. 730, a pronoun has been omitted. Solomon's crown, like Solomon himself, was credited with occult power.

[3] The twelve stones listed are identical, except for the *carbunculus*, with those said by Marbod to form the floor of heaven (*De duodecim lapidibus. P.L.* clxxi,

In cuius dextra leua quoque parte locata
Est ametisti lux, cui color est geminus.
Ethereus ueluti propulsis nubibus axis
   Insitus ignitis sẏderibus rutilat,   780
Aurea lucifluis distincta corona lapillis
   Vndique sic renitet[a] lumine clarifico.
Sceptrum cum uirga componit post diadema,
   Commoda quę pariter significant patrię;[1]
Nam sceptro tumidę regni moderantur habenę,   785
   Dispersos uirga colligit ac reuocat.
Tempore disposito quo rex sacrandus habetur,
   Terrę magnates et populosa manus,
Pontificale decus, uenerabilis atque senatus
   Vndique conueniunt regis ad officium.   790
Ex his eligitur presul celeberrimus unus,[2]
   Moribus insignis et probitate cluens,
Qui regem sacret, simul et sacrando coronet,
   Et regale caput stemmate nobilitet.[b]
Illius imperio, solito de more priorum,   795
   Bini ponuntur magnificare Deum.[3]
Ordo cucullatus, clerus cum pontificali
   Nobilitate, petunt templa beata Petri:
Anteferendo cruces sequitur processio cleri;
   Post clerum pergit pontificale decus.   800
Rex, multa comitumque ducum uallante caterua,
   Vltimus incedit cum strepitu populi.
Illius et dextram sustentat metropolita;
   Ad leuam graditur alter honore pari.[4]
Taliter ęcclesiam laudes modulando[5] requirit   805
   Rex, et regalem ducitur ad cathedram.
Laudibus expletis, turba reticente canora,
   Indixit pacem cantor et ut sileant.
Conticuit clerus; compescuit ora senatus;
   Non est auditus ullus ab ore sonus.   810

---

   [a] retinet A; renitet *edd.*   [b] nobilitate A; nobilitet *edd.*

---

col. 1772); they were thought to possess certain virtues and to enhance them in
the wearer. *Carbunculus* is a name used of any red gem; Marbod's alternative,
the amethyst, was also considered red ('totus rubeus').

highest point, above all, stood a pearl that filled the stones below itself with light, placed on the right and on the left of which there gleamed twin amethysts, perfectly matched. As with the clouds dispelled the wheel of heaven turns, studded with blazing stars, so the golden crown, adorned with precious stones glorious with light, flashed upon all sides with a dazzling radiance.

After the diadem, (the artificer) prepared the sceptre and the rod, which alike symbolize the weal of the realm;[1] for by the sceptre the tossing reins of the kingdom are controlled, and the rod gathers and recalls the scattered.

At the holy season in which it was ordained that the king should be consecrated, the high men of the land and a multitude of the people, the dignity of the episcopate and the venerable Witan, assembled from all sides for the royal rite. From these was chosen one most renowned bishop,[2] peerless in character and famed for righteousness, who would consecrate the king, and in consecrating also crown him and dignify the royal head with the diadem; both dedicated together to the glory of God by his authority, in the manner customary with those of yore.[3]

The monastic order, the clergy with the episcopal nobility, sought the blessed church of Peter. Crosses borne on before, the procession of the clergy followed; after the clergy proceeded the dignity of the episcopate. Last, to the shouts of the people, the king advanced, surrounded by a great troop of counts and captains. A metropolitan supported his right hand; at his left walked the other of equal rank.[4]

In this manner, to the chanting of the *Laudes*,[5] the king sought the church and was conducted to the royal chair. The *Laudes* ended and the chanting throng hushed, a precentor enjoined silence and bade them remain quiet. The clergy ceased utterance, the Witan did not speak; not a sound was heard from any mouth.

---

[1] *Commoda . . . patriȩ.* See the note to v. 689.

[2] No doubt Aldred, archbishop of York, is meant, but the omission of a name may be significant. See above, p. xxii.

[3] For a discussion of the coronation rite as presented in the *Carmen* see above, pp. liv–lix.

[4] Aldred and Stigand of Canterbury. That they are styled metropolitans of equal rank shows that the poem must have been written before 1072. See above, pp. xxi f.

[5] *Laudes* preceded the Christmas service in Normandy at this period. Cf. E. H. Kantorowicz, *Laudes Regiae* (Berkeley, 1958), pp. 166, 178.

Normannus quidam presul¹ mox pulpita² scandens,
Famosis Gallis talia uerba dedit:
'Oblatus uobis si rex placet, edite nobis,
Arbitrio uestri nam decet hoc fieri.'
Concessit populus, clerus fauet atque senatus;   815
Quod sermone nequit, innuit et manibus.
Sermo peroratur³ post illum metropolite;ᵃ
Hęc eadem lingua protulit Angligena.
Spirat utroqueᵇ manus; laudat; spondet famulari;
Annuit ex toto corde subesse sibi.   820
Conuertens sanctam se summus presul ad aram,
Ante suam regem constituit faciem;
Ad se pontifices accitos congregat omnes,
Et cum rege simul membra dedere solo.
Inchoat incentor stans rectus Kyrieleison;   825
Sanctorum pariter poscit habere preces.
⟨Sed⟩⁴ postquam Sanctorum sitᶜ Letania peracta,
Presule cum summo pontificalis honor
Erigitur, solo prostrato rege relicto.
Incentor siluit; omnis et ordo tacet.   830
Summus et antistes populo precepit ut oret;
Incipit et proprium protinus officium.
Collectam dixit; regem de puluere tollit;
Crismate diffuso regis et ipse caput
Vnxit, et in regem regali more sacrauit.   835

*   *   *   *   *₅

ᵃ metropolite A; metropolita P., C.   ᵇ utq̃ A, edd.; but this does not
scan. M suggested utrinque   ᶜ fit A; sit P., C.

Thereupon a certain Norman bishop,[1] mounting the dais,[2] addressed such words as these to the renowned men of France: 'If the king presented please you, declare it to us, for it is fitting that this be done by your free choice.' The people thus addressed consented; the clergy and also the Witan applauded, intimating by their hands what they were unable to say. Afterwards a speech was delivered[3] by the metropolitan; this set forth the same thing in the English tongue. On both sides the throng drew breath, hailed William, vowed to be his subjects, promised with a whole heart to be obedient to him.

Turning himself towards the holy altar, the archbishop made the king stand facing it. He gathered to him all the bishops who had been summoned, and together with the king they prostrated themselves upon the ground. Standing upright, the precentor began the *Kyrie eleison* and also invoked the intercession of the saints. But[4] after the Litany of the Saints was completed, the episcopal order rose with the archbishop, the king alone being left prostrate. The precentor had ceased chanting; every order was silent. The archbishop bade the people pray and forthwith began the rite itself. He said the collect and raised the king from the dust. Then, with the chrism poured forth, he himself anointed the king's head, and consecrated him king in the royal manner. . . .[5]

---

[1] Geoffrey of Coutances.

[2] *Pulpita*, usually the singular *pulpitum*, is used of the raised dais upon which the king's throne was placed. See above, p. lvi n. 3.

[3] For *peroro*, 'deliver (a speech)', cf. Tacitus, *Dial.* 38. 4; *Annales* 2. 30. 2; and Vulgate, 2 Macc. 15 : 24. An excellent example occurs in *Draco Normannicus*, v. 1334 (ed. H. Omont, Rouen, 1884, p. 53).

[4] Unless the first three vowels of *letania* are long, a scansion for which we can find no precedent, a word has been lost at the beginning of the line. We suggest *S; (Set)*, as pointing the contrast between the recumbent position of the clerics in vv. 824–6 and their rising in vv. 828–9.

[5] At least a pentameter is missing. See above, p. lxii, for a conjecture as to the probable original length of the poem.

APPENDIX A

OATHS AND CLAIMS TO THE CROWN
OF ENGLAND IN 1066

At the death of Edward the Confessor on 5 January 1066, there were three principal claimants to the crown of England: Edward's great-nephew, Edgar, still very young; Edward's brother-in-law and the most powerful noble in England, Harold Godwinson; and Edward's first-cousin once removed, William, duke of Normandy.[1] On what the supporters of Edgar or Harold would have based their claims is clear enough. Edgar was the sole remaining male of the line of Cerdic, which, save for the periods of Danish rule between 1013 and 1042, had furnished the kings of Wessex and then of England for centuries. Against him, however, were his extreme youth,[2] his foreign birth, and perhaps his character.[3] Even more telling must have been the memory of the reign of the last 'boy-king', Ethelred.

Harold had been named by the dying Edward to succeed him,[4] a nomination legally superseding any earlier choice, and had been confirmed as king-elect by the Witan.[5] He had for years led Edward's

---

[1] Sweyn Estrithsson of Denmark and Harald Hardrada of Norway also had claims of a kind, and Harald put his forward later in the year, but these are unlikely to have been supported by any faction in England at the time of Edward's death.

[2] Edgar was apparently still alive about 1125 (*GR* ii. 310), and is called *puer* by the early sources for the Conquest. Had he been other than very young at the time of his father's death in 1057, one would have expected some mention of him in the *ASC* as the heir next in blood.   [3] Cf. below, p. 59.

[4] *ASC*, 1066 (MSS. C, D; E is silent); *VE*, p. 79; *GG*, pp. 172–4 (where this claim by Harold is not denied or mentioned by the duke) and p. 208 (where it is explicitly admitted by William of Poitiers); Eadm., p. 8; *BT*, Pls. 33, 34, VI (where those offering the crown to Harold point back to the scene of Harold with the dying Edward). Queen Edith, who is not known to have favoured her brother's accession, was present at Edward's deathbed (*VE*, p. 79; *BT*, Pl. 33), hence a witness of any last designation by him. It is therefore significant that the *VE*, written for her, and completed after the Conquest, none the less makes no mention at all of William and agrees with the *ASC* that the kingdom was entrusted to Harold. That William of Poitiers does not contradict but rather endorses this statement is a telling admission. (The *GND* is silent.) We therefore reject the contrary view of T. Oleson (*EHR* lxxii (1957), p. 227), who advances no new evidence to support his opinion.

[5] The consecration of Westminster Abbey at Christmas 1065 brought to London a great concourse of nobles and ecclesiastics, who were thus present at

armies and acted almost as his 'Mayor of the Palace'.[1] Together with his
brothers Gyrth and Leofwin he controlled the richest part of England.
His weakness lay in his lack of connection with the old royal house (save
by marriage), although he was related by blood to the Danish kings of
England.[2]

The claims of William, of which we have no statement before the
Conquest, were based on: his supposed nomination at some time as heir
by Edward, a nomination said to have been made with the consent of the
Witan; hereditary grounds; the oath said to have been taken to him by
Harold before Edward died; and the divine approval implicit in his
victory.

Edgar's claim being self-evident, and Harold's admitted even by
William's most zealous propagandist, it is the claims of William that
have been most often examined. As the material provided by the *Carmen*
has been neglected in such studies, we have thought it useful to re-
appraise the entire question in the light of its testimony.

Guy of Amiens derives William's claim *hereditario jure* from ancestors
who had held England (v. 37) and from the fact that William's father,
Duke Robert, had subjugated the English (v. 332). These statements
merit examination, for while Guy may be simply exaggerating William's
claim, he was closely connected to him by marriage, and writing at a
time when William's objections to Harold's accession were fresh. It is
remarkable that William of Poitiers, far more fervent in his praise of his
master, founds his hereditary title only on the fact that Edward's mother
was William's great-aunt,[3] overlooking both William's bastardy,[4] and
the fact that Emma, a foreign queen consort, could not, in her own
person, transmit a right to the crown of England.[5]

the time of Edward's death and Harold's election. Cf. *VE*, pp. 71 f.; *Historia
Ramesiensis*, p. 178; that Harold was the popular candidate is also reproachfully
admitted by the Norman chroniclers (*GND*, p. 133; *GG*, p. 146).

[1] Cf. his titles, *dux Anglorum* (*BT*, Pls. 1–2) and *subregulus* (*FW*, 1066). The
former implies judicial as well as military authority (Niermeyer, *Med. Lat. Lex.*,
p. 363); the latter is common with the meaning, 'Mayor of the Palace' (ibid.,
p. 999).

[2] See genealogical table II.

[3] *GG*, p. 222.

[4] Cf. the canons of A.D. 786–7, no. 12: 'nec christus Domini esse valet . . . qui
ex legitimo non fuerit connubio generatus' (Haddan and Stubbs, *Councils and
Ecclesiastical Documents* iii. 447–62). Kings begotten in a marriage *more Danico*
had been accepted in England (Edmund Ironside, Harold I), but William's
parents were, seemingly, not married in any way. This may have been because
Robert was already married to Estrith at the time that he began his liaison
with Herleva.

[5] The phrase, *quem Edwardi regis mariti sui adoptio, filii loco* (*GG*, p. 168), is
not to be understood literally: William himself describes Edward only as his
kinsman (*consanguineus*) a little later (ibid., p. 174), and there is no suggestion of

Early in the eleventh century, the chronicler Dudo of St. Quentin had made the surprising claim that an English king, called by him 'Alstemus', had entered into an irrevocable pact (*indissolubilis amicitiae foedus*) with Rollo of Normandy,[1] and that, having been aided against rebels by Rollo, he asked him to share his realm. The story is repeated shortly after the Conquest by William of Jumièges,[2] in whose account 'Alstemus' becomes *Athelstanus*. The king in question cannot, on the dates, have been Athelstan the Great (although both chroniclers may have wished to think that he was), but was apparently Guthrum, the erstwhile opponent of King Alfred, who had been granted the Danelaw on his conversion to Christianity, and had taken the baptismal name of Athelstan. We have thus a story by which the ducal house of Normandy possesses an irrevocable claim to at least part of England. That it remained a popular tale appears from its elaboration by Robert of Torigny,[3] whose interpolations to William of Jumièges's text expand the latter's summary version of Dudo and restore the verses in which 'Alstemus' makes his surprising offer.

Dudo's story gives a strong impression that the dukes of Normandy early thought it worth while to record a claim on England, torn by war for some years before Canute's sole rule, but still immensely wealthy. It was not much of a claim, it is true, but it appears to have been strengthened by the successive marriages of Emma, daughter of Richard I of Normandy, with Ethelred and Canute. Apparently, the children of Ethelred by Emma were to have precedence over his older sons.[4] Certainly Emma's encomiast asserts this for her second contract, with Canute.[5] It is, therefore, not improbable that the story of 'Alstemus's' grant to Rollo arose at the end of the tenth century, at the time of Emma's

a formal adoption by Edward in any of the diplomata of William's reign. Of the other eleventh-century sources, the *Carmen* does not mention Emma or adoption; William of Jumièges (*GND*, p. 133) bases William's claim on his nomination by Edward and the oath taken by Harold at Edward's command; Baudri says that Edward announced his grant to William by writing and sent Harold with the envoys to swear that he would observe this bequest (BB, vv. 267–74, 281–4); the Tapestry shows Harold taking an oath (*BT*, Pl. 29). Hariulf of Saint-Riquier, however, tells the astonishing story that William invaded England to restore Edgar, whose claim Harold had sworn to Edward to support (Hariulf, pp. 240 f.). Hariulf does not explain why William, and not Edgar, then became king, but hastily abandons the subject, saying that the events are recent and well known.

[1] Dudo, pp. 147 ff. 'Alstemus' says:
> Sis, peto, pars animae semperque meae comes, atque
> Finibus in nostris temet deposco morari.

[2] *GND*, pp. 19, 25. [3] Ibid., pp. 210 ff.

[4] The *VE*, pp. 7 f., has Edward looked for as the king-to-be even before his birth, although it is not stated in so many words that Ethelred's older sons are to be passed over.

[5] *EE*, p. 12.

first marriage, as a justification for the conditions laid down for the succession.

It is also possible, we consider, that the actual terms of the arrangements into which Emma entered with her husbands were vague enough to give some support to William's claim through her. Could the line with prior claim to the throne have been defined simply as *ex sanguine* or *ex genere Emmae*? Such a phrase could later have been interpreted as 'of Emma's race or stock',[1] and the old story told by Dudo would lend it support. As it turned out, William's resounding military victory made it possible for him to gain the crown without having to have recourse to legend, but, had the throne been a matter for negotiation, as it must have seemed likely to be at various times between 1035 and 1066 (and indeed had been in 1016), this tale and Emma's marriage contracts would have given the dukes of Normandy an advantageous argument, if no more.[2]

Edward was apparently regarded as his prospective heir by Hardicanute.[3] Was this the result of a pact like that in the time of William III and Mary II, whereby the joint issue of king and queen (in this case Hardicanute) would succeed before any children of but one or the other of them? If so, it is quite possible that Emma's sons by Ethelred would not have been excluded from their inheritance, failing any sons at all of Canute, a situation that existed on the death of Hardicanute. Were any such arrangements made and phrased loosely, as we have suggested, it would hardly have been surprising if William had regarded them as forming a hereditary claim.

The ignoring of the line of Edmund Ironside is noteworthy in all of the negotiations involving Canute, Harold I, and Hardicanute. While the exile of Edmund's sons as infants and the subsequent residence in Hungary of Edward the Exile go far toward explaining this, it is none the less odd that so little claim was put forward for Edgar. The *Carmen* (vv. 647 ff.) says that the Londoners elected him king as a last flicker of resistance to William; the *ASC*, William of Poitiers, and William of Jumièges mention him fleetingly;[4] the Tapestry and Eadmer ignore

---

[1] In the *GG*, p. 222, William's claim as Emma's great-nephew is actually described as *ratio sanguinis*.

[2] As, for example, Edward I later based his claim to the lordship of Scotland on the legend of the conquest of Britain by Brutus of Troy.

[3] *ASC* (1040); *EE*, p. 52.

[4] *ASC* (1066); *GG*, p. 214, pp. 236 f.; *GND*, p. 140 (not until 1069). Hariulf's story (p. 56 n. 5 above) inclines us to think that Edgar may have had a faction at court, possibly headed by Queen Edith, who showed no enthusiasm for either Harold or (despite William of Poitiers's assertions) William. Saint-Riquier had enjoyed the warmest of relations with Edward and Edith; Hariulf may, therefore, in a garbled form, preserve the record of the queen's feelings in this matter. The claim by William of Malmesbury (*GR*, ii. 297) that Edgar was named by the

him. As well as being very young, Edgar was an ineffectual and unin-
spiring figure, or he would not have been tolerated as a potential menace
during the next three reigns. Yet even a *statua regis* can be a nuisance,
if only as a focus for rebellion. Was his apparent immunity to suppres-
sion by the Norman kings due, partially at least, to the fact that in their
view his line had long since been removed by Emma's marriage contracts
from succession to the throne?

The story of the offer of Guthrum/Athelstan to Rollo is a reminder
that an actual division of England had already occurred by the date at
which Dudo's tale must be set. Guthrum himself had been given by
Alfred that portion of England lying beyond Watling Street, a partition
of the country that endured beyond the lives of both.[1]

Agreements to share England or to allow its reversion were frequent
among the Danish and half-Danish kings of the eleventh century:
Canute made such a pact with Edmund Ironside;[2] Harold I and Hardicanute were appointed to govern England jointly in 1036;[3] and in 1041
Edward returned to England and was 'sworn king', sharing Hardicanute's residence, if not his rule.[4] Hardicanute had also made an earlier
pact with Magnus the Good of Norway that, should either of them die
without sons, his kingdom would revert to the other.[5]

It is perhaps in the light of such agreements that we must investigate
the confused account of Robert of Normandy's attempt to restore to
the athelings Edward and Alfred at least half their inheritance.[6] This
attempt appears to have followed on a quarrel between Canute and
Robert over the latter's treatment of his wife, Estrith, who was Canute's
sister, and to have taken place in 1035, the year in which both Robert
and Canute died.[7] If Robert knew of Canute's failing health, it is

---

dying Edward, a statement that conflicts with his account elsewhere, possibly
echoes the same feeling, which, however, finds no place in the *VE*, written for
Edith.

[1] Cf. *EHD*, i. 380f., for the references.

[2] *ASC* (1016). Edmund was to have Wessex and Canute Mercia. MS. D adds
that they became sworn brothers and comrades.

[3] *ASC* (1036), followed by FW (1035), who adds that Harold was to have the
north and Hardicanute the south.

[4] *ASC* (1041); FW (1041); *EE*, p. 52.

[5] *Heimskr.*, 'Magnus the Good', vi. Hardicanute was then (1036) king of only
Denmark, which he had earlier offered to divide (ibid. iv) with Sweyn Alfivasson
(ob. 1035). Both agreements included a pact of brotherhood, but only the second
is reported as having been solemnly ratified by the nobles of the countries
concerned.

[6] *GND*, p. 109; *GR*, i. 218; *RR*, vv. 2740 ff.

[7] 'Non fuerat ei (sc. Roberto Normannorum duci) proles matrimonio aliqua
ad regimen suscipiendum provinciae, quamlibet sororem Anglorum regis Canuc
manifestum est duxisse uxorem, quam odiendo divortium fecerat' (Rodulf
Glaber, *Historia*, iv. 6, § 20, ed. M. Prou, Paris, 1886). The Roskild Annals have

possible that he thought the athelings more useful to Normandy as successors, especially if helped to the throne by Norman arms, than Hardicanute, reared in Denmark.

The story told by William of Jumièges is that Robert sent to Canute, asking for a half share in England for Edward and Alfred; that Canute contemptuously refused; that Robert launched an attack by sea on England, but, driven by storms to Jersey, in the end raided Brittany instead; and that, despite this, he found on his return messengers from Canute, offering half of England to the athelings after his death.

On the face of it, this tale is most unlikely. Canute already had an heir, with prior claims by a marriage contract agreed to by Normandy. No explanation is given of Canute's sudden interest in the athelings or of his volte-face, but it is hard to believe that Robert's abortive expedition had either frightened him or softened his heart. (We cannot, however, understand the suggestion of Freeman that Hardicanute is the heir really meant in this story.[1]) Canute was dying and Harold Harefoot, who had no links with Normandy, powerful. Robert's fear was perhaps the well-founded one that Harold would seize England, perhaps even that Canute would abrogate his contract with Robert's sister to avenge his own sister's repudiation by Robert.

William of Jumièges follows up this story by an account of a dual expedition against England by Edward (who was very successful in a raid on Southampton, but, realizing that he had not enough men to take England, sensibly went home with much booty) and Alfred, who landed at Dover, fell into the hands of Godwin, was blinded, and died.[2] It is, however, worth noting that the earliest descriptions of Alfred's invasion do not mention any expedition by Edward,[3] which is found first in William of Jumièges, whom William of Poitiers follows.[4] Furthermore, the *ASC* records no great battle in or about Southampton in this year. Against its silence, however, is the curious statement in the *Carmen* (v. 332), that William's father 'set the necks of the English under the yoke'.

Is it not possible that Alfred's single expedition of 1036 was preceded in 1035 by a joint effort of Edward with Robert? If their raid on Southampton had been sharp enough to disquiet Canute, who is said

the same story (*SRD*, i. 377), except that Estrith's husband is wrongly given as Duke Richard; Adam of Bremen and Saxo Grammaticus have confused versions. We see no reason to doubt Rodulf Glaber's account; he was contemporary and disinterested. Such a pre-contract with Estrith would also explain why Robert of Normandy seems not to have entered into even a marriage *de more Danico* with Herleva, of whom he showed the greatest fondness.

[1] *NC*, i. 528.　　　　[2] *GND*, pp. 120 ff.　　　　[3] *ASC, EE, VE*.
[4] *GG*, pp. 4 f. In this version of the story, which today begins with the death of Canute, no negotiations between him and Robert are mentioned (indeed, Robert does not appear at all), and Edward sails a little before Alfred.

to have been very ill, it is possible that he might indeed have made an offer that he himself would not have to keep. Raids on ports are not necessarily recorded in the *ASC* in every instance, and such an expedition by Edward and Robert would explain William of Poitiers's admission that the English asked Edward in 1041 to bring but few Normans with him, as they feared that the duke would take England.[1] A fairly successful raid would also have given some basis to v. 332 of the *Carmen*, and would have left Edward to some extent in Robert's debt, if only morally.

That Robert did not launch a war-fleet solely to replace one cousin by another in the English succession or to indulge family affection almost goes without saying. It would appear that the athelings had been treated very much as poor relations during Canute's reign. Barlow has pointed out that Edward and Alfred sign low on the list when witnessing charters in Normandy, indicating that they had hardly the precedence of princes.[2] And William of Malmesbury describes their situation as one of humiliation and poverty.[3] Probably, as Barlow remarks, Edward had no reason to feel grateful to Normandy.[4] It had been the Norman contract with Canute on Emma's second marriage that had kept him an exile for over twenty years, and it was by the invitation of Hardicanute that he returned in 1041, not by the aid of Duke William's guardians. Although her encomiast associates Emma with Hardicanute in the invitation, her fall from favour and power soon after Edward's coronation supports the statement in the *ASC* for 1043 that she had done less for him than he could have wished. One text goes so far as to state that she had incited Magnus of Norway to take England from him.[5]

It is to be assumed that, had Robert succeeded in restoring the athelings to even a share of the heritage, he would have expected (and demanded in advance) a portion for himself. Even later, when Edward returned to England as heir presumptive to Hardicanute (as Hardicanute himself seems to have regarded and treated him), he must have been uneasily aware that, were Hardicanute to have sons of his own, his position would be gravely weakened. A pledge of Norman support, were this eventuality to occur, would not have been unwelcome to him.

---

[1] Ibid., p. 30. As William was hardly of an age to be a threat to England at this time, the fear that the English apparently expressed suggests that Duke Robert's expedition may have had some success.

[2] *The English Church, 1000–1066*, p. 44 n. 1.

[3] 'Nam filii Ethelredi jam fere omnibus despectui erant' (*GR* i. 228), and 'Siquidem aliquantos Normannos rex (sc. Edwardus) accersierat, qui olim inopiam exulis pauculis beneficiis levarant' (ibid. i. 239).

[4] *William I and the Norman Conquest*, pp. 17 f.

[5] 'ipsa eius genetrix accusabatur regem norðuuegorum Magnum nomine ad inuadendum anglicum imperium concitasse · suosque thesauros infinitos secum illi dedidisse' (*Translatio . . . B. Mildrethae*, MS. Cotton Vesp. B. xx, f. 177ᵛ).

The foregoing recapitulation will, we think, be of some service as establishing the background of the circumstances under which Edward, and later Harold, would have secured the crown of England to William. The date at which Edward promised England to William is doubtful. That often cited, 1051, has as its basis: (1) a statement found in one manuscript of the *ASC*, that William visited England in that year;[1] (2) the claim by William of Jumièges that Robert, archbishop of Canterbury, brought such a pledge from England to Normandy;[2] and (3) the inherent likelihood that any such pact during Edward's reign would have been made during the year in which the Godwin family was in exile.

The statements of the *ASC* and William of Jumièges are not incompatible in themselves, for the former does not say that William received such a promise on his visit. A secret offer might have been conveyed by Robert. Yet Florence of Worcester, following MS. D, does not suggest such an offer,[3] and the pseudo-Ingulf, despite being an apologist of William, admits, 'de successione autem regni spes adhuc aut mentio nulla inter eos fuit'.[4] Even more remarkable is the silence on any visit by William in the accounts of the eleventh-century French and Norman writers.[5] Had William received any intimation at all during his visit of becoming Edward's heir, one would hardly have expected them to suppress it.

It is worth noting, however, that those sources that mention a visit say nothing of a promise; those that speak of a promise record no visit.[6] It has therefore been questioned whether either took place. We consider the description of a visit in the *ASC* probably reliable, for, had it been interpolated after the Conquest, there would have been every reason to make it less non-committal. The objections to the visit set out by Douglas[7] are not themselves unchallengeable. His argument that MS. E of the *ASC* would hardly have overlooked William's state progress from Dover through southern England rests on the assumption that William made such a progress, of which no indication is given in the *ASC*. We

---

[1] MS. D, a post-Conquest recension: 'Ða sone com Willelm eorl fram geondan sæ. mid mycclum werode Frenciscra manna. 7 se cyning hine underfeng. 7 swa feola his geferan swa him to onhagode. 7 let hine eft ongean.'

[2] *GND*, p. 132. Robert is known to have left England only twice during his archiepiscopate: in 1051, when he went to Rome for his pallium, and in 1052, when he was outlawed, with many other Normans. We think it most unlikely that he brought any such offer to William at the latter date.

[3] FW (1051).

[4] *The Chronicle of Croyland Abbey*, ed. W. de Gray Birch (London, 1883), p. 113.

[5] i.e. the *Carmen, GND, GG*, BB.

[6] MS. D, FW, and 'Ingulf' mention no promise, and the last denies one; the sources cited above, n. 5, give promises at various dates, but record no visit.

[7] D. C. Douglas, 'Edward the Confessor, Duke William of Normandy and the English Succession', *EHR* lxviii (1953), pp. 526–45.

have it only from pseudo-Ingulf. Douglas's view that the Norman chroniclers would have recorded their duke's state visit would be better founded if we knew it to be, in fact, a state visit, and if the Norman chroniclers did not elsewhere remain silent on important matters when they felt these to reflect no credit on William.[1] That William had neither the time nor the opportunity to visit England in 1051, because of his campaigns in France, cannot be proved, for the exact dates of his sieges are unknown. Circumstances may well have dictated, however, that any visit paid by him to Edward be brief.

Indeed, circumstances cannot have been such themselves as to augur well for William's reception in England. He either had allied or was manœuvring to ally himself by marriage with Baldwin V of Flanders, against whom Edward was aiding the emperor and the pope.[2] Furthermore, he was persisting in this marriage in defiance of a papal prohibition.[3] One can see why William might have wished to discuss both his alliance and the papal opposition to it with his cousin in England; it is less easy to see how either would have gained him favour with Edward.

For the promise of the crown, presumably in 1051, and seemingly conveyed by Robert of Jumièges when he went to Rome for his pallium, we have only the word of one Norman chronicler, and one given to special pleading.[4] The estrangement that clearly existed between Edward

[1] e.g. the successive papal prohibitions of his marriage.

[2] *ASC* (1049, MSS. C, D). The struggle between the emperor and Baldwin V continued intermittently until 1054, and there was fierce fighting in 1051 (*Ann. Elnon. Maior.*, *MGH SS* v. 13; *Ann. Laub.*, *MGH SS* iv. 20).

[3] By Leo IX at the council of Rheims, October 1049 (Anselm of St. Rémi, *P.L.* cxlii, col. 1437c). The canonical basis for the prohibition has not been established; on this see H. Prentout, 'Le mariage de Guillaume', *Mém. de l'acad. nat. . . . de Caen*, N.S. vi (1931), pp. 29–56, and Körner, op. cit., pp. 163–88. Prentout does not completely establish the connections through which William and Mathilda may have been fourth-cousins, and, in any case, as late as 1063 relationship within the forbidden degrees was not so construed as to preclude such a marriage (cf. Alexander II, *Ad sedem apostolicam* and *De parentelae gradibus*, *P.L.* cxlvi. 1379 and 1402; *Regesta pontificum Romanorum*, ed. P. Jaffé, 2nd rev. edn., Leipzig, 1885, nos. 4500 and 4506). An affinity arising from the second marriage of Baldwin IV with Judith, William's aunt, or from the betrothal of Mathilda's mother as a child to Richard III, William's uncle, seems a more likely pretext. Pretext it was; the pope's opposition was probably on political grounds—to prevent an alliance between the rebel Baldwin V and his powerful neighbour, himself at odds with his suzerain (cf. O. Delarc, *Saint Grégoire VII et la réforme de l'Église au XIᵉ siècle* (Paris, 1889), p. 164 n. 1). A little later the marriage of Mathilda of Tuscany with her foster-brother was, equally for political reasons, welcomed and encouraged by the papacy.

[4] Cf. the appraisal of his editor, Marx (*GND*, p. xx): 'Guillaume de Jumièges n'a rien d'un historien impartial. Sous des apparences moins dithyrambiques que Guillaume de Poitiers, c'est tout de même un panégyriste au service des ducs de Normandie chargé d'apprendre aux gens ce que les ducs veulent qu'on sache et de taire ce qui doit être ignoré.' On the passage in question, Marx adds (*GND*,

and Robert on the latter's return to England[1] weakens the case for him as the successful negotiator of a delicate piece of secret diplomacy, unless—and we consider this possible—he had greatly exceeded his authority from the king.

Yet William of Jumièges's story of a personal promise brought from Edward by Robert, even if it could be shown to be true, would leave us with the difficulty that nowhere is there documentary confirmation of the story that William's nomination was public and formal. The *ASC* had habitually recorded arrangements in the eleventh century for the partition or reversion of the kingdom, and it would be remarkable that the solemn endorsement by the Witan of William as heir be missing from it—the more so in that one recension, at least, was copied in his reign. Similarly, there is no pre-Conquest charter or deed recording or referring to either Edward's bequest or William's expectations. It will be seen below that we consider the evidence of the *Carmen* on this point carefully equivocal (p. 69); in any event, the *Carmen* places Edward's decision in a later year, for Harold himself is the emissary (vv. 291-6). Baudri, likewise, places the bequest at the very end of Edward's reign.[2]

Yet, without the approval of at least the most powerful nobles in the Witan, Edward's promise would have been worth little. It is doubtless for this reason that William of Poitiers improved on the story of William of Jumièges, first alleging the consent of the nobles, and later making Archbishop Stigand and the great earls Godwin, Leofric, and Siward, by name, witness and approve the nomination.[3] The choice of names is

p. 132 n. 1): 'Nous nous trouvons ici en présence d'une version officieuse, arrangée par l'entourage de Guillaume le Conquérant, et destinée à établir les droits du duc de Normandie à la succession du trône d'Angleterre.' William of Poitiers follows, but alters and elaborates this story of William of Jumièges; see below, p. 64 n. 3.

[1] *ASC* (1051, MS. E), in which Robert's refusal to consecrate Sparhavoc bishop of London is met with opposition by the king; Sparhavoc was, in fact, invested for a time with the temporalities of London. Edward failed even to attend Robert's installation as archbishop.

[2] BB, vv. 281-4. The *BT* suggests that Edward's death followed soon after Harold's return from Normandy.

[3] *GG*, pp. 30 f., 174 f. In the first of these passages, the verbal echoes of the *GND* are clear, but there are alterations, too: it is not Edward's childlessness that moves him to name William, but his gratitude to the duke for aid given him both earlier and in 1040-1 (when William was hardly so placed as to aid anyone) and the thought of their kinship. He is said to owe his crown to William ('coronae, quam per eum (sc. Guillelmum) adeptus est'); in the *GND*, he owes it to God ('regno sibi a Deo attributo'). In this first passage, William of Poitiers adds magnates to the story told by William of Jumièges, but without naming them: 'Optimatum igitur suorum assensu per Rodbertum Cantuariensem archipraesulem ... obsides ... ei direxit.' The 'optimates' are identified in the second passage (purportedly a verbatim report of William's speech to Harold's envoy): 'suorum optimatum consensu, verum consilio Stigandi archiepiscopi, Godwini comitis, Leofrici comitis, Siwardi comitis ...'

suspicious, for even if William of Poitiers is here antedating Stigand's archbishopric (as he later does his primacy, cf. p. xxi), why was he included? Barlow has shown that at the mid-Lent council of 1051, at which Robert of Jumièges was elevated, Cynsige obtained York and Sparhavoc London.[1] It seems more likely that William of Poitiers has lied carelessly than that the witnesses to Edward's promise included the bishop of Winchester, while omitting York and London—and for that matter, Harold, earl of East Anglia.

Our impression from the confused and contradictory accounts is that William received no promise on his visit, and that any mission sent hopefully to Edward on the news of Godwin's downfall misfired completely. Barlow has pointed out the advantages to Edward of being able to dangle the inheritance of England before the dazzled eyes of his contemporaries without irrevocably committing it.[2]

Further, there was a severe check to any continued hopes that William may have entertained, when, in 1052, the house of Godwin was restored to favour, Robert of Jumièges exiled, and the greater part of the Normans at Edward's court sent packing.[3] Although Godwin himself died the next year, the influence of his family was undiminished. It may even have been enhanced, for there is reason to think that Edward was uneasy in his relations with Godwin, whether because he believed him to have been in part responsible for Alfred's death, or because it is uncomfortable for a king to be conscious of owing his crown to one of his subjects. Apparently, no such tension existed between Edward and Godwin's sons.[4] The efforts to recall Edward the Exile in the following years also argue against any plan of Edward's to leave his crown to William.[5] It is true that William of Malmesbury says that, after the Exile's death, the king promised the succession to William, his only remaining relative,[6] but there is not a shred of evidence to support this claim, and the elevation of Gyrth and Leofwin to earldoms in that year (1057) argues strongly against it. It shows, however, how utterly in conflict chroniclers were as to exactly when in Edward's reign to place this important bequest. There is also the objection raised above (and this must apply to any date at which the pledge is said to have been given), that there is no evidence whatsoever of any confirmation of it by

---

[1] *The English Church, 1000–1066*, p. 48 and n. 2.
[2] *William I and the Norman Conquest*, p. 18.
[3] *ASC* (1052). MSS. C and D: 'buton swa feala swa hig geræddon þ þam cynge gelicode mid him to hæbenne · þe him getreowe wæron 7 eallum his folce', an interesting and illuminating statement.
[4] MS. D of the *ASC* (1051) calls them: 'þæs cynges dyrlingas'.
[5] The first overtures were made to Edward the Exile in 1054 (*ASC*, MSS. C and D). He died shortly after his arrival in England in 1057 (ibid., MSS. D and E). The Norman and French sources do not mention him at all.
[6] *GR*, i. 278.

F

the Witan.[1] It is most unlikely to have been forthcoming, for the English did not want a foreign king; they particularly did not want William.[2]

We should, therefore, probably seek any designation of William before 1051, but here again there is no evidence for confirmation. In any case, the disgrace of Queen Emma soon after Edward's coronation shows a diminution of Norman influence, rather than the reverse, as does the steady rise of the Godwin family.

The likelihood is therefore that the promise was made before Edward's accession, and the account given by Eadmer of a promise made by Edward to William while the former was still in Normandy seems to us the most probable version and to fit perfectly the circumstances in which Edward then found himself.[3]

Of the earliest sources for the Conquest, the *ASC* is silent about any promise made by Edward to William at any time; the *Vita Aedwardi*, written for Queen Edith, does not even mention William's name; and the Bayeux Tapestry seems to bear out Eadmer's description of the warning given Harold by Edward.[4] The accounts in French and Norman sources (the *Carmen*, William of Jumièges, the *Gesta Guillelmi*, and Baudri of Bourgueil) cannot agree at all upon the date or circumstances of this important event, and (apart from William of Jumièges) claim for the promise a formal and public affirmation for which there is no evidence.

Eadmer (1064(?)–1144) is therefore the earliest authority to present a credible account of Edward's promise. The weight of his evidence is the greater in that he: (1) is not an apologist of Harold or William—or even of Edward; (2) had excellent sources of information for what had passed years before between William and Harold. He was not only the

[1] We agree with the thesis of C. N. L. Brooke in his excellent study of the Old English succession (*The Saxon and Norman Kings*, London, Batsford, 1963, pp. 28–58) that designation by the reigning king was the weightiest single factor in deciding the heir, but it was not the sole factor. The consent and approval of the Witan, though in most cases a formality, was none the less a necessary one, the more so when, as in Edward's case, any successor except Edgar would be a man not of the blood royal. For England in the eleventh century, we can find no instances of designation without this consent before the Conquest. Hardicanute's promises of his realm successively to Sweyn Alfivasson and Magnus of Norway (see above, p. 59 n. 5) involved only Denmark, and at least the second of these was solemnly confirmed by the chief nobles of both kings.

[2] *Carmen*, vv. 193–4, 371–2; *GG*, pp. 100, 104, 186, 214, 228.

[3] Eadm., p. 7 (William is addressing Harold during the latter's stay in Normandy): 'Dicebat (sc. Willelmus) itaque regem Edwardum, quando secum juvene olim juvenis in Normannia demoraretur, sibi interposita fide sua pollicitum fuisse, quia si rex Angliae foret jus regni in illum jure haereditario post se transferret.'

[4] *BT*, Pl. 1 (where Edward is apparently giving a warning to the departing Harold) and Pl. 31 (where Harold, having returned, is listening in a hangdog attitude to an admonishing Edward, enlarged in colour at Pl. V).

correspondent of Nicholas, prior of Worcester, the favourite pupil of St. Wulfstan, Harold's close friend and confessor, but also acquainted with Lanfranc, and the intimate companion himself of St. Anselm, as well as being the constant associate of older monks at Canterbury who could remember many of the events in question and the claims made at the time. His manuscript, a transcript, is pointed to be read aloud to the monks, and his account cannot, therefore, have been unacceptable to his superiors.

Freeman discounted Eadmer's story chiefly because of the word *iuuenis*, which he denied could have been at any given time applicable to both Edward and William,[1] but he erred. *Iuuenis, adolescens*, and *puer* overlap in medieval Latin to the extent that all can be used of the same person and the first two can apply to any age from puberty to forty.[2] At the time that he returned to England at Hardicanute's invitation, Edward was about thirty-seven and William in his fourteenth or fifteenth year. We are therefore of the opinion that the famous pledge was given no later than 1041.

The historical situation, such as we know it, supports this hypothesis: Normandy would wish for some return for harbouring Edward and Alfred for over twenty years, however meanly, and for the expenses in money and men incurred by Duke Robert's attack on Canute. Normandy would also be loth to part with the heir presumptive to England, unless and until an affirmation of continued Norman influence could be gained. Edward, for his part, had every reason to be nervous, after Alfred's end, and would have wanted hostages kept for his own safety. He may also have been glad of an assurance of help against Magnus of Norway, should he attempt to seize England. All of these matters may have been the subjects of negotiations among Emma, Hardicanute, Edward, and the Normans during 1040.[3]

According to Eadmer's account, Edward promised William not half the kingdom in his own lifetime, as had so often been the case in the recent past, but the reversion of the whole. But how could the Normans

---

[1] *NC*, iii. 673.

[2] Cf. *EE*, p. 42, where both athelings (then in their thirties) are called *regiis adulescentibus*, but Alfred, immediately below, is *iuuenis*. Earlier, Sweyn Fork-beard is *iuuenis* at the time of his revolt against Harald Bluetooth (according to the *Jómsvíkinga Saga*, ed. N. F. Blake, ch. 11, he was fifteen), and Campbell remarks (*EE*, p. 9 n. 5) on the vagueness of this word in medieval Latin. Cf. also Rodulf Glaber, *Historia* iii. 9 where Hugh, eldest son of Robert II of France, then in his middle teens, is called successively *puer, adolescens, iuuenis, puer* again, and *iuuenis* again.

[3] Hardicanute is said to have gone to England through Normandy (*GR* i. 228), and Edward to have met his mother in Flanders and declined a part in the kingdom previously (*EE*, p. 48). The story may not be true (we doubt that the last bit is), but there is no actual evidence against it.

have been sure that Edward would not have sons of his own? The successive contracts of Emma with Ethelred and Canute showed how easily a prior arrangement could be set aside when circumstances changed. Edward was at this time close to forty; if he could not, for some reason, beget children, the fact may have been known. We have no evidence for his private life before his accession.[1]

If, however, Edward's agreement with William followed the lines of what little is known of Harold's, Edward may conceivably have promised to marry William's sister Adelaide, then presumably still a child. If this indeed happened, and Edward jilted her for Edith (and the support of Godwin), William's fury at Harold's 'adultery' is readily understandable; it would be the second time that this had happened to him. That Edward certainly thought William a hard bargainer appears in Eadmer's story,[2] and may also be reflected in his attitude as shown in the Bayeux Tapestry on Harold's return.[3]

But if Edward made his promise of the succession in 1041, he did so without endorsement by the Witan, before he himself was king, and probably under a certain amount of pressure.[4] These are also the conditions that would have obtained when Harold took his famous oath to William.

A certain amount of light is cast upon the vexed question of Harold's oath by the *Carmen*, but in using it, one must, we think, distinguish between two (possibly among three) levels of information. William's claim to Harold's allegiance and the crown of England is stated clearly in a number of speeches, some by William himself, others by one or another of his envoys. The same is true of Harold's defence. In other words, the parties to the quarrel make their own cases. Guy himself is relatively reticent, and but few references to William's claims occur in the narrative portions of the poem:

William is *regia proles* (v. 21), and has reclaimed by valour a stolen realm (vv. 23–4). Birth and prowess have brought him the royal title, for which he has given up that of count (vv. 30–1). He is another Caesar, whose victory he has repeated, and compels a froward race to love the yoke (vv. 32–3). The realms he sought were left him by his ancestors (v. 37), but he also comes as the avenger of Tostig (v. 140). Although the foolish English denied him to be king (v. 147), he sought the whole realm (v. 655), and God aided him in this endeavour (v. 656), which

---

[1] It is perhaps worth noting that none of Emma's sons had offspring, so far as is known, and only one of her grandsons (Ralph, earl of Hereford).

[2] Eadm., p. 6 (Edward to Harold): 'Nec enim ita novi comitem mentis expertem, ut eos aliquatenus velit concedere tibi, si non praescierit in hoc magnum proficuum sui.'   [3] Cf. p. 66 n. 4.

[4] Cf. *GR* i. 238: 'Nihil erat quod Edwardus pro necessitate temporis non polliceretur.'

he accomplished by conquest, not arguments (v. 658). Although he told Ansgar secretly that the name alone of king would suffice him (vv. 687-8), this was a blind; by guile, dissimulation, and bribery (vv. 724-8) he tricked the English into becoming his vassals (vv. 751-2).

It is possible that the foregoing represents all that Guy himself knew of William's claim, and that the details of it given in speeches are put in the mouths of William and his men as a disclaimer on the part of the poet for Norman representations. Certainly, this picture of William's regaining an ancestral, but hostile kingdom *iure belli*, but *arte adiuuante*, is not that of the accepted canon. It has, however, an obvious connection with the tale told by Dudo, and amounts to saying that William had ancestral claims on England, which he enforced by arms and guile, despite the resistance of the English. It is interesting that an immediate *casus belli* would seem to be the death of Tostig, which had not yet occurred at the time that William assembled his fleet.

Harold is charged openly only with adultery (v. 261) and fratricide (v. 137). He is wily (vv. 168, 248); he steals (v. 280) and cheats (v. 279) and is wicked (v. 129), but no details are given of his iniquity. Guy seems to know a great deal more about William (little as he says) than he does about Harold.

It is, further, noticeable that William himself is made to voice a far less definite claim than his envoy makes for him: the duke begins by speaking of the pact of friendship between himself and Harold (v. 233), and adds that Harold is breaking secret oaths sworn to him (vv. 239-40). He is, however, willing to grant to Harold all of the lands that Godwin had held (v. 245), if Harold will be his man, as he was formerly (v. 246). After sending off his messenger to Harold, he encourages his troops only by extolling their several national reputations, telling them nothing more of his cause than that Harold is forsworn and an adulterer (v. 261). He is none the less willing to continue negotiating with him (vv. 269-72).

Unlike the envoys in classical and Carolingian epics, those in the *Carmen* deliver messages noticeably different from what they were told to say. Is it possible that Guy has differentiated not only between what he knows himself and what William's supporters claim, but also between that portion of their claim that he thinks the duke himself may have voiced and that which is mere bombast? In any case, the speech of William's messenger is by no means as conciliatory as William's own; he says nothing of negotiation, friendship, or grants, but declares that all know that Edward named William his heir, for the Witan and people approved this,[1] and, further, that Harold himself had come to Normandy

---

[1] The claim of a formal bequest, endorsed by the Witan, is made again at vv. 737-8, again by an envoy, the messenger whom the remnant of the Witan had sent to William and who had been suborned by him.

to deliver to William the sword and ring sent him as tokens of his nomination (vv. 294–300). Harold must, he adds, keep his sworn allegiance or suffer the consequences.

Leaving aside the envoy's claim of a formal public bequest, which we have shown above to be highly improbable, we are left with William's own claim: that Harold and he had made a pact of friendship involving secret pledges, including one of marriage, which Harold is breaking or has broken; but that if Harold is still willing to acknowledge him his lord, as he once did, he will give him most of southern England. In any case, he wishes to negotiate.

Harold, in turn, makes no actual denial of William's claim, but bases his appeal to his army on what England will suffer under Norman rule (vv. 185–8). The army refuse to accept a foreign king (vv. 193–4), and Guy, speaking as himself, repeats their dislike of foreigners at vv. 371–2. Harold, like William, is willing to negotiate peace (vv. 197–202), if William will leave England and seek what new lands he wants overseas. To the speech of William's messenger he replies only that God will judge between the duke and himself.

Harold's envoy, however, while conceding the pact between his master and William (v. 218), and emphasizing to William the distaste of the English for his rule (vv. 221–2), adds the intriguing item that Harold has grievances against William other than the invasion itself (*cetera dampna*), which, however, he is willing to overlook, if William will only leave (v. 216).

The oath of Harold to William, as described by Guy of Amiens, thus apparently reduces to a pact of mutual assistance, like that sworn between Hardicanute and Magnus and perhaps between Canute and Edmund;[1] the possible betrothal of Harold, presumably to a relative of William; and Harold's agreeing to become in some sense William's vassal.

Exactly what this last entailed may be explained by the astonishing offer made by William to Ansgar, as reported by Guy (vv. 689–90), which is most unlikely to have been the invention of anyone writing to please William. Ansgar may have the rule and revenues of England, so long as William has the style of its king. Taken in conjunction with the reiteration in the *Carmen* of English aversion to foreign rule and the admission in the *Gesta Guillelmi* that Harold would have had to use all of his influence and fortify England as well to hold it for the duke,[2] this offer may echo an original intention (or pretence) on the part of William to content himself with the style and precedence of a joint king, so long as Harold set a Norman queen by his own side. Arrangements to share the rule of England in this fashion had been common in preceding

---

¹ Cf. p. 59 n. 2, and n. 5 above.   ² *GG*, pp. 100, 104.

reigns: Edward himself had shared the title of king with Hardicanute and Hardicanute with Harold I.

The secrecy of such a pact would arise partly from the necessity to conceal from the English the prospect of having William as even a titular king; partly, we suspect, to enable William later to exaggerate, if he wished, what Harold had promised. Harold, in abrogating this agreement, did no more than Edward had done, who, having promised the reversion of his throne to William, left it in the end to Harold. Like Edward, in our opinion, Harold had entered into the pact no free agent; like Edward, he could not pledge the consent of the Witan; like Edward, he was not yet king; but unlike Edward, he was not even heir presumptive by blood, nor have we any reason to think that at the time of the oath Edward had offered him that hope of the succession which Edward himself had had from Hardicanute.

Then, too, there are the *cętera dampna*, of which Harold speaks. These are nowhere defined, but, if he and William had entered upon the *fędus amicicię* both acknowledge in the *Carmen*, William's failure to restrain Tostig from attacking England would certainly have amounted to a breach of it.[1]

That whatever Harold agreed, he agreed privately, and not in a solemn public ritual, appears from the inability of the French and Norman chroniclers to agree upon the location of the oath-taking or to name even one witness to it, although both William of Jumièges and William of Poitiers were in excellent positions to learn exactly what had occurred. Guy of Amiens states explicitly that the oaths were secret. The Bayeux Tapestry shows a hasty and informal scene, in which Harold is being urged to sail even as he swears, and two attendants of the duke make gestures of admonition or warning. There is no assembly of notables and, most surprising of all, no clerical witness whatsoever.[2] Further,

---

[1] That William actually aided Tostig is claimed by both Robert of Torigny and Orderic Vitalis in their interpolations to William of Jumièges (*GND*, pp. 192, 257), and by Benoît de Saint-Maure (*Chronique des ducs de Normandie*, vv. 36816 ff.). Orderic repeats the charge in his own history, OV, p. 142 (ii. 123). It is also possible that the *cętera dampna* refer to the otherwise omitted incident of Harold's removal from the hands—or the hospitality—of Guy of Ponthieu, the poet's nephew. Compare as well with this passage the words of Harold's envoy to William in the *GG* (p. 174): 'Quapropter de terra juste cum tuis te regredi postulat. Alioquin *amicitiam* et *cuncta pacta* per ipsum in Normannia tibi firmata solvet, penes te omnino relinquens ea.'

[2] Even if C. R. Dodwell be right in considering the Tapestry an essentially secular 'document' ('The Bayeux Tapestry and the French Secular Epic', *Burlington Magazine* cviii (1966), pp. 549–60), it by no means omits clerics from scenes where they are appropriate and might be expected (e.g. Edward's death-bed and Harold's coronation), and even where they are inexplicable (*BT*, Pl. 19: *Ubi unus clericus et Aelfgiva*). The absence of a clerk at the all-important oath-taking is remarkable.

William of Poitiers is vague even about the terms of this most important undertaking,[1] and, apart from the bequest of the kingdom, the only item generally agreed upon by later writers is the promise of Harold to marry one of William's daughters—a part of the agreement mentioned only much later, and in passing, in the *Gesta Guillelmi*.[2]

Harold makes no attempt in the *Carmen* to answer William's charge that he had become his vassal. Guy of Amiens, however, can hardly have been unaware that men of power, once in William's hands, might emerge his subjects: his nephew, Guy of Ponthieu, had had the same experience. Of the three, then, who had claims to succeed Edward the Confessor, Edgar had the strongest by modern standards (but these were not the standards of eleventh-century England); Harold had the dying king's nomination and the election of his peers; and William of Normandy had: (1) a legendary family right in England and a great-aunt who had been twice its queen; (2) an early promise of the succession from Edward; and (3) an oath of friendship and loyalty from Harold. The deciding factor, however, without which none of these others would have availed him, was the victory that has given him the lasting title, William the Conqueror.[3]

---

[1] William of Poitiers makes the promise to help William to the throne by every means a voluntary one on Harold's part, and the last in a series of oaths (*GG*, p. 104), but he gives no details of the others, which were presumably not voluntary. Cf. also p. 71 n. 1, end.

[2] *GG*, p. 230, in an apostrophe to England.

[3] Professor Frank Barlow, in his fine biography, *Edward the Confessor* (London, 1970), argues many of the questions raised in this Appendix, not always to the same conclusions. We regret that his work appeared only after this edition was in the press.

APPENDIX B

THE BATTLE OF HASTINGS

I. THE PRELUDE TO THE BATTLE

'IF detailed narratives are to be fitted into their historical place, the first question that suggests itself is why battles were fought where they were. The exact site is usually a matter of deliberate choice on the part of one combatant or the other, the assailant seizing his enemy at a disadvantage . . . or the defendant selecting what seems to him the best position in which to await attack; and what position is most favourable obviously depends on the tactics of the age. Of the latter, Hastings and Waterloo furnish conspicuous examples . . .'[1]

Military historians are agreed that the English position in the battle of Hastings was most formidable in terms of this definition.[2] To say this implies that Duke William committed his men on terrain that in every way favoured the enemy,[3] yet it is clear that he could not afford to give his opponent the advantage of the ground, for the battle was savagely fought till nightfall.[4] Such considerations make the statement in MS. D of the *ASC*—that the duke came against Harold 'on unwær ær his folc gefylced wære'[5]—sound suspiciously like an excuse for defeat. Duke William's panegyrists make no claim that he surprised the enemy,[6] and the Bayeux Tapestry shows the English receiving the first attacks in perfect formation.[7]

[1] H. B. George, *Battles of English History* (London, 1904), p. 4.

[2] The consensus of opinion may be summed up in the words of Lt.-Col. C. H. Lemmon, D.S.O., whose knowledge of the terrain must be unrivalled ('The Campaign of 1066', in *The Norman Conquest: its setting and impact* (London, 1966), p. 100): 'From every point of view the position must have been ideal for an army of foot soldiers to hold against an army strong in cavalry and archers.'

[3] Cf. Vegetius, op. cit. III. xiii: 'In subiectos enim uehementius tela descendunt, et maiore impetu obnitentes pars altior pellit. Qui aduerso nititur cliuo, duplex subit cum loco et hoste certamen.' Cf. *GG*, p. 188.

[4] According to the *GND* (p. 135), the battle began at the third hour. The alleged duration of the battle of Hastings has perplexed a number of military historians.

[5] *ASC*, MS. D, 1066. Some factual basis for this incident may be postulated, but the chronicler must exaggerate its significance in regard to the issue of the battle.

[6] *GND*, p. 135 (see below, pp. 108 f., where the text is quoted); *GG*, pp. 186 ff. (see below, pp. 87–9, where this text is collated with the *Carmen*).

[7] *BT*, Pls. 62–3.

The solution to these problems is to be found, we believe, in neglected passages in the *Carmen*, for this is the only source to explain how the English got possession of the hill. Guy of Amiens describes in convincing detail the seizure of the position by tactical surprise (vv. 363–8), and also mentions an incident which may illuminate the statement in MS. D of the *Chronicle*.[1] When the Norman writers are examined, it will be found that, despite their reticence on the king's initial success, they provide evidence which would account for his *coup de main*.[2]

According to William of Jumièges and William of Poitiers, two things would have made the surprise possible; Harold had accelerated his advance by an all-night march with mounted men,[3] and when the alarm was sounded in the Norman camp early on 14 October most of the duke's *socii* were foraging and those in camp were unarmed.[4] In the *BT*, indeed, one of the knights who sight the English scout appears to be a forager.[5]

---

[1] And that in MS. E: 'éar þan þe his here come eall.'

[2] The significance of these passages is salient when they are read in conjunction with the *Carmen*.

[3] *GND*, p. 134. There are good reasons for accepting this statement, which is consistent with the evidence of the *Carmen* and the *GG*. It will be remembered that it was by such marches that Harold had achieved surprise against the Norsemen (*ASC*, MS. C, 1066): 'þa for he norðweard dæges 7 nihtes . . .' For the variants in *GR* ii. 302 see below, p. 77 n. 4.

[4] *GG*, p. 180 (see below, pp. 85–6 for collated texts). William of Poitiers is speaking of the morning of the battle, not that of the previous day, as some scholars have believed. In the foregoing scene, the interview between Harold and the duke's envoy, the king predicates that God may judge between him and William *hodie*. The scene of the alarm in the camp opens with the words, *Interea exploratum* . . . In the *Carmen*, the interview must be read as taking place before midnight on the night of 13/14 October, for here Harold says that God will judge between the claimants to the kingdom *cras* (v. 303). When the monk returns to Duke William in the poem, the latter has advanced to within sight of the future field and is marshalling his knights; hence this scene presupposes an earlier alert in the camp. The two accounts are, therefore, complementary. For the likelihood that William had an advanced camp near the isthmus, as well as his *castra marina* (*Carmen*, v. 575), see below, p. 77 n. 4.

[5] *BT*, Pl. 57. As Charles Gibb-Smith comments (*BT*, 'Notes to the Plates', p. 173), one knight in this scene wears no helmet, but only a mail coif. This is certainly important, for the designer conveys much information simply by meticulous attention to detail, and, in showing foragers immediately after the landing (Pls. 46–7), he depicts them as coifed or bare-headed. (Note also that in the earlier campaign in Brittany (Pls. 20–6) few of the duke's knights are fully armed till they have passed the border at Dol and are in hostile territory. Every knight is afterwards mail-clad and helmeted.) Some degree of unpreparedness is indicated, in our view, by the coifed knight in Pl. 57, and two other coifed figures are casualties, in Pl. 63 and in the lower margin of Pl. 67, the latter beside his horse. The margins above and below the sequence showing the advance from Hastings may also contain references to the foragers and to Harold's intention of surprising the enemy. It is always hazardous to attempt an inter-

In seeking to interpret the evidence, two neglected factors must be borne in mind; the influence of geography on strategy and Duke William's supply problems. Both have received the attention of Mr. J. A. Williamson, whose valuable contributions have too often been passed over or undervalued in modern studies of the campaign. Briefly, in 1066 Hastings lay in a peninsula, 'the ideal invader's camp, fifty square miles of it, fit to feed him while he was settling in, fit to support the cattle he would collect from far afield, with a good seaport, and a narrow isthmus as the only means of access. There was nothing so good on the whole coastline for his (William's) purpose.'[1] This excellence must be considered, however, as qualified in certain respects at the date of the battle. Duke William was not the first commander to have an army to feed in this region in 1066; in the spring Tostig had ravaged the south-east coast, and Harold had later stationed the fyrd there throughout the summer till supplies failed about 8 September.[2] Moreover, the Weald constituted a natural refuge for

pretation of the enigmatic scenes which appear at intervals in the margins of the Tapestry, but these look very like a commentary. Thus, the erotica in the upper margin of Pl. 54 seem to show English peasants roused from sleep and taking leave of their women, suggesting, perhaps, the urgency of Harold's call to arms; in the lower margins of Pls. 55 and 61, an eagle pursues a hare, and two small animals carry off a goose and other quarry, all moving from the left, as does the Norman advance; above Pl. 55, a grazing ass, facing in the same direction, is stalked from behind trees by a carnivore, which cranes forward to watch, and the same figures recur in the lower margin of Pl. 57, directly below the coifed knight, as the Normans and English sight each other—here the hunter is nearer, and crouched to spring. If, as seems likely, the marginal scenes have reference to the main story, they may be read as a pictorial gloss for the informed spectator.

[1] J. A. Williamson, *The English Channel* (London, 1959), pp. 80 f. It would be hard to overestimate the importance of the data provided here and in Williamson's earlier study, *The Evolution of England* (Oxford, 2nd edn., 1944). He is certainly right in believing that 'a wide survey of the geographical situation of 1066 must form the setting for a true appreciation of what took place' (*Eng. Chan.*, p. 74), and his deduction that Duke William's invasion plan combined viking strategy with the use of a continental army, on a mercenary, not a feudal basis, as well as a propaganda campaign designed to give victory in months rather than years, commands respect. Williamson condemns the narrative sources *en bloc* for their inadequacy (with an honourable exception in favour of the *BT*), yet he himself has provided a criterion by which the value of their individual contributions may now be tested. In the geographical context, for example, the neglected prelude to the battle in the *Carmen* gains in military significance, and the derivative account in the *GG* is shown to be tendentious (see below, collated texts, pp. 83 ff.). Conversely, in deducing William's strategy from the different coastal geography of Sussex 900 years ago, Williamson says (*The Evolution of England*, p. 72): 'It is all supposition, but it explains the facts, and the fact of that landing at Hastings needs explanation.' But the facts of the campaign, such as are known, derive from the sources, and it is above all the *Carmen*'s evidence which demands attention. See below, p. 110, for Williamson's map of the district in 1066.

[2] *ASC*, MS. C, 1066.

men and cattle. Hence after half a month the situation might well have approached that which had forced William, according to his biographer, to abandon his Brittany campaign: 'Si quid residuum erat inopi terrae . . . id in tutis locis incolae cum pecoribus abdiderant.'[1] Further, to be secure, William had to have command of the sea, and lastly, the narrow isthmus was not merely the only means of access for an army; it was also the invaders' only exit.[2] Therefore, under certain conditions the peninsula could become a trap, and it seems not impossible that the existence of such conditions dictated the speed of Harold's movements.[3]

The *Carmen* and the *GG* state that it was only on the morning of the battle that Duke William had intelligence of his enemy's strategy; namely, that the king was preparing to blockade him by sea and surprise him in great strength on land.[4] Both sources say that William gave battle the same morning with the advantage of the ground against him.[5] What they do not say is that the king had barred the 'gate of the peninsula'.[6]

Guy of Amiens's story is extremely interesting in the geographical setting. He conveys that neither commander fought as he had hoped to fight, because his opponent counter-moved. In vv. 280–2 of the poem, Harold briefs his men by night, ordering them to ambush the duke's men on the move, *si ualeant*. An alternative plan is implied, and it is this which Guy depicts being put into action. We infer that the king had

[1] *GG*, pp. 110–12.

[2] *The English Channel*, pp. 78 f. For an excellent and detailed description of the terrain see Lt.-Col. Lemmon's *The Field of Hastings* (St. Leonards, 4th edn., 1970), pp. 20–2.

[3] The geographical data obviously lend support to the view advanced by many scholars that Harold had studied the potentialities of the terrain earlier. Orderic notes that Pevensey and Hastings had been guarded throughout the summer watch on the coast (OV, p. 168; ii. 143). The reference to dismantled fortifications in v. 143 of the *Carmen* may therefore be significant. When the king was forced in September to disband his watch and ride against the Norse invaders, an invitation to the Normans to land where they could be contained would have been sound strategy, and 'there was nothing so good on the whole coastline' for William's purposes. It is worth attention that monks of the ducal abbey of Fécamp holding land in Hastings itself and in the great neighbouring manors of Rameslie and Brede were not expropriated, though lands to which Fécamp had a claim at Steyning in west Sussex were in Harold's hands at the beginning of his reign (cf. D. Matthew, *The Norman Monasteries and their English Possessions* (Oxford, 1962), pp. 19–21). According to the *GG*, p. 210, Romney to the east was defended, and both the *Carmen* and the *GG* depict Dover castle as a great fortress (see above, p. xlvi and n. 3). William, perhaps, took a calculated risk, the outcome of the campaign in the north being an unknown factor.

[4] *Carmen*, vv. 317–22; *GG*, p. 180 (see collated texts).

[5] *Carmen*, vv. 365–6; *GG*, pp. 186–8.

[6] Williamson, *The Evolution of England*, p. 73; *The English Channel*, p. 88. The hill is usually considered merely as a strong tactical position; Williamson has demonstrated that it was also a strategic key point. This throws new light on the movements of both commanders; see the map, p. 110.

probably hoped to intercept the foragers at dawn beyond the isthmus,[1] leaving the remnant of the Normans at his mercy. Conversely, it seems clear that the speed of the English advance caught the duke unprepared, giving him barely time to muster his knights.[2] When his envoy returns from his mission to Harold, William is in sight of the field and has ridden ahead of his foot, who are in battle-line, to call in the knights (foragers?), whom he curtly orders to fall back and marshals in close order by hand-signals (vv. 307–10).[3] This scene evidently takes place on Telham Hill, 'the defence of the peninsula against incursion from the Weald'.[4] Here the English could have attacked only at great cost (see the map, p. 111). Once disordered by archers and crossbow-men, they could have been tumbled into the marshes by the knights. The duke, however, could not wait to check the intelligence received; he had to fear that Harold would make a stand beyond the isthmus, forcing a battle on his own terms.[5]

[1] Geffrei Gaimar (*L'Estoire des Engleis*, ed. A. Bell (Oxford, Anglo-Norman Texts xiv–xvi) vv. 5221 f.) says that Harold came upon the Norsemen plundering cattle at Stamford Bridge. The story need not conflict with that in the *ASC*, MS. C, that they were expecting hostages. Cf. *GG*, p. 180.

[2] The *Carmen* (vv. 305–20, 335–40) indicates that William changed his plan of battle immediately on receiving intelligence of the king's strategy, and again when he sighted the enemy forces. There is no hint of this in the Norman writers, but his action in the *Carmen* is logical (cf. note 5 below, and pp. 79 f.), and the swiftness of his decisions impressive. In the twelfth century, it was believed at Bec that the duke had intended to let a tired enemy take the offensive (cf. Stephen of Rouen, op. cit., vv. 1415 ff.).

[3] For another example of the interesting detail on hand-signals see v. 447. The references to them in the *GG* (pp. 184, 190) are less explicit.

[4] Williamson, *The English Channel*, p. 79. Telham is evidently the hill splendidly drawn in Pl. 57 of the *BT*. Pls. 56–7, in which the armies sight each other and the knight Vital gallops back to report to William, bear a resemblance to the *Carmen*'s story. Professor Foreville (*GG*, p. xxv) identifies Vital with the monk, William's envoy, described in the *Carmen* as of warlike character (vv. 273–5). Compare similar scenes in the anonymous *Brevis relatio* (Giles, *Scriptores*, pp. 6–7) and the related *Chronicon monasterii de Bello*, p. 3. Williamson reasonably postulates that the duke had an advanced camp on Telham (op. cit., p. 88), and passages in the sources can be understood best on this premiss (cf. *Carmen*, vv. 261–8 and *GND*, p. 135). It is hard to believe that Duke William, having seized the peninsula in the first place, should then have left the isthmus unguarded, even before he had any intelligence of the enemy's approach. We think, therefore, that an advanced camp did exist, and that it was this camp which was alerted against surprise after the duke received Harold's envoy, the alert then being relaxed because the speed of the king's advance was misreckoned. The story told by William of Malmesbury (*GR* ii. 302) that the English and Normans encamped near each other may be accepted only on the premiss that both sides had such camps of observation—which seems highly probable. This writer (an Anglo-Norman with divided sympathies, familiar with the *ASC*, the *GND*, and the *GG*) purposely slows the action, passing over all evidence that represents either commander as taken at a disadvantage.

[5] Williamson, op. cit., p. 89: '. . . time had gone over to Harold's side and delay would make the Normans grow hungry.' This is said here without reference

It appears later in the *Carmen* that the English were still in the forest (v. 344). The envoy's statement that Harold's standards could be seen (v. 314), suggests that the king himself had ridden forward to interrogate his scouts (see the *BT*, Pl. 58) and view the field. Between Caldbec and Telham lay the low hill which barred 'the gate of the peninsula', and it would seem from Guy's account that there was a race for it.[1]

On this hypothesis, the story in MS. D of the *Chronicle*, that William attacked unexpectedly, before the king's men were in array, assumes new interest, for it could relate to a preliminary skirmish; a last-minute attempt by the Normans to gain the strategically vital hill and repulse the enemy. Our hypothesis would also explain the related statement in MS. E, that Harold gave battle before all his army had come up. Lastly, it would explain why the Norman panegyrists are silent, for if such an attempt was made by the duke, it failed.

Now the *Carmen*, in a sequence which evidently embarrassed Guy of Amiens, actually describes a hastily improvised attack launched by William *before* the English had seized the hill and formed their phalanx. On receiving his envoy's report that the king's standards are in sight, with alarming intelligence as to his numbers and strategy, the duke is briefly silent, and then orders forward his archers to engage the enemy, settling crossbow-men in the midst, with instructions to aim at the faces of the English and then retire.[2] A significant passage, which has received

to the threat from the sea, which in our view was the decisive factor. Whether the king had a fleet at sea on 14 October cannot be established in default of evidence; in the *Carmen* the news is qualified by *fertur*, suggesting that it could have been 'planted'. If so, it was timed perfectly, calculated to bring the duke to battle forthwith outside the peninsula, yet without depleting his garrisons at Pevensey and Hastings. It could also be expected to cause alarm and despondency among the Normans. It will be noticed that William of Poitiers (*GG*, loc. cit.) omits *fertur*, antedates the reception of the news, augments the number of the ships by two hundred, and describes them impressively as *classis armata*, though Guy speaks only of *carinas* (see the collated texts).

[1] For a close analogy see *De bello civili*, i. xliii, where Caesar and Afranius race for a lower feature of strategic importance, lying between two hills. Caesar's men, repulsed, fell back on the main body. Guy of Amiens uses the verb *praeripio* (Lewis and Short, 'I. In gen., to *take away* a thing *before another*, to *snatch* or *tear away*, to *carry off*'). The derivative passage in the *GG* (p. 186) contains a *suggestio falsi*, the verb being changed to *praeoccupo* and panic being the enemy's alleged motive in occupying higher ground before the battle. Anyone conversant with the importance of the hill, however, would read here a more flattering variant of the *Carmen*'s story (see the first literal example of *praeoccupo* in Lewis and Short, 'A. Lit.: hic ne intrare posset saltum, Datames praeoccupare studuit, Nep. Dat. 7, 2'). William of Poitiers is telling his patron that the English, who would have trembled to meet him, even on level ground, seized the hill lest he should get it first. The *BT* (Pls. 62–3) suggests the hill only by the English stance, a break in the ground line, and the angle of weapons.

[2] *Carmen*, vv. 335–40. The military detail in this passage is of great interest. The duke's purpose is, seemingly, to check the enemy's further advance, so that

little attention, follows (vv. 341–4): William had hoped to establish the knights in the rear of the foot,[1] but the onset of battle did not permit this, for he perceived companies of the English appearing not far off, and could see the forest glitter, full of spears.[2]

At this crisis in the narrative, Guy of Amiens suddenly blots out the whole scene, inserting the great rhetorical apostrophe to the god of war (vv. 345–62). The incident is cut in the *GG*, pp. 182–4, and yet evidence of haste and confusion emerges: the duke's mail is put on wrongly, and his speech to hearten the knights, 'qua pro tempore breviter', had not been fully reported (see below, p. 80 n. 1). Supplying an address in *oratio obliqua*, full of borrowed rhetoric, William of Poitiers includes one pregnant phrase, possibly Duke William's: 'Jam non id agi quis regnans vivat, sed quis periculum imminens cum vita evadat.' The duke, *autem*, advances in befitting order (compare the *Carmen*, vv. 337 ff.); bringing up the rear are the squadrons of knights, William himself riding in the centre amidst the flower of his chivalry (see collated texts below). Only later does the reader learn that the terrified foe holds a hill—the slopes of which the Normans slowly ascend, 'neque loci territus asperitate'. In the *Carmen*, we see the move that gave Harold the hill.

After rhetoric designed to lessen the shock (see above, p. xxxvii), Guy of Amiens depicts the English army suddenly (*ex inprouiso*) breaking cover in strength and surging forward in massed ranks to seize the positions held in the battle. What action the knights took when the duke was forced to commit them is nowhere stated, but we learn later in the *Carmen* that Harold's advance guard, at least, was mounted (v. 377).[3] It

he may anticipate the seizure of the hill—causing panic with his missiles, notably his bolts (see Appendix C), while the enemy is in the act of concentration upon Caldbec (see map, p. 111). Since the range of these weapons was not great, it would be necessary for the foot to advance beyond the lower hill to achieve this. They would then fall back on that position, the duke in the meantime having brought up the knights in support (v. 341). The text may, however, be construed to mean that only *balistantes* in the centre were to retire, opening a way for the knights to press home the attack, with archers upon the two flanks ready to enfilade any attempted counter-attack. The duke's presumed objective, in this case, would have been to carry Caldbec Hill, pushing the English back in disorder from the high ground and so assuring himself freedom of manœuvre.

[1] The remarkable reference to the knights was noted by Sir James Ramsay (*The Foundations of England* (London, 1898), ii. 30). Ramsay, however, misread it as relating to a period after the battle had been joined: 'William had hoped to carry the day with his infantry, without engaging his precious cavalry, but he soon found that all the three arms of his force had to be sent to the front.' Guy's statement has barely been noticed elsewhere, but its significance becomes evident in the light of Williamson's data.

[2] Cf. BB vv. 395 ff. Baudri of Bourgueil says that at the sudden presence of an enemy whose strength was unknown, there were 'Frigida corda'.

[3] See also the *GG*, p. 186. Guy of Amiens carefully distinguishes three stages of the English advance: (*a*) the standards are in sight (v. 314); (*b*) armed bands

would seem, therefore, that it was the sight of armed bands of horsemen on Caldbec, with the advance-guard of the English close behind them at the edge of the forest, that forced William to change his plans. His foot, we infer, would have moved too slowly to accomplish their mission; hence the duke's only hope was to launch his knights against Harold's mounted infantry in a last attempt to win the strategic race and establish himself outside the peninsula. The tentative failed, as Guy shows, because the king moved too fast. 'Florence' of Worcester's story that there were heavy desertions among the English early in the day may denote the initial effect of *balistae*, but William could not dislodge the enemy.[1]

emerge from the Weald, with the army massing behind them (vv. 343–4); (c) a sudden mounted charge wins the hill (vv. 363–8). Against (a) and (b), Duke William's counter-moves are given (vv. 335–42), but between (b) and (c) comes the long passage of rhetoric. By another literary device, Guy then distracts attention from the knights and from Duke William by making the English the subject in describing the tactical surprise and introducing the duke's opponent (vv. 373–6) as he makes his dispositions. When the poet returns to Duke William (vv. 379 ff.), as the duke slowly advances against the phalanx, there is still no reference to the knights; archers and crossbow-men are once again in the van. There is, therefore, no doubt that the smoke-screen of rhetoric conceals an action in which the *ordo militum* failed to prevent the king's seizure of the hill.

[1] Cf. FW (1066). Something remarkably like the incident veiled by Guy of Amiens appears—equally veiled—in the history of Henry of Huntingdon. The passage was interpolated in the second edition (1135) of his history, and retained in later editions (*Historia Anglorum*, ed. T. Arnold (London, 1879; *RS* lxxiv), pp. 200–2). Although in the context this interpolation appears to make no sense, it was embodied by Henry's friend, the distinguished Norman historian, Robert of Torigny, in his additions to the chronicle of Sigebert of Gembloux, written after 1152 ('Accessiones ad Sigebertum', in R. Howlett's *Chronicles of the Reigns of Stephen, Henry II and Richard I* (London, 1889; *RS* lxxxii, v. 4), pp. 36 f.). The passage begins with William haranguing his marshalled knights before the battle, implying with suitable circumlocutions that they have already been in trouble (*Historia Anglorum*, pp. 200 ff.). Robert omits this speech, but says that the knights were addressed, 'ut si segnes antea viderentur, omnibus audaciores postea probarentur'. No explanation of the speech is given in either text, but its effect is spectacular: while William is speaking, the knights charge, 'ira accensi ultra quam credi potest', though what they achieved is not mentioned. Here the interpolation of 1135 ends and the original text records that shortly before the warriors encountered, a certain Taillefer did feats of arms (see below, pp. 81 ff.) and met his death. Yet the battle begins with clouds of arrows, and the close fighting follows. Should the inserted passage have come here (cf. *GG*, p. 188), the knights burning to avenge their first failure (cf. *De bello gallico*, II. xix, xxvii)? Or is it rightly placed before the battle—the knights (blamed for William's dilemma) charging as the enemy breaks cover? Compare Guy's story, vv. 341–4.

Neither Henry of Huntingdon nor Robert of Torigny provides verbal echoes of the *Carmen*, but the word *alloquor* (*Hist. Anglorum*, p. 200) is conceivably an echo of *alloquitur* over Pl. 59 of the *BT* (see below, p. 108), and here the knights seem to charge as Duke William addresses them. But if Henry of Huntingdon used the Tapestry, he knew more than is there explicit (see below, p. 81 n. 2), for in the caption, Pls. 59–62, the duke only exhorts his knights to fight *viriliter et sapienter*; and Robert of Torigny is more candid than the *Carmen* or the *GG*.

This attempt failing, the Normans would have had to fall back and regroup, and one would expect a considerable period of confusion and delay while the duke had to revise his whole plan of action. Such an interval would mean that the main battle began much later than commonly supposed, and this would seem to justify those critics who have found difficulty in accepting its recorded duration.[1] A long delay is, in fact, clearly indicated by Guy of Amiens; for the king is able to make his dispositions unhindered (vv. 373–6), and his men dismount, form their phalanx, and sound trumpets for the battle, before Duke William makes any move (vv. 377–8).[2] Compare the *GG*, pp. 186–8.

An initial reverse carrying such devastating implications for the invaders would necessarily have had a shattering effect on Norman morale, already, it would seem, none too high.[3] When the duke resumes his advance in the *Carmen*, the poet again has recourse to rhetoric; a vivid analogy likens the temper of the English to that of a wild boar turning upon the hunter, but there is no corresponding passage in praise of the Normans.[4] Instead, two verses, hinting that the battle looked ominous, introduce the first account of Taillefer's legendary ride;[5] but here there is only the raw material of legend—courage. To put it in modern terms, in the *Carmen* Taillefer is a man with a job, not a figure of high romance. His ride is necessary because of the events which have preceded it. He heartens his own side and confounds the enemy (v. 393),[6] whom he

[1] Vegetius (op. cit. III. viiii) declares that the issue of a pitched battle cannot be in doubt for more than two or three hours, 'post quem partis eius, quae superata fuerit, spes omnes intercidunt'.

[2] According to one of the anonymous chroniclers of Battle Abbey (*Chronicon Monasterii de Bello* (London, 1846), p. 4), William parleyed with the king three times immediately before the armies engaged, his peace-offers being three times rejected. Parleying is perhaps indicated in the upper margin of Pl. 61 of the *BT*, where the fable of the wolf and the goat appears. One reading of this fable would be highly applicable—the wolf tried in vain to induce the goat to descend from his crag. The *Chronicon* hides an earlier action, the battle beginning *denuo*.

[3] Between the landing and the battle, the invaders appear to have suffered from some degree of 'nerves' (cf. *Carmen*, vv. 247–72, 311–12; *GND*, p. 135 (where the Normans stand to arms on the night before the battle from dusk, 'ad gratissimam usque lucem'); and the *GG*, p. 180–2). For William of Poitiers's account of the duke's reception of the news of Stamford Bridge cf. ibid., p. 170, and compare Pl. 51 of the *BT*.

[4] Contrast the conventional approach of Geffrei Gaimar, describing the same scene in the next century (op. cit., vv. 5263–4):

> Mult i ot gent d'ambes [dous] parz,
> De hardement semblent leuparz.

[5] A number of works relating to Taillefer are cited by E. Faral, *Les Jongleurs de France* (Paris, 1910). There is a considerable literature on the subject, but, so far as we know, the significance of his story in the *Carmen* has escaped comment.

[6] According to Henry of Huntingdon (op. cit., p. 203), the English were

G

insults by juggling with his sword—an invitation to the insulted to break ranks and chastise such impudence.[1] The *histrio* is one of the few named characters in the poem, and Guy salutes him as a hero.[2] The scene which follows is the end and climax of the prelude to the battle. The poet introduces another character, an unknown warrior among the English; brave as his opponent,[3] he springs forward to take Taillefer's challenge and falls to the player's lance (vv. 395–402). Taillefer hews off his head stupefied by Taillefer's sleight of hand. Gaimar, who augments the player's feats, gives a glimpse of the scene from the English side (op. cit., vv. 5284–6):

> L'un dit a l'autre qui ço veit
> Que ço esteit enchantement
> Que cil faiseit devant la gent.

[1] Baudri of Bourgueil, though he names no one in the battle except William and Harold, depicts the situation which was the *raison d'être* of Taillefer's ride (BB, vv. 405–8):

> Hostis, equo abjecto, cuneum densatur in unum,
> Qui, nisi disperet, intemerandus erat;
> Nam neque Normannus consertos audet adire,
> Nec valet a cuneo quemlibet excipere.

Gaimar (op. cit. v. 5300) and Wace (*RR*, vv. 8043 ff.) knew that Taillefer had asked for the honour of the first blow, but in these twelfth-century accounts the reason for his ride is either unknown to the writers or suppressed. Hence, if the authority of the *Carmen* be overlooked, the incident assumes a mythical character, which has perplexed some scholars and led others to reject it.

[2] *Carmen*, v. 391.

[3] Ibid., vv. 395–8. No later account takes note of Taillefer's opponent; the passage reads like the memory of a chivalrous eyewitness. According to Henry of Huntingdon (op. cit., loc. cit.), the player cut down three Englishmen, the first being a standard-bearer, before he himself fell. Gaimar also gives Taillefer three victims before the English kill him (op. cit., vv. 5280–99). The most famous account is that of Wace (*RR*, vv. 8035 ff.):

> Taillefer, qui mult bien chantout,
> Sor un cheual qui tost alout,
> Deuant le duc alout chantant
> De Karlemaigne e de Rollant
> E d'Oliuer e des uassals,
> Qui moururent en Renceuals . . .

It is perhaps worth noting in connection with the prelude to the battle in the *Carmen*, that Taillefer's song, according to Wace, celebrated the death of heroes trapped and fighting against odds. Wace gives Taillefer two victims (vv. 8054–58), and then quotes him:

> Pois a crie: 'uenez, uenez!
> Que faites uos? ferez, ferez!'

Benoît (op. cit., vv. 39725 ff.) singles out Taillefer as one of those who did the enemy most harm that day, and represents him as taking great prizes, riding coolly in among the press of the English and fighting still more gallantly when mortally wounded. The poet declares that he is following an earlier account (vv. 39732 ff.), but his version answers to none of those that survive. Indeed all of these appear to be independent, each contributing original material. William

The photographs reproduced here by kind permission of the Phaidon Press do not cut the action of the Tapestry at the precise points shown in Sir Frank Stenton's edition, but may be identified by the plate numbers. We have supplied brief sub-titles and added notes and page-references. The original Latin captions are given in full in the Parallel Texts (pp. 108–9 above).

(Excellent reproductions may also be studied in Mademoiselle Simone Bertrand's beautifully produced book, *La Tapisserie de Bayeux* (see Bibliography). For an unfolding reproduction of the Tapestry in colour, there is no substitute for the *dépliant, Telle-du-Conquest dite Tapisserie de la reine Mathilde*, obtainable from the Musée de la Tapisserie, Bayeux, France 14. Montfaucon (see Bibliography) provides the earliest reproductions of the Tapestry. These engravings are of great value, as showing the state of the work before modern restorations. The artist, in general exquisitely exact, has made a few minor slips.)

a. (*BT*, plates 54–5) *The advance from Hastings* (see pl. 74 n. 5 and p. 77 n. 4 above)

Only horsemen are shown in the advance. The borders may have relevance to the story, cf. Harold's intended surprise and the duke's foragers. The grazing ass in the upper border is stalked under cover by a predator; below, an eagle (?) pursues a hare

b. (*BT*, plate 57) *Knights and an English scout sight one another* (ref. as above)

The first knight (a forager?) wears no helmet. In the lower border the ass and its hunter reappear; the beast of prey prepares to spring. (In the preceding and following scenes, not shown here, reports are carried to both commanders. The knight Vital gallops back to William, Harold is close to his scout)

a. (*BT*, plate 59) *The knights charge as the duke harangues them* (see p. 80 and n. 1 above)

The designer cuts to this scene without showing the English army. Only one knight turns to hear William. He carried no shield. In the lower border, the Fable of the Pregnant Bitch (who asked help only to betray her benefactor) may relate to a theme of the speech—namely Harold's perfidy. (This fable first appears under plate 5, as the earl sails from Bosham)

b. (*BT*, plate 59) *Knights overtaking archers* (refs. as above and pp. 78–81 and notes, and Appendix C below)

The mailed archer, unique in the Tapestry, is discussed in Appendix C. The Fable of the Wolf and the Goat above may refer to parleying, and the two archers to the right may belong to the next scene. Foraging animals appear in the lower border

a. (*BT*, plate 62) *Knights charge the phalanx* (see p. 74 n. 5, and p. 81 n. 2 above)

A hiatus earlier in the narrative seems implied here; the fallen show that the duke's foot have attacked and been repulsed with loss. Two fighting birds in the lower border symbolize the fury of the encounter. (Such birds first appear over plates 51–2, where William has news of Harold's advance after the bloody victory of Stamford Bridge)

b. (*BT*, plates 62–3) *The phalanx attacked and counter-attacking* (for the counterattack, see above, p. 96 and n. 1)

The hill is symbolized, not represented. Two actions are depicted. The English facing left have the advantage of the ground—skilfully conveyed by their stance and exaggerated stature, the incidence of weapons, and the break in the ground-line under the first horseman. In the second action (the arrows have been exhausted), the knights have gained the summit— note the changed angle of weapons and the size of the English—but a counter-attack is beginning. The standard has been taken up (see the ferrule) and is advanced, following an axeman who must be the king. It is of interest that there are no captions

IV

a. (*BT*, plates 68–9) *The Norman rout checked; William and Eustace charge* (see Parallel Texts, pp. 100 ff.)

(No feigned flight appears in the Tapestry. Plates 64–7, omitted here, show a mêlée, in which Harold's brothers fall to unnamed opponents, and knights are overthrown at a ditch below a hillock defended by English light-armed (see Map 2 and v. 429). In contrast to the hill itself, this feature is realistic.) In plate 68, a single knight, threatened by Odo, represents the rout. Charging ahead with banner, Eustace points back to the duke, who turns to show his followers a furious face—the caption gives no explanation. In the lower border archers appear. (These continue under plate 70 and part of plate 71, not given here. The English weaken)

b. (*BT*, plates 71–2) *Harold's death in last stand* (see pp. 94, 97 and n. 4, and Appendix D)

These are companion pieces to plates 62–3 above. The hill is again symbolized. The ferrule of the Dragon is planted in the ground for a last stand. (For Harold's reputed eye-wound see *BT*, Fig. 1, facing p. 32, and p. 176, note to plate 62.) The leg-wound mentioned in the *Carmen* (v. 549) is depicted. In the following action, the knights are carrying the hill against opposition. Seen in full, these two scenes show only four (unidentified) knights engaged. In the lower border, as in the *Carmen* (vv. 531–5), plundering has begun before the king falls. (Plate 73 shows the English light-armed flying, and pursued)

and holds it up to show his comrades that the prognosticon of the battle favours them (vv. 403–4). It is hard to believe that their recorded reaction was not reported by a man who had shared it. To the Normans, familiar with judicial trial by combat in which God was held to give judgement for the innocent party, the player's victory would have seemed clear proof that Heaven was after all on William's side.[1] Exulting that the first blow was theirs, Taillefer's comrades rejoiced and honoured God. A tremor and a thrill ran through them, and at once they closed their ranks for the attack (vv. 405–8). Thanks to the *histrio*, that is, the duke's men got themselves in hand. Only then, according to Guy of Amiens, did the battle of Hastings really begin.

I. THE PRELUDE TO THE BATTLE IN THE *CARMEN* AND IN THE *GESTA GUILLELMI* PARALLEL TEXTS

(Military information in the two works is collated below and subtitled for reference, from the sending of William's envoy to the king to the ride of Taillefer. In the *Carmen* (vv. 261–8) the duke has earlier warned his men against Harold as a crafty commander and ordered them to guard the camp. For clarity we have excised or summarized non-military material in collating the texts. Short rhetorical clauses have been put in parentheses. Passages in which the two texts are clearly related—though not necessarily verbally identical—have been italicized.)

[*Footnote cont. from p. 82*]

of Malmesbury, writing earlier, does not mention Taillefer, but speaks of the *Song of Roland* (*GR* ii. 302). His account of the battle begins after William's mail has been put on back-to-front ('ministrorum tumultu loricam inversam indutus, casum risu correxit'; cf. *GG*, p. 182). William interprets this omen to mean that valour will change his county to a kingdom. Malmesbury continues: 'Tunc cantilena Rollandi inchoata, ut martium viri exemplum pugnaturos accenderet, inclamatoque Dei auxilio, praelium consertum, bellatumque acriter, neutris in multam diei horam cedentibus.' If these narratives are read in conjunction with the *Carmen*, they appear to us to contain many passages that gain in value, and their silences are not less significant.

[1] Taillefer's existence has been doubted by some writers on the ground that he is not mentioned by William of Poitiers, but, as we have shown, the biographer had a clear motive for suppressing the *histrio*'s valiant exploit. Yet Taillefer is not wholly absent in the *GG*. Just as the tactical surprise described in detail in the *Carmen* could be implied by William of Poitiers in the single word, *praeoccupo* (see above, p. 78 n. 1), so a single phrase could recall to every man who had fought the duke's battle how two champions had seemed to try the cause of William versus Harold before Hastings. The biographer, with the text of the *Carmen* before him, cut the episode of Taillefer and the events leading up to it, and on p. 188 of the *GG* words and ideas borrowed from Guy of Amiens are twisted to suit his purpose (see the collated texts below, p. 90). Here it is not the *histrio*, '*cor audax*', who has the first blow, but *Normannorum alacris audacia* which takes the initiative—'just as, when a case of robbery is tried in law, it is the prosecutor who speaks first'.

CARMEN

The king lays stratagems by night, but William is vigilant

vv. 279–86

Interea, (sedes fuscatę fraudis et heres,)
Nocte sub obscura, (furis in arte uigens,)
Rex acies armare iubet, ducis atque latenter
Mandat ut inuadant agmina, si ualeant.
Estimat inuigiles prosternere fraudibus hostes;
(Fallere dum querit, falliter atque ruit,
Dux quia, directo legato, peruigil exstat;
Eius et ingenio conscius artis erat.)

The envoy finds the king in the wilds

vv. 287–8

Diuertens legatus iter per deuia terrę,
Nescius accessit rex ubi furta facit.

The monk delivers William's message

(For claims variously presented see Appendix A, pp. 68–70. The passage here runs from v. 289 to v. 300.)

Harold's answer

vv. 301–4

Heraldus, uultu distorto, colla retorquens,
Legato dixit, 'Vade retro, stolide!
Iudice *cras* Domino regni, pars iusta patebit:
Diuidet ex equo sacra manus Domini.'

GESTA GUILLELMI

The monk delivers William's message

p. 178

Ut ergo mandata eadem Heraldo appropinquanti per monachum sunt relata, stupore expalluit, atque diu ut elinguis obticuit.
(The duke has offered to submit his case to Norman or English law, or to meet Harold in single combat.)

Harold's answer

pp. 178–80

Roganti autem responsum legato semel et iterum, primo respondit: 'Pergimus continenter'; secundo: 'Pergimus ad pretium.' Instabat legatus ut aliud responderetur, repetens: non interitum exercituum, sed singulare certamen Normanno duci placere.

Tum levato Heraldus in caelum vultu ait: 'Dominus inter me et Guillelmum *hodie* quod justum est decernat.'

CARMEN	GESTA GUILLELMI

The monk returns as he came

vv. 305–6

Ille retro gressum uertens per deuia
　rursum,
　A quo missus erat huic maledicta
　refert.

Meanwhile the alarm is sounded in the Norman camp

p. 180

Interea exploratum directi jussu probatissimi equites, hostem adesse citi nuntiant.

The king's march had been speeded

Accelerabat enim eo magis rex furibundus, quod propinqua castris Normannorum vastari audierat.

Harold's reported strategy

Nocturno etiam incursu aut repentino minus cautos opprimere cogitabat. Et ne perfugio abirent, classe armata ad septingentas naves in mari opposuerat insidias.

Hasty call to arms; most of the duke's men were foraging

Dux propere quotquot in castris inventi sunt—pleraque enim sociorum pars eo die pabulatum ierat—omnes jubet armari.

(*Spiritual preparations*)

pp. 180–2

(The duke hears Mass with great devotion and communicates. He humbly hangs round his neck the relics on which Harold had been forsworn. By this act the king had forfeited the protection of the saints. Odo of Bayeux, Geoffrey of Coutances, priests and monks with the army, prepare to fight with spiritual weapons.)

The duke's mail put on wrongly

p. 182

Terreret alium loricae, dum vestiretur, sinistra conversio. (Hanc conversionem risit ille ut casum, non ut mali prodigium expavit.)

CARMEN

GESTA GUILLELMI

William's speech to hearten his men, necessarily brief, not fully reported

Exhortationem, qua pro tempore breviter militum virtuti plurimum alacritatis addidit, egregiam fuisse non dubitamus; etsi nobis non ex tota dignitate sua relatam.

(*Summary of the duke's speech*)

pp. 182–4

(Professor Foreville (p. 184 n. 1) notes general resemblance to the address by Catilina (Sallust, *Catilina*, lviii. 5–21); and the *Carmen*, v. 324 and v. 458, has been laid under contribution. A phrase we have not identified is, perhaps, what William of Poitiers had heard: 'Jam non id agi, quis regnans vivat, sed quis periculum imminens cum vita evadat.')

On the return of his envoy, William has advanced; calling in his knights, he orders them to fall back and marshals them in close order

vv. 307–10

(Imperiale decus,) dux, (pax et gloria regni,)
   Preuius incedens ante suas acies,
Aggregat et strictim compellit abire quirites,
   Et faciles hasta conglomerare facit.

The envoy is terrified; he is interrogated and reports the enemy at hand

vv. 311–14

Legati facies natiuo cassa rubore,
   Pallor et ostendit proxima bella fore.
Dux ait, 'Est ubi rex?' 'Non longe,' monachus inquit.
   Dixit in aure sibi, 'Signa uidere potes.'

He reports Harold's strategy

vv. 315–20

('Plurima uerba fero quę censeo non referenda;
   Illa tamen dicam quę reticere nocet:)

CARMEN

Ex inprouiso sperat te fallere posse;
Per mare, per terram prelia magna
    parat.
In mare quingentas fertur misisse
    carinas,
Vt nostri reditus preprediatur iter.'

(*His rhetorical description of the huge*
size of Harold's army)

vv. 321–2

(forests of spears, rivers run dry
where the king's host passes)

(*The monk heartens Duke William*)

vv. 323–34

(Perhaps the duke fears numbers?
Valour is more in war. Harold's knights
are effeminate. Let William recall the
deeds of his forebears. What is there
for him but to excel them?)

The duke's dispositions

vv. 335–40

Paulo conticuit; faciens et se remo-
    ratum,
Armatas acies ordinat imperio.
Premisit pedites committere bella sagit-
    tis
    Et balistantes inserit in medio;
Quatinus infigant uolitancia uultibus
    arma
(Vulneribusque datis, ora retro
    faciant.)

The duke is forced to change his tactics

vv. 341–4

Ordine post pedites sperat stabilire
    quirites,
Occursu belli set sibi non licuit:
Haut procul hostiles cuneos nam
    cernit adesse,
Et plenum telis irradiare nemus.

(*Rhetorical apostrophe of the god Mars*)

vv. 345–62

(For the importance of this passage
see above, p. xxxvii.)

GESTA GUILLELMI

The duke's dispositions

p. 184

Hac autem commodissima ordinatione
progreditur, vexilla praevio quod
apostolicus transmiserat. *Pedites in*
fronte locavit, sagittis armatos et
balistis, item pedites in ordine secundo
firmiore et loricatos; ultimo turmas
equitum, quorum ipse fuit *in medio*
cum firmissimo robore, unde in
omnem partem consuleret manu et
voce.

(*Rhetorical description of the huge size*
of Harold's army)

pp. 184–6

(Professor Foreville (p. 185 n. 4)
draws attention to the close analogy
between this passage and vv. 321–2 of
the *Carmen* and notes verbal resem-
blances to Juvenal, x, vv. 176–8.
She postulates also the influence of
Lucan, *Pharsalia,* iii, vv. 394–452).

CARMEN

GESTA GUILLELMI

The text continues (p. 186): 'Maximae enim ex omnibus regionibus copiae Anglorum convenerant.'

(*The author's comment on the English*) (Studium pars Heraldo, *cuncti patriae praestabant, quam contra extraneos,* tametsi non juste, *defensare volebant.*)

Denmark had sent auxiliaries
Copiosa quoque auxilia miserat eis cognata terra Danorum.

The English suddenly break cover and seize a hill near the forest

The English, terrified of William, seize a hill near the forest

vv. 363–8

Ex inprouiso diffudit silua cohortes,
   Et nemoris latebris agmina pro-
   siliunt.
Mons silu̧e uicinus erat, uicinaque
   uallis,
   Et non cultus ager asperitate sui.
Anglis ut mos est, densatim pro-
   gredientes,
   Hęc loca preripiunt Martis ad
   officium.

Non tamen audentes cum Guillelmo ex aequo confligere, plus eum quam regem Noricorum extimentes, *locum editiorem praeoccupavere, montem silvae per quam advenere vicinum.*

(*The author's comment on the English*)

vv. 369–72

(Nescia gens belli *solamina* spernit
   equorum,
Viribus et fidens, heret humo pedi-
   bus;
Et decus esse mori summus diiudicat armis
   Sub iuga ne tellus transeat alterius.)

Harold's dispositions

vv. 373–6

Ascendit montem rex bellaturus in
   hostem,
Nobilibusque uiris munit utrumque
   latus.
In summo montis uexillum uertice
   fixit,
Affigique iubet cętera signa sibi.

The English dismount and form their battle-order; their trumpets sound

The English dismount and form up in the closest order

vv. 377–8

p. 186

Omnes descendunt et equos post terga
   relinquunt;
Affixique solo, *bella ciere tubis.*

Protinus *equorum ope* relicta, cuncti pedites constitere densius conglobati.

CARMEN	GESTA GUILLELMI
The duke advances less precipitately and boldly approaches the hill	*The duke and his men, undismayed by the terrain, slowly ascend the hill. The clarions sound on both sides*

vv. 379–80

pp. 186–8

Dux, (humilis Dominumque timens,)
   moderantius agmen
Ducit, et audacter *ardua montis adit.*

Dux cum suis neque loci territus asperitate, *ardua clivi sensim ascendit.* Terribilis *clangor lituorum pugnae signa cecinit utrinque.*

The armies prepare to engage

vv. 381–4

Prelia precurrunt pedites miscere
   sagittis;
(Quadratis iaculis scuta nihil faciunt.)
Festinant parmas galeatis iungere
   parmis;
Erectis hastis hostis uterque furit.

Ferocity of the English

vv. 385–8

Vt canibus lassatus aper stans dente
   tuetur
Oreque spumoso reicit arma pati,
Non hostem metuit nec tela minancia
   mortem,
Sic plebs Angligena dimicat inpauida.

While the impending battle looks ominous, Taillefer rides out alone

vv. 389–94

Interea, dubio pendent dum prelia
   Marte,
Eminet et telis mortis amara lues,
Histrio, cor *audax* nimium quem
   nobilitabat,
Agmina precedens innumerosa
   ducis,
Hortatur Gallos uerbis et territat
   Anglos:
Alte proiciens ludit et ense suo.

An Englishman breaks ranks to challenge him

vv. 395–8

Anglorum quidam, cum de tot milibus
   unum
Ludentem gladio cernit abire procul,
Milicię cordis tactus feruore decenti,
Viuere postponens, prosilit ire mori.

CARMEN	GESTA GUILLELMI
Taillefer kills his challenger and heartens his comrades	*The valour of the Normans gives them the initiative*
vv. 399–408	p. 188

Incisor-ferri mimus cognomine dictus Vt fuerat captus, pungit equum stimulis. Angligenę scutum telo transfudit acuto; Corpore prostrato distulit ense caput. Lumina conuertens sociis hęc gaudia profert, Belli *principium* monstrat et esse suum. Omnes letantur, Dominum pariter uenerantur; Exultant *ictus* quod *prior* exstat eis, Et tremor et feruor per corda uirilia currunt, Festinantque simul iungere scuta uiri.	Normannorum alacris *audacia pugnae principium* dedit. (Taliter cum oratores in judicio litem agunt de rapina, *prior ferit* dictione qui crimen intendit.)

II. THE ROLE OF THE FRENCH AT HASTINGS IN THE CARMEN AND IN THE GESTA GUILLELMI

Of the primary sources celebrating the Norman Conquest, only two, the *Carmen* and the Bayeux Tapestry, make this their sole subject and have the battle as their climax,[1] and only these and the *Gesta Guillelmi* describe the battle itself in any detail.[2] In the work of Guy of Amiens, the French play a role which is all-important at Hastings; in William of Poitiers's work, the Normans completely eclipse the Manceaux, the French, the Bretons, and the Aquitanians;[3] and in the *GND* the story of the Conquest is summarized without any reference to Duke William's allies. The Tapestry and the *ASC* (MS. D, 1066), on the other hand, refer only to the French, using the word in a generalized sense to mean all those who fought for William.[4]

[1] The *Carmen* and the *BT* seem to be independent and original authorities, but their treatments of the subject show some affinity. Both lack the whole-hearted partisanship of the Norman panegyrists (see above, p. xxvii f. and *BT*, p. 11). It is of some interest that Eustace of Boulogne figures prominently in the battle in both these sources (*Carmen*, vv. 519 ff.; *BT*, Pls. 68–9).

[2] The *GND* reduces the account of the whole period from the sailing to the coronation to seventeen sentences, of which only three are devoted to the battle. William of Poitiers makes some use of this exiguous material, but his chief literary source—one might rather say target—is the *Carmen*. He does not, in our opinion, use the *BT*.   [3] *GG*, p. 192.

[4] The word 'French' is never used in this wide sense by the Norman pane-gyrists, though it occurs in Anglo-Norman diplomata *post* 1066, when the king distinguishes between his English and foreign subjects in this country. Norman

None of these works is objective, and all the authorities who celebrated the duke's triumph had their own motives for presenting the story with more than one public in mind. Thus, on one level, they wrote for the victors, and particularly for men who had a first-hand knowledge of the battle and had provided oral information.[1] But, on another level, they wrote for posterity and for uninformed contemporaries, to whom they wished to convey a calculated picture of events.[2] In the cases of the *Carmen* and the Tapestry, where the creators' sympathies were ambivalent, an even more complex process may be divined.

It is by no means easy to attempt an analysis of these sources, the modern student finding himself among those whom the authorities set out to indoctrinate and sometimes to mislead. It is usually impossible to control these narratives by documentary evidence, but it is clear that much could be learnt from a comparative study of the conflicting sources, weighing the contrasting biases against each other.[3]

sources show that the writers took pride in the non-Frankish origin of their race and treated Hastings as a Norman victory.

[1] See below, next note.

[2] The Norman authorities had a literary exemplar in Dudo of St. Quentin, whose specious history of the Norman dukes was commissioned by Duke Richard I. Cf. D. C. Douglas, 'The Ancestors of William FitzOsbern', in *EHR* lix (1944), 62–79; Douglas writes (p. 73): 'Dudo had considerable assistance from the ducal dynasty he served, and, in particular, he confessed his debt to Count Rodulf whom he actually described as "hujus operis relator".' His work was abbreviated and continued by William of Jumièges, who wrote at the express command of the Conqueror (*GND*, p. 1), and it was also known to William of Poitiers (*GG*, pp. 108, 116 n. 2). It would be surprising if Dudo's work had been unknown to the authors of the *Encomium Emmae* (*EE*, p. xxii) and the *Vita Aedwardi* (*VE*, p. xxiv). Campbell observes (op. cit., p. xxxv) that Freeman called Dudo one of 'a very bad class of writers, those who were employed, on account of their supposed eloquence, to write histories which were intended only as panegyrics of their patrons', and comments that 'the Encomiast belongs undeniably to this class of writers, who have to find a middle way between obvious lies and truths unpalatable to their employers . . .'. The anonymous author of the *VE*, William of Jumièges, and William of Poitiers all pertain to this school and the two last are known to have written in the hope of preferment. The attitude of Guy of Amiens, an independent magnate averse to Normans, using literary skill almost disdainfully to plead a political cause under the guise of a panegyric, is essentially different, as is that of the enigmatic designer of the *BT*. Their work need not be more trustworthy, but the inherent value of such departures from the norm is evident.

[3] On the urgent necessity for such analytical work see Körner, op. cit., pp. 82 ff. Körner, however, ranks the *Carmen* and the *BT* with the Norman sources. What they certainly have in common, whatever their attitude, is an intention to deceive posterity in some degree, while refraining if possible from verbal untruth (see Campbell, op. cit., p. xlvi and xlvi n. 4, where this practice in the *Encomium Emmae* is admirably illustrated and analysed). Unfortunately, a considerable degree of skill in these black arts appears to have been attained by our authorities for the Conquest.

A comprehensively comparative study of the sources is not possible here. We have therefore selected a single aspect of the battle in the *Carmen* for comparison with its treatment in the derivative text of William of Poitiers: namely, the role played by Duke William's French allies.[1]

Nowhere in the work of Guy of Amiens is the French bias so marked as in his account of the battle of Hastings. This is of great interest, for the whole of the first part of the poem builds to the battle as its great climax, and it is here that the poet introduces his 'second hero', Eustace of Boulogne.[2]

The narrative of the conflict falls naturally into three distinct parts: (1) the general tactics, up to the time when Duke William saves the day;[3] (2) the duke's personal combats and hazards in the desperate fighting that follows;[4] (3) a précis of the onslaughts subsequently led by Eustace and William in conjunction, and a detailed account of the death of Harold at the hands of these two, aided by Hugh of Ponthieu and 'Gilfardus'—an event decisive in giving victory to the duke.[5] In contrast to the great length of the prelude, the immediate sequel to the battle—the events of the night following—occupies only six lines.[6] The defeated fly, the victor takes his rest among the dead, and Count Eustace mercilessly pursues the fleeing till it is day.

This presentation of the battle shows that Guy is not merely reporting. In his account of the general tactics his evident purpose is to highlight the achievements of the French by contrast with the Normans. Sarcasm, if not malice, is evident in his treatment of the latter.[7] Duke William himself, however, appears as a titanic figure at the crux of the action (vv. 445 ff.). As in the prelude (vv. 335 f.), he emerges as a commander who meets adversity undaunted and with presence of mind, and now he is shown in action as a matchless warrior.

In the first part of the battle, the terse military detail resembles that in the prelude, standing in sharp contrast to the occasional passages of rhetoric and poetic diction. There can be little doubt, we think, that Guy's informant was a French commander of experience and ability—possibly Eustace of Boulogne himself.[8] The 'literary' interpolations,

---

[1] The Latin texts of these works have not previously been collated at length, and the sequences relating to the battle are therefore given below, rhetorical passages being set in parentheses, or, if of great length, summarized. Following these parallel texts, we give the captions of the *BT* and the brief accounts of the battle in MSS. D and E of the *ASC* and in the *GND*.

[2] See above, p. xxii.   [3] Vv. 409–66.   [4] Vv. 467–524.

[5] Vv. 525–60.   [6] Vv. 561–6.   [7] Cf. vv. 444–9.

[8] That Eustace himself briefed Guy must, of course, remain a hypothesis, but that the two men should have been in communication seems possible, and even probable. From whatever source it emanates, the excellent military detail in the

which we surmise to be the poet's personal contribution, have their own interest. They are invariably introduced to obscure or manipulate preceding factual statements.[1] Taken without these passages, the narrative throughout Part 1 of the battle makes a clear and credible story; whether or not the informant of Guy of Amiens was telling the truth, he knew the ground, and his account is that of a professional soldier.

The *Carmen* ceases to be concerned with tactics at this point, and takes up the story of Duke William's exploits. Part 2 begins with a simile: the advancing army of English, terrified at the sight of the duke, melts away before him as wax melts before a fire (vv. 467 f.). The whole sequence that follows builds up the image of Duke William as a warrior. When Gyrth brings down his horse, William slays the king's brother and holds his own in the ensuing mêlée alone and on foot (vv. 471–84); when the terrified knight of Maine refuses to dismount for him, the duke drags him headlong from the saddle and seizes his horse (vv. 485–94); the poet calls to heaven to witness what destruction then overtakes the English (vv. 495–500). Again unhorsed by 'Helloc's son' and half stunned, William recovers himself, and rushes among the enemy to kill his assailant (vv. 503–18). It is a magnificent picture, and an epic scene follows. Eustace of Boulogne, surrounded by great squadrons of knights, sweeps to the rescue and gives the duke his own destrier, to be horsed in turn by one of his own household (vv. 519–24).

The picture, as we have said, is magnificent, and it is hard to believe that it is pure invention.[2] But if this picture be set in the wider context of the battlefield, one is forced to ask how it is that the duke appears to be involved alone in such desperate combats. The enemy is not melting

---

Carmen has attracted attention. Köhler (op. cit., p. 32 n. 3) praises Guy's description of the terrain, and Dr. Engels (op. cit., p. 10) writes with reference to the battle: 'De veldslag wordt zeer levendig en tot in details beschreven (vs. 363–566). Dank zij bijzonderheden over de opstelling en de tactiek kan men het verloop van de strijd goed volgen.'

[1] See vv. 415 ff., vv. 436–8, and vv. 465 f. On interior evidence Guy consistently exaggerates the English losses to create a more favourable impression of the course of the battle. The most striking example occurs at vv. 495 ff. where the poet's appeal to the Deity to witness William's slaughter of the English conceals the deadly peril of the duke himself.

[2] These single combats have been thought improbable, but it will be remembered that the account was written for the Conqueror himself. Earl Gyrth's slayer is not named in the *BT*, and his death is not described elsewhere, except in the *RR*, where it is set later. Wace, who shows no knowledge of the *Carmen*, says that Duke William struck Gyrth down and heard a rumour that he had killed him, but did not know if it was true (vv. 8851–4). The incident of the knight of Maine is found only in the *Carmen*, yet it has a vivid realism which inspires confidence and could have been retailed by William himself. Nothing is known of 'Helloc's son', but the name is obviously corrupt, suggesting that here Guy may have followed a story reported by some English hostage.

away before him, as Guy has alleged; on the contrary, William is fighting
for his life. Further, he cannot turn for help to the Normans—it is a
vassal from Maine to whom he vainly appeals—and when he is rescued,
it is by Count Eustace.[1] This second sequence in the battle implies that
furious fighting followed the duke's attempt to repulse the massive
English counter-attack which had demoralized his men (vv. 439–44).
The Normans' commander is the target of his opponents, whom he
appears to attack with the fury of despair, unsupported by his own men. It
would be extraordinary that anyone should have dared to present such
a version of events to the Conqueror, had the story had no factual basis.
We therefore think that Part 2 of the battle, as reported in the *Carmen*,
is of more interest than has usually been supposed, and that the account
of William's rescue by Eustace of Boulogne cannot lightly be dismissed.

The last part of Guy's version of Hastings begins with an astonishing
reversal of the order of precedence: the count and the duke renew the
battle together, fighting wherever the conflict is most furious (vv. 525 f.)[2]
A rhetorical description of the havoc they create does not inspire confidence (vv. 527, 529–30), but the statement that a number of the English
deserted, tottering with exhaustion, may be accepted (v. 528). According
to Guy of Amiens, it was when the French had almost won the day and
plundering had begun that the duke sighted Harold in the distance,
cutting to pieces his Norman assailants (vv. 531–4).[3] Duke William,
fighting alongside the French, calls Eustace to him[4] and leaving the
battle there to his allies, goes to the aid of his own men (vv. 535 f.). The
death of Harold (see below, Appendix D) is credited to William and
Eustace, Hugh of Ponthieu (another Frenchman), and 'Gilfardus'
(a Norman),[5] these four succeeding where the Normans had failed. The
report of the king's death breaks the stubborn resistance of the English;

---

[1] We suspect that Count Eustace's loyal knight may be maliciously contrasted
with the knight of Maine who refused William his mount.

[2] This passage seems to imply that there had been a lull in the battle and that
the duke's forces had regrouped. The enemy is clearly not in flight.

[3] Guy's treatment of William's opponent is dramatically most skilful. Harold
appears only twice, each time in a brief vignette. In the prelude, he is shown as
the commander who has out-generalled his rival; holding the hill, he can make
his dispositions with the duke powerless to hinder (vv. 373 ff.). At the end of the
battle, William sees him, still with the advantage of the ground (v. 533), seemingly about to snatch victory from defeat by personal prowess. Both protagonists
are assessed as a soldier would rate them, and emerge as worthy of each other's
steel.

[4] Cf. *La Chanson de Roland*, ed. J. Bédier (Paris, 1960), vv. 1691 f.:

> Le quens Rollant des soens i veit grant perte,
> Sun cumpaignun Oliver en apelet . . .

[5] The Giffard caput was at Longueville-sur-Scie, within a few miles of the
Bresle, which divides Normandy from Vimeu. In mentioning the role of local
magnates in the battle, Guy sets a precedent to be followed by later authorities.

at evening the duke is victorious,[1] and the defeated take refuge in the forest.[2] There follows the brief rhetorical sequel in which the duke rests while Eustace ceaselessly pursues the English, engaged in conflicts throughout the night. The brevity of this closing passage, the obscure reference to conflicts, and the intrusion of rhetoric suggest that what the poet had described as a rout was, in reality, a withdrawal, covered by a fierce rearguard action, which held the pursuit in check. A description of such a reverse for the count would hardly have furthered Guy's claim that King William had already triumphed, thanks to Eustace and the French. Nevertheless, this claim—coming as it does in a panegyric addressed to the Conqueror himself—is too daring to be dismissed as pure invention.[3] A degree of truth must be presumed to underlie the story told by Guy of Amiens,[4] and this may well explain the failure of his ill-fated epic. It could also explain the 'revised version' of the battle in the *Gesta Guillelmi* of William of Poitiers, and the misfortune of the poet may prove to be a blessing to students of the battle. The royal chaplain was undoubtedly in a position to know the facts. His handling of Guy's material may, therefore, make it possible to control both narratives, weighing the bias evident in each story against the other.

The parallel texts given below show that William of Poitiers had studied the battle in the *Carmen* minutely. His revision is intended: (*a*) to exalt the Conqueror's qualities still further;[5] (*b*) to vindicate the Normans, and especially the *ordo equitum*, of which he had formerly been a member;[6] and (*c*) to cry down the role of their allies, in particular that of Eustace of Boulogne.[7]

---

[1] The reference to *corda superba* (v. 552) indicates a stubborn resistance up to the time of the king's death. Rhetorical passages conveying that the battle was almost won previously must therefore be considered suspect.

[2] In the prelude to the battle, Guy of Amiens is alone in stressing that the forest afforded cover to the English till they were within striking distance of the hill (vv. 343 f., 363 ff.). At the close, when the forest gives refuge to the defeated, v. 364 is echoed with dramatic irony in v. 560.

[3] To have advanced such a claim in defiance of all the evidence would have been madness.

[4] The poet's fear as to the reception of his work is evident in the Proem addressed to 'L.'. He may have been thinking chiefly of his temerity in describing the battle. Cf. vv. 6–8, where Guy is anxious about potential rivals, and *Boreas* may well be used in its familiar connotation as a synonym for the Normans.

[5] This is achieved partly by eliminating the figure of King Harold, who plays no role in William of Poitiers's version of the battle, a circumstance unique in an account of such detail.

[6] Compare the *GG*, p. 188: 'subveniunt equites . . .', and Caesar, *De bello gallico*, II. xxvii. The fury of William's knights reflects the shame of their reverse in the prelude to the battle (see above, Appendix B, i). Caesar's horse had been similarly repulsed.

[7] Compare the detailed account of the sequel to the battle in the *GG* (pp. 202–4). Pouncing on this weak passage in Guy's account, William of Poitiers

In the first part of the battle, the *Carmen* and the *GG* are in general agreement, save that William of Poitiers deletes the feigned flight initiated by the French and palliates the Norman flight (p. 190), caused, as in the *Carmen*, by a powerful English counter-attack.[1] In the second part, the biographer avoids showing his hero fighting on foot,[2] and gives a panoramic picture of the conflict. When the texts are collated, it is clear that a young Norman commander on the right wing, Robert of Beaumont,[3] has been substituted for Eustace of Boulogne, as a personage singled out for special praise (*GG*, p. 192). Robert's deeds, however, are not enumerated, and William of Poitiers declares that he is in haste to end his praise of William the count in order to celebrate the glory of William the king.[4] Thus, he avoids reference to the duke's rescue by Eustace of Boulogne, but makes no attempt to refute the story.

In the last part of the battle (*GG*, pp. 194–200), comes the famous story of multiple feigned flights, inspired by the destruction of the pursuers after the genuine flight, when William saved the day.[5] This passage (*GG*, p. 194) contains a verbal echo of the *Carmen*, at the point where Eustace and William join forces and renew the battle—a circumstance buried in the *GG* (loc. cit.) under a reference to 'the Normans and their allies'. William of Poitiers claims that the stratagem was repeatedly successful, but the narrative then gives place to a long digression. A select list of magnates present in the battle is given, headed by

describes the English resistance at length, brings Duke William himself to the rescue, and depicts Eustace as a coward. It emerges incidentally, however, from this version that the count, not William, had been heading the pursuit, and for this the biographer offers no explanation. Benoît de Saint-Maure, who knew the *GG*, sets this scene much earlier, at the time when the duke was endeavouring to stem the rout (Benoît, op. cit., vv. 39643–53), and notes elsewhere the importance of Eustace's contribution to the duke's cause.

[1] In both the *Carmen* and the *GG* (p. 190), the importance of this counter-attack is stressed, and it is difficult to see why it is very generally ignored in modern histories. Certain scholars, however, mostly military historians, have accepted that it was the obvious explanation of the Norman rout.

[2] For a knight to fight on foot was ignominious, and an interesting passage in the *GG* (p. 198) mentions the amazement of the Norman *equites* at the sight of their duke fighting as a foot-soldier. Why none of them gave him a horse is not explained.

[3] Robert was a son of Roger of Beaumont, in whose fief William of Poitiers had been born, and whose kinsman he may have been (*GG*, p. vii).

[4] See the parallel texts. William of Poitiers excuses himself from describing individual deeds, and declares that the most fluent writer, if an eyewitness, could not recount each action. The evasion is obvious, and 'Count William' is a most significant slip. Rarely in the *GG*, and nowhere else in the battle is the Conqueror called *comes*. William of Poitiers is thinking of Count Eustace, in the *Carmen*; if he could have refuted the story that the count rescued William, he would not have been so careful to avoid the subject.

[5] The *Carmen*'s story is here generally accepted as the more reasonable.

Eustace of Boulogne.[1] All were excelled, however, by Duke William, and a summary of his leadership and personal courage follows—mentioning, incidentally, that three horses were killed under him (pp. 196–8).[2] In avoiding the subject of Harold's death, William of Poitiers (GG, p. 198) has a verbal echo of *Hectorides*[3] and again digresses. The collated texts show that the classical parenthesis has been created to fill the lacuna. There is, again, no *démenti*, merely evasion. To assure the reader that William would not have feared to meet Harold in single combat does nothing to disprove the *Carmen*'s story;[4] yet one may be sure that here, even more than in the case of Eustace's rescue of the duke, William of Poitiers would have disproved the story had it been possible.[5] Once again, however, he insists that he is anxious to press on with his history, and so must hasten to end his brief and truthful account of the battle.[6]

At this point (p. 200), the GG ceases to give a revised version of the *Carmen*, and William of Poitiers now rewrites his other source, the GND (p. 135).[7] He elaborates William of Jumièges's plain statement that it was the report of the king's death which put the English to flight, reducing this news to the status of one contributory factor among many which broke the spirit of the enemy. The English fled at last, because the Normans were fighting more fiercely than in the morning, and because it was seen that the fury of the duke, which spared no opponent, could find rest only in victory.[8] Finally, after describing the desperate flight of the defeated and the merciless Norman pursuit, the biographer recounts the rearguard action, in which Eustace is derided and Duke William consummates his victory against great odds.[9] The English, who in terror of the duke had occupied the hill that morning, are now depicted as the most formidable of opponents.[10]

If Guy of Amiens is guilty of exaggeration in the cause of the French, it is clear that William of Poitiers cannot shake the fundamental thesis

[1] This tacit witness to the count's importance supports Guy's view of Eustace. The men named are given as the most outstanding among many valiant warriors. It may be noticed that Robert of Beaumont is not included.

[2] This exaggeration of Guy's figure has been noted with scepticism by a number of writers. William of Poitiers, it will be seen, leaves Duke William without a mount.

[3] *Carmen*, v. 537.

[4] The *BT* shows four unidentified knights in the scene of Harold's death, one of whom slashes the king's thigh (Pls. 71–2) (see Appendix D). William of Jumièges, though he places Harold's death in the first encounter of the knights (GND, 135), says that he died 'vulneribus letaliter confossus'.

[5] See the GG, p. 178. In this passage, allegedly giving the duke's own words, the biographer had made Duke William challenge Harold to single combat before the battle.

[6] GG, p. 200. [7] See below, collated texts. [8] GG, loc. cit.
[9] Ibid., pp. 202–4. [10] Ibid., pp. 186, 202.

of his story, though he distorts it to the greater glory of his duke and his nation. It must be accepted, we believe, that the French contribution at Hastings was much more important than was agreeable to Norman pride.[1]

II. THE BATTLE IN THE *CARMEN* AND IN THE *GESTA GUILLELMI*, PARALLEL TEXTS[2]

CARMEN	GESTA GUILLELMI
Archers and crossbow-men attack the English phalanx	*The duke's foot attack with missiles; the English resist strongly*
vv. 409–12	p. 188
Inuadunt primi peditum cetus pharetrati, Eminus et iaculis corpora trahiciunt. Et balistantes clipeos, ad grandinis instar, Dissoluunt, quaciunt ictibus innumeris.	Pedites itaque *Normanni* propius accedentes provocant Anglos, missilibus in eos vulnera dirigunt atque necem. Illi contra fortiter, quo quisque valet ingenio, resistunt. Jactant cuspides ac diversorum generum tela, saevissimas quasque secures, et lignis imposita saxa. Iis, veluti mole letifera, statim nostros obrui putares.
General assault: the order of attack	*The knights charge to the rescue and fight at close quarters*
vv. 413–14	
Set leuam *Galli*, dextram peciere *Britanni*; Dux cum *Normannis* dimicat in medio.	Subveniunt equites, et qui posteriores fuere fiunt primi. Pudet eminus pugnare, gladiis rem gerere audent.
The English phalanx fights furiously	*The battle rages for some time*
vv. 415–16	
Anglorum stat fixa solo densissima turba, Tela dat et telis et gladios gladiis.	Sic aliquandiu summa vi certatur ab utrisque.

---

[1] According to Eadmer (Eadm., pp. 8 f.), French survivors were alleging some forty years after Hastings that so great had been the slaughter and flight of the Normans that their ultimate victory could only be ascribed to a miracle, God's judgement on the perjury of Harold.

[2] Material is collated as above, pp. 83–90, save that italics are here used to emphasize the prominence given to one nationality or the other in the battle by the two writers. The brief account of William of Jumièges, the equally brief captions of the Bayeux Tapestry accompanying the battle scenes, and the relevant passages of the *ASC*, MSS. D and E (1066), are appended (pp. 108 f.).

CARMEN

The ranks are so close, the dead cannot fall

vv. 417-20

Spiritibus nequeunt frustrata cadauera
    sterni,
Nec cedunt uiuis corpora militibus.
Omne cadauer enim, uita licet euacua-
    tum,
    Stat uelut illesum, possidet atque
    locum.

The French feign flight on the right wing

vv. 421-4

Nec penetrare ualent spissum nemus
    Angligenarum,
Ni tribuat uires uiribus ingenium.
Artibus instructi, *Franci*, bellare periti,
Ac si deuicti fraude fugam simulant.

*The English light-armed charge on both
flanks*

vv. 425-32

Rustica letatur gens, et superasse
    putabat;
Post tergum nudis insequitur gladiis.
(Amotis sanis, labuntur dilacerati,
    Siluaque spissa prius rarior efficitur.)
Conspicit ut campum cornu tenuare
    sinistrum,
    Intrandi dextrum quod uia larga
    patet:
Perdere dispersos uariatis cladibus
    hostes
    Laxatis frenis certat utrumque
    prius.

*The French wheel and cut off their
pursuers*

vv. 433-8

Quique fugam simulant instantibus
    ora retorquent;
    Constrictos cogunt uertere dorsa
    neci.
Pars ibi magna perit—pars et densata
    resistit—
    Milia namque decem sunt ibi passa
    necem.

GESTA GUILLELMI

Many factors aid the English

loc. cit.

Angli nimium adjuvantur superioris
loci opportunitate, quem sine procursu
tenent, et maxime conferti; ingenti
quoque numerositate sua atque vali-
dissima corpulentia; praeterea pugnae
instrumentis, quae facile per scuta vel
alia tegmina viam inveniunt. Fortis-
sime itaque sustinent vel propellunt
ausos in se districtum ensibus impetum
facere. Vulnerant et eos qui eminus in
se jacula conjiciunt.

The Bretons fly on the left

pp. 188-90

Ecce igitur hac saevitia perterriti aver-
tuntur pedites, pariter atque equites
Britanni, et quotquot auxiliares erant
in sinistro cornu;—

CARMEN

Vt pereunt mites bachante leone
　　bidentes,
Sic compulsa mori gens maledicta
　　ruit.

*The main body of the English charges,
routing the Normans in a massive
counter-attack*

vv. 439–44

Plurima quę superest pars bello acrior
　　instat,
Et sibi sublatos pro nichilo reputat.

Anglorum populus, numero superante,
　　repellit
Hostes, uique retro compulit ora
　　dari,
Et fuga ficta prius fit tunc uirtute
　　coacta.
Normanni fugiunt; dorsa tegunt
　　clipei.

William confronts the fugitives in fury

vv. 445–7

Dux, ubi perspexit quod gens sua
　　uicta recedit,
Occurrens illi signa ferendo, manu
Increpat et cedit; retinet, constringit
　　et hasta.

*The duke addresses the French and
shames them; they wheel to face the
enemy*

vv. 448–61

Iratus, galea nudat et ipse caput.
Vultum *Normannis* dat; uerba pre-
　　cantia *Gallis*
Dixit, 'Quo fugitis? Quo iuuat ire
　　mori?
Quę fueras uictrix, pateris cur uicta
　　uideri
Regnis terrarum Gallia nobilior?

GESTA GUILLELMI

Almost the whole of the duke's army flies

p. 190

... cedit fere cuncta ducis acies, (quod
cum pace dictum sit *Normannorum*
invictissimae nationis. Romanae
majestatis exercitus, copias regum
continens, vincere solitus terra mari-
que, fugit aliquando, cum ducem
suum sciret aut crederet occisum.
Credidere *Normanni* ducem ac dominum suum cecidisse. Non ergo nimis
pudenda fuga cessere; minime vero
dolenda, cum plurimum juverit.)

*William confronts the fugitives in fury,
seeing a great part of the enemy in
pursuit*

Princeps namque prospiciens multam
partem adversae stationis prosiluisse,
et insequi terga suorum, fugientibus
occurrit et obstitit, verberans aut
minans hasta.

*The duke addresses the Normans, who
recover their courage*

Nudato insuper capite detractaque
galea exclamans, 'Me', inquit, 'cir-
cumspicite. Vivo et vincam, opitu-
lante Deo. Quae vobis dementia fugam
suadet? Quae via patebit ad effugien-
dum? Quos ut pecora mactare potestis,
depellunt vos et occidunt. Victoriam
deseritis ac perpetuum honorem; in

CARMEN

Non homines set oues fugitis, frustraque timetis;
Illud quod facitis dedecus est
nimium.
Est mare post tergum; maris est iter
ad remeandum
Pergraue, quod uobis tempus et
aura negat.
Ad patriam reditus grauis est, grauis
et uia longa;
His uobis nullum restat et effugium—
Vincere certetis, solum si uiuere
uultis.'
Dixit, et extimplo serpit ad ora
pudor;
Terga retro faciunt; uultus uertuntur
in hostes.

*William heads a charge; the enemy is
repulsed with heavy losses*

vv. 462-70

Dux, ut erat princeps, primus et ille
ferit;
Post illum reliqui feriunt. Ad corda
reuersi,
Vires assumunt reiciendo metum.
Vt stipulę flammis pereunt spiranti-
bus auris,
Sic a *Francigenis*, Anglica turba,
ruis.
Ante ducis faciem tremefactum labitur
agmen,
Mollis cera fluit ignis ut a facie.
Abstracto gladio, galeas et scuta recidit;
Illius et sonipes corpora multa facit.

*William, unhorsed by Gyrth, kills the
king's brother and fights on foot in the
furious mêlée*

vv. 471-84

*A knight of Maine refuses to give the
duke his horse; William pulls him down
headlong and mounts. He rages among
the enemy*

vv. 485-94

GESTA GUILLELMI

exitium curritis ac perpetuum opprobrium. Abeundo, mortem nullus
vestrum evadet.' His dictis receperunt
animos.

*William heads a charge; the enemy is
repulsed with heavy losses*

pp. 190-2

Primus ipse procurrit fulminans ense,
stravit adversam gentem (quae sibi,
regi suo, rebellans commeruit mortem). Exardentes *Normanni* et circum-
venientes aliquot millia insecuta se,
momento deleverunt ea, ut ne quidem
unus superesset. Ita confirmati, vehe-
mentius immanitatem exercitus in-
vaserunt,—

*Despite such losses, the vast army of the
English seems unweakened and fights
savagely, keeping order*

p. 192

—qui maximum detrimentum passus
non videbatur minor. Angli confi-
denter totis viribus oppugnabant, id
maxime laborantes, ne quem aditum
irrumpere volentibus aperirent. Ob
nimium densitatem eorum labi vix
potuerunt interempti.

*Some inroads made by the bravest
knights, chiefly Normans*

CARMEN

GESTA GUILLELMI

(Rhetoric, calling on God to witness the slaughter of the English)

vv. 495–500

Attacking furiously, William is again unhorsed, by 'Helloc's son' and half-stunned. The duke rushes among the English to kill his assailant

vv. 501–18

Eustace of Boulogne is first to the duke's aid with a great following

vv. 519–24

At comes Eustachius, generosis patri-
   bus ortus,
   Septus bellantum multiplici cuneo,
Ad ducis auxilium festinat primus
   haberi;
   Efficiturque pedes dux ut abiret
   eques.
Miles erat quidam comitis, nutritus
   ab illo,
   Fecerat ut domino, fecit et ille sibi.

Together, Eustace and William resume the battle, where the fight is hottest

vv. 525–6

Talibus auspiciis, comes et dux
   associati
   Quo magis arma micant, bella simul
   repetunt.

Patuerunt tamen in eos viae incisae per diversas partes fortissimorum militum ferro. Institerunt eis *Ceno-manici, Francigenae, Britanni, Aqui-tani*, sed cum praecipua virtute *Normanni*.

Special valour of Robert de Beaumont, who led a thousand knights on the right wing

Tiro quidam *Normannus* Rodbertus, Rogerii de Bellomonte filius, Hugonis de Mellento comitis ex Adelina sorore nepos et haeres, praelium illo die primum experiens, egit quod aeter-nandum esset laude: cum legione quam in dextro cornu duxit, irruens ac sternens magna cum audacia.

The author cannot relate all the deeds that were done, nor would this be to his purpose. The most gifted writer, had he been present, could not have set down all that happened. The biographer hastens to conclude his praise of Count William, in order to extol the glory of William the king

The Normans and their allies hold a council of war and feign flight

p. 194

Animadvertentes *Normanni* sociaque turba, non absque nimio sui incom-modo hostem tantum simul resistentem superari posse; terga dederunt, fugam ex industria simulantes. (Meminerunt quam optatae rei paulo ante fuga dederit occasionem.)

The English roar and pursue

Barbaris cum spe victoriae ingens laetitia exorta est. Sese cohortantes exultante clamore nostros maledictis increpabant, et minabantur cunctos illico ruituros esse. Ausa sunt ut superius aliquot millia quasi volante cursu, quos fugere putabant, urgere.

<table>
<tr><td>CARMEN</td><td>GESTA GUILLELMI</td></tr>
</table>

CARMEN / GESTA GUILLELMI

The Normans wheel and cut off their pursuers

Normanni repente regiratis equis interceptos et inclusos undique mactaverunt, nullum relinquentes.

The ruse twice repeated, they attack the surviving enemy with zeal, but can make little impression

Bis eo dolo simili eventu usi, reliquos majori cum alacritate aggressi sunt; aciem adhuc horrendam, et quam difficillimum erat circumvenire.

The enemy stands fast against all attacks

Fit deinde insoliti generis pugna, quam altera pars incursibus et diversis motibus agit, altera velut humo affixa, tolerat.

Eustace and William gradually wear down the English; many desert, exhausted

The English are gradually worn down and become exhausted

vv. 527–30

Amborum gladiis campus rarescit ab Anglis,
Defluit et numerus, nutat et atteritur.
Corruit apposita ceu silua minuta securi,
Sic nemus Angligenum ducitur ad nihilum.

Languent Angli, et quasi reatum ipso defectu confitentes, vindictam patiuntur. Sagittant, feriunt, perfodiunt Normanni: mortui plus dum cadunt, quam vivi, moveri videntur. Leviter sauciatos non permittit evadere, sed comprimendo necat sociorum densitas. (Ita felicitas pro Guillelmo triumpho maturando cucurrit.)

Magnates in the battle

pp. 194–6

(List of eight names, headed by Eustace of Boulogne and including Aimery of Thouars)

William excelled them all

p. 196

He led his men in every sense

pp. 196–8

Nobiliter duxit ille cohibens fugam, dans animos, periculi socius; saepius clamans ut venirent, quam jubens ire. (Unde liquido intelligitur virtutem illi praeviam pariter fecisse militibus iter et audaciam. Cor amisit absque vulnere pars hostium non modica, prospiciens hunc admirandum ac terribilem equitem.)

CARMEN

GESTA GUILLELMI

He lost and avenged three horses

p. 198

His feats of arms on foot

His knights, amazed to see him fight as a foot-soldier, took heart. The wounded urged their comrades not to follow the duke faintheartedly or let victory slip from their grasp

Gaul was almost victorious and plundering had begun, when William sighted the king on the hill destroying his Norman assailants

vv. 531–4

Iam ferme campum uictrix effecta regebat,
  Iam spolium belli Gallia leta petit,
Cum dux prospexit regem super ardua montis
  Acriter instantes dilacerare suos.

William summons Eustace and goes to the rescue

William rescued many

vv. 535–6

Aduocat Eustachium; linquens ibi prelia *Francis*,
  Oppressis ualidum contulit auxilium.

Auxilio ipse multis atque saluti fuit.

William, Eustace, and two others ride to kill the king

The duke would not have feared to meet Harold in single combat

vv. 537–40

Alter ut Hectorides, Pontiui nobilis heres
  Hos comitatur Hugo, promtus in officio;
Quartus Gilfardus, patris a cognomine dictus:
  Regis ad exicium quatuor arma ferunt.

(Cum Heraldo, tali qualem poemata dicunt Hectorem vel Turnum, non minus auderet Guillelmus congredi singulari certamine, quam Achilles cum Hectore, vel Aeneas cum Turno.)

Many were seeking to kill Harold; these four excelled them—witness their achievement, for the king was slaughtering the rightful victors

Tydeus needed help against fifty enemies; William would not have feared to meet a thousand single-handed

vv. 541–4

Ast alii plures? Aliis sunt hi meliores.
  Si quis in hoc dubitat, actio uera probat:

pp. 198–200

(Tydeus adversum insidiatos quinquaginta rupis petivit opem; Guillelmus

CARMEN	GESTA GUILLELMI

Per nimias cedes nam, bellica iura
    tenentes
Heraldus cogit pergere carnis iter.

par, haud inferior loco, solus non
extimuit mille.)

*Statius and Virgil, who, in the manner
of poets, exaggerate great deeds, would
have found a worthier subject in William*

The four cut down the king

vv. 545–50

p. 200

Per clipeum primus dissoluens cuspide
    pectus,
Effuso madidat sanguinis imbre
    solum;
Tegmine sub galeę caput amputat
    ense secundus;
Et telo uentris tertius exta rigat;
Abscidit coxam quartus; procul egit
    ademptam:
Taliter occisum terra cadauer habet.

*Such writers, fired by their subject,
would have raised William to the stature
of their gods by the nobility of their style.
But the author's humble prose seeks only
to stress (for the benefit of other rulers)
his devotion to the one true God . . .
Hence the biographer will hasten on to
end his truthful, brief account of the
battle, which William won as valiantly
as justly*

*Rumour of the king's death breaks the
English*

vv. 551–8

Fama uolans 'Heraldus obit!' per
    prelia sparsit;
  Mitigat extimplo corda superba
    timor.
Bella negant Angli. Veniam poscunt
    superati.
  Viuere diffisi, terga dedere neci.
Dux ibi per numerum duo milia misit
    ad orcum,
  Exceptis aliis milibus innumeris.

*Knowledge of their losses, exhaustion,
and despair of support break the English*

pp. 200–2

Vesper erat; iam cardo diem uoluebat
    ad umbras,
  Victorem fecit cum Deus esse
    ducem.

Jam inclinato die haud dubie intel-
lexit exercitus Anglorum se stare
contra *Normannos* diutius non valere.

CARMEN	*GESTA GUILLELMI*
	Noverunt se diminutos interitu multarum legionum; regem ipsum et fratres ejus, regni primates nonnullos occubuisse; quotquot reliqui sunt prope viribus exhaustos; subsidium quod expectent nullum relictum. Viderunt *Normannos* non multum decrevisse peremptorum casu, et quasi virium incrementa pugnando sumerent, acrius quam in principio imminere; ducis eam saevitiam quae nulli contra stanti parceret; eam fortitudinem quae nisi victrix non quiesceret. In fugam itaque conversi quantotius abierunt, alii raptis equis, nonnulli pedites; pars per vias, plerique per avia. Jacuerunt in sanguine qui niterentur, aut surgerent non valentes profugere. Valentes fecit aliquos salutem valde cupiens animus.

Only night and the forest afford refuge to the defeated	*Many seek the forest only to die; others fallen along the roads hinder the pursuit*
vv. 559–60	p. 202
Solum deuictis nox et fuga profuit Anglis Densi per latebras et tegimen nemoris.	Multi silvestribus in abditis remanserunt cadavera, plures obfuerunt sequentibus per itinera collapsi.

The duke rests that night among the dead

vv. 561–2

Inter defunctos noctem pausando peregit
Victor, et exspectat lucifer ut redeat.

Eustace pursues furiously	*The Normans pursue in unknown country*
vv. 563–4	
Peruigil Hectorides sequitur cedendo fugaces; Mars sibi tela gerit; mors sociata furit.	*Normanni*, licet ignari regionis, avide insequebantur, caedentes rea terga, imponentes manum ultimam secundo negotio. A mortuis etiam equorum ungulae supplicia sumpsere, dum cursus fieret super jacentes.

Eustace is involved in conflicts till it is day	*Difficult ground halts the pursuit; the enemy stands*
vv. 565–6	
Duxit ad usque diem uario certamine noctem; Nec somno premitur; somnia nec patitur.	Rediit tamen fugientibus confidentia, nactis ad renovandum certamen maximam opportunitatem, praerupti valli et frequentium fossarum.

CARMEN   *GESTA GUILLELMI*

Only the greatest valour could have beaten the English, descendants of the Old Saxons, the fiercest of men. They had recently vanquished with ease the king of Norway, with a powerful and warlike army.

William, although he thought the enemy had received reinforcements, presses on

Cernens autem felicium signorum ductor cohortes inopinato collectas, quamvis noviter advenire subsidium putaret, non flexit iter neque substitit, (terribilior cum parte hastae quam grandia spicula vibrantes)—

He shouts to Eustace, who is about to sound the recall, to stand fast

—Eustachium comitem cum militibus quinquaginta aversum, et receptui signa canere volentem, ne abiret virili voce compellavit.

Eustace, remonstrating with the duke, is wounded

pp. 202–4

Ille contra familiariter in aurem ducis reditum suasit, proximam ei, si pergeret, mortem praedicens. Haec inter verba percussus Eustachius inter scapulas ictu sonoro, cujus gravitatem statim sanguis demonstrabat naribus et ore, quasi moribundus evasit ope comitum.

The duke scorns to turn back and consummates his victory, but the terrain causes heavy losses

p. 204

Dux formidinem omnino dedignans aut dedecus, invadens protrivit adversarios. In eo congressu *Normannorum* aliqui nobiliores ceciderunt, adversitate loci virtute eorum impedita.

William returns to the field and views the slaughter with compassion

Sic victoria consummata, ad aream belli regressus, reperit stragem, quam non absque miseratione conspexit (tametsi factam in impios; tametsi

CARMEN

GESTA GUILLELMI

tyrannum occidere sit pulchrum, fama
gloriosum, beneficio gratum).

*GESTA NORMANNORUM
DUCUM*

(*GND*, pp. 134 f.)

Quem (sc. Willelmum) Heroldus in-
cautum accelerans preoccupare . . .
tota nocte equitans, in campo belli
mane apparuit.
Dux vero, nocturnos precavens ex-
cursus hostis, inchoantibus tenebris,
ad gratissimam usque lucem exercitum jussit esse in armis. Facto autem
diluculo, legionibus militum in tribus
ordinibus dispositis, horrendo hosti
intrepidus obviam processit.

BAYEUX TAPESTRY

(Pls. 52–73)

Pls. 52–5:

Hic milites exierunt de Hestenga et
venerunt ad prelium contra Haroldum
regem.

Pls. 55–7:

Hic Willelm dux interrogat Vital si
vidisset exercitum Haroldi.

Pl. 58:

Iste nuntiat Haroldum regem de
exercitu Wilelmi ducis.

Pls. 59–62

Hic Willelm dux alloquitur suis militibus ut prepararent se viriliter et
sapienter ad prelium contra Anglorum
exercitum.

Pls. 62–3:

Cum quo sub hora diei tertia com-
mittens bellum,

(Two scenes, no captions: (*a*) The
English phalanx attacked; (*b*) a
counter-attack begins.)

Pls. 64–5:

Hic ceciderunt Lewine et Gẏrð
fratres Haroldi regis.

Pls. 66–7:

in cedibus morientibus usque ad
noctem protraxit.

Hic ceciderunt simul Angli et Franci
in prelio.

Pls. 67–8:

Hic Odo episcopus baculum tenens
confortat pueros.

Pls. 68–9:

Hic est dux Wilel[m]   E[usta]tius

GESTA NORMANNORUM
DUCUM
(*GND*, p. 135)

BAYEUX TAPESTRY
(Pls. 52–73)

Pls. 69–71:

Hic Franci pugnant et ceciderunt qui erant cum Haroldo.

Pls. 71–2:

Heroldus etiam ipse in primo militum congressu occubuit vulneribus letaliter confossus.

Hic Harold rex interfectus est.

Pls. 72–3:

Comperientes itaque Angli regem suum mortem oppetiisse, de sua diffidentes salute, jam nocte imminente, versa facie, subsidium appetierunt fugae.

Et fuga verterunt Angli.

(Here the Tapestry ends, incomplete)

Fortissimus igitur dux, ab inimicorum strage reversus, nocte media, ad campum belli est regressus.

ASC, MS. D, 1066

MS. D

Ða com Wyllelm eorl of Normandíge ínto Pefneseá . on Sc̄e Michǽles mæsse ǽfen . 7 sona þæs hi fére wæron . worhton castel æt Hæstinga port . þis wearð þa Harolde cynge gecydd . 7 he gaderade þa mycelne here . 7 com him togénes æt þære háran apuldran . 7 Wyllelm him com ongean on unwær . ær his folc gefylced wære . Ac se kyng þeah him swiðe heardlice wið feaht . mid þam mannum . þe him gelæstan woldon . 7 þær wearð micel wæl geslægen on ægðre healfe. Ðær wearð ofslægen Harold kyng . 7 Leofwine eorl his broðor . 7 Gyrð eorl his broðor . 7 fela godra manna . 7 þa Frencyscan ahton wælstowe geweald . eallswa heom God uðe for folces synnon.

ASC, MS. E, 1066

MS. E

þa hwile com Willelm eorl úpp æt Hestingan . on Sc̄e Michǽles mæssedæg. 7 Harold com norðan . 7 him wið gefeaht éar þan þe his here come eall . 7 þær he feoll . 7 his twægen gebroðra . Gyrð 7 Leofwine . and Willelm þis land geeode.

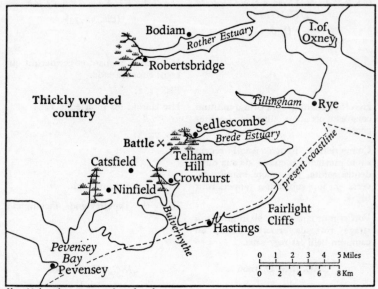

MAP 1. The Hastings District in 1066

From: J. A. Williamson: Evolution of England (Clarendon Press)

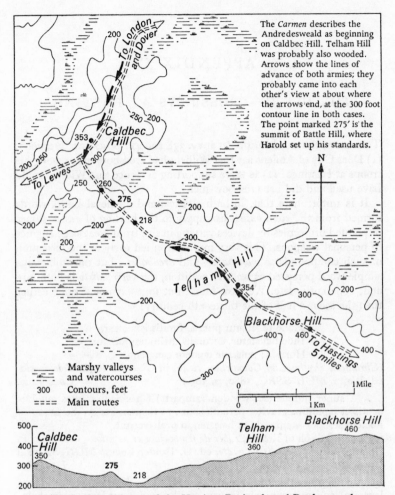

The *Carmen* describes the Andredesweald as beginning on Caldbec Hill. Telham Hill was probably also wooded. Arrows show the lines of advance of both armies; they probably came into each other's view at about where the arrows end, at the 300 foot contour line in both cases. The point marked 275′ is the summit of Battle Hill, where Harold set up his standards.

MAP 2. The Isthmus of the Hastings Peninsula and Battleground

Adapted, by the kind permission of Patrick Thornhill, Esq., from the map reproduced on p. 38 of his *The Battle of Hastings*, London, Methuen & Co. Ltd., 1966

APPENDIX C

THE USE OF CROSSBOWS AT HASTINGS

THE use of the word *balistantes* at vv. 338 and 411 poses two questions: (1) Does Guy of Amiens say that William had crossbow-men among his troops at Hastings? (2) Is there supporting evidence that William could have used and did use crossbow-men? It is unfortunate that, in both classical and medieval Latin, words formed from the stem *balist-* can apply to the hurling of either stones or pointed projectiles by devices varying in size from great siege engines to personal weapons. This very imprecision led early to the formation of such compounds as *manubalist-* and *arcubalist-*, but the ambiguous simple word persisted as well. In addition, the verb *balisto* is both rare and, apparently, late. We have found but four examples, none earlier than the second half of the thirteenth century:

> Mane rebellatur pueris, fundis iaculatur,
> Inde balistatur, accursus utrimque minatur
> Horrida; pulsatur tandem campana.

(*Chronicon rhythmicum Coloniense*, v. 46, in *Chronica Regia Coloniensia*, ed. Waitz, *MGH SSRG*, 1880, p. 305.) *Circa* 1260.

. . . super quibus (sc. wooden ramparts) Christiani stantes sudibus acutis et lapidibus graviter percutiebant . . . Sequenti enim die usque ad noctem semper sagittando et balestando preliaverunt.
(Albertus Milioli of Reggio, *Liber de temporibus et aetatibus*, cap. ccxx, in *Gesta obsidionis civitatis Damiate*, ed. O. Holder-Egger, *MGH SS* xxxi (1903), p. 363.) *Ante* 1265.

Et in die Martis siderunt (sc. the besieging Genoese) usque ad Tertiam levando laudem communis Januae, et illos, qui erant in turribus, balestando, turrim etiam Veronicae diruentes.
(Caffarus, *Annales Genuenses*, lib. x, ed. A. Muratori, vi. 583D.) *Post* 1283.

viriliter se defendebant ballistendo circumquaque et lapides projiciendo.
(*Annales Edwardi I, RS* xxviii. 484) 1303.

Mittellateinisches Wörterbuch, now in progress under the editorship of Dr. Otto Prinz, defines *balisto* as, 'ballistâ missilia jacere'. It would be impossible, in the light of the above examples, to assign a more precise meaning to the verb. In the final case, either crossbows or a mechanical sling may be meant; the other three instances are all of large engines for hurling sizeable stones.

None the less, in the *Carmen* the *balistantes* are clearly crossbow-men. Guy describes the movements of William's archers three times: in vv. 337–8, the first reference, he adds that *balistantes* were set in their midst; at v. 381 the archers are mentioned again in much the same terms as in v. 337, but instead of naming the *balistantes* this time, Guy describes the effect of their squared bolts:

> Prelia precurrunt pedites miscere sagittis;
> (Quadratis iaculis scuta nihil faciunt).

Lastly, archers and *balistantes* are again coupled in vv. 409–12, the last two lines of which read like a gloss on v. 382:

> Inuadunt primi peditum cetus pharetrati,
> Eminus et iaculis corpora trahiciunt.
> Et balistantes clipeos, ad grandinis instar,[1]
> Dissoluunt, quaciunt ictibus innumeris.

Quadrata iacula can be nothing but crossbow bolts (see the note to v. 382), and the substitution of these words for *balistantes* makes it certain what weapons Guy is describing. There remains, however, the question of whether his description is accurate. Was it possible for William to have had crossbow-men? Do any other contemporary sources for the battle support Guy of Amiens in this statement?

Perhaps because of the ambiguity of the stem *balist-*, it has been claimed that crossbows ceased to be known, or at least to be used, soon after the fall of the Western Empire, reappearing only at the time of the First Crusade. If this were so, it would obviously be most unlikely that William the Conqueror had employed them thirty years earlier. But it is not so. Both the word *arcubalista* (whose meaning is not in doubt) and the word *balista* (in a context implying or requiring that it refer to a bow, not a sling) occur, sparsely, but significantly, in texts throughout the early Middle Ages:

(1) Si quis in terris suis foveas fecerit, ut feras in eisdem foveis conprehendat, aut laqueos vel arcos protenderit seu ballistas in locis secretis vel desertis . . .

(Laws of Reccaswinth, in *Leges Visigothorum Antiquiores*, ed. K. Zeumer, viii. 4. 23.) Seventh century.

---

[1] For *grando*, used of arrows, cf.:

> Undique tela volant, circumtegit aëra totum
> Grando sagittarum . . .

(William of Apulia, *De Gestis Normannorum in Sicilia, Appulia et Calabria*, in Muratori v. 264D.)

. . . donec Haroldus, ictu unius sagittarum, quarum multitudo ad instar hiberni grandinis volando perstrepuit . . . expiravit. (*Flores Hist.* i. 596.)

(2) Est autem id genus arboris aptum spiculis et arcubalistis, vulgo enim dicitur ivus.

(Miracula Martini Abbatis Vertavensis, ed. B. Krusch, *MGH SSRM* iii. 571. 1.)   Ninth century (*post* 878).

(3) Belgae vero quia ab urbanis nimium arcobalistis impetebantur, resistere quiescunt.

(Richer, *Historia* ii. 92 (ed. J. Guadet, Paris, 1845, 2 vols.; also ed. R. Latouche, Paris, 1930, 2 vols.).)   995–6

(4) Et quia aperta fronte stare animo non fuit, sagittarii cum arcubus et balistis per montana dispositi sunt.

(Ibid. iii. 98.)   996–8

(5) Missaeque sagittae et arcobalistae. . . tam densae in aere discurrebant, ut a nubibus dilabi, terraque exsurgere viderentur.

(Ibid. iii. 104.)   996–8

(6) Fulcherius arcibalister.

(Witness to a confirmation at Courdemanche, 4 August 1060, by Duke William of a donation by Richard de Reviers to Saint-Père de Chartres. *Recueil des Actes des Ducs de Normandie, 911–1066*, no. 147 (ed. M. Fauroux, Caen, 1961. (*Mém. de la Soc. des Antiq. de Normandie* xxxvi).)
4 August 1060

Early crossbows were relatively less effective than short-bows or long-bows against any but a sizeable and static target, but much more powerful, though considerably slower to operate.[1] They were, therefore, of greatest use against an enemy massed in close formation, like the 'boar's snout' popular with the Germanic tribes encountered by the Romans up to the fourth century. After Adrianople, however, as tactics came increasingly to be based on the use of cavalry,[2] the crossbow dropped out of favour as a military weapon (though it apparently continued to be employed in hunting). At Hastings, however, William confronted a nation which, as Guy tells us, clung to the traditional close formation of its ancestors (v. 367) and fought on foot (vv. 369–70). He could certainly have used Fulcherius and his brethren in such unfamiliar warfare, and he would have needed their help. Two other eleventh-

---

[1] Cf. R. Payne-Gallwey, *The Crossbow* (London, 1958), pp. 9, 37.

[2] An exception to the growing emphasis on cavalry after the fourth century occurs in the kingdom of the Franks; they continued for over a hundred years to fight mostly on foot. Their opponents, however, chiefly other Germanic peoples, either had not the technical skill to manufacture reliable crossbows, or (more probably) considered these long-range weapons beneath the dignity of a warrior. We have found no record or depiction of their use in France before the ninth century, and then not by native Franks. Indeed, the last four examples cited above hint strongly that they were popular chiefly in Flanders. They were perhaps introduced into Normandy only after William's alliance with Baldwin V.

century sources for the Conquest bear out the *Carmen*. While neither the *ASC* nor William of Jumièges gives any details of the arms used, William of Poitiers says: 'Pedites in fronte locavit, sagittis armatos et balistis' (*GG*, p. 184); and although he does not specify further what the *balistae* were, he clearly means 'bolts'—sometimes so called, cf. example 5, above, p. 114. Foreville translates this word as 'arbalètes', without comment: '. . . armés de flèches et d'arbalètes;'

Baudri of Bourgueil (born 1046), writing for William's daughter, Adela of Blois, is most explicit:

> Arcubus utantur, dux imperat atque balistis,
> Nam prius has mortes Anglia tunc didicit;
> Tunc didicere mori quam non novere sagitta:
> Creditur a coelo mors super ingruere. (BB, vv. 409–12.)

The arrow by which the English learned to die, which they had not known before, and which fell from heaven, was not that used with the English bow, but rather the crossbow bolt, often called *sagitta* (cf. the note to v. 382), and usually fired upward in a steep trajectory. Some confirmation that the English were ignorant of it may be found in the *ASC* for 1079 (MS. D):

> Her Rotbert feht wið his fæder. 7 hine on þa hand gewundade. 7 his hors wearð under ofscoten. 7 se þe him oðer to brohte wearð þærrihte mid ánan arblaste ofscoten.

The English chronicler, writing thirteen years after the Conquest, uses a French word for this still unfamiliar weapon.

Finally, the remaining eleventh-century source, the Bayeux Tapestry, perhaps suggested a crossbow-man as one of the four archers in Pl. 61 and Pl. X. The bow itself is normal and yet the archer is unique. His stance (looking upward, feet together) and his dress (mail shirt, quiver hung at belt, not shoulder) are quite different from those of the other three archers, and conform with the practice of crossbow-men, who fired upward, whose legs did not have to brace them for the shot, who wore their quivers at the waist, the bolts point up, and whose slowness in reloading required them to wear more defensive armour than the archers. This figure is one of the mysteries of the Tapestry. Perhaps here, as often elsewhere, the designer suggests more than he shows. The crossbow was considered a barbarous weapon (its use in warfare between Christian nations was banned at the Second Lateran Council in 1139), and it is significant that the *French* sources have most to say on William's *balistae*. Was the designer of the Tapestry ordered to observe discretion? And has he also given us the ratio of *balistantes* to archers at the outset of the battle?

APPENDIX D

THE DEATH OF HAROLD IN THE *CARMEN*

> Iam ferme campum uictrix effecta regebat,
> Iam spolium belli Gallia leta petit,
> Cum dux prospexit regem super ardua montis
> Acriter instantes dilacerare suos.
> Aduocat Eustachium; linquens ibi prelia Francis,   535
> Oppressis ualidum contulit auxilium.
> Alter ut Hectorides, Pontiui nobilis heres
> Hos comitatur Hugo, promtus in officio;
> Quartus Gilfardus, patris a cognomine dictus:
> Regis ad exicium quatuor arma ferunt.   540

The text of the manuscript is not punctuated, apart from a dot (occasionally a semicolon) at the end of each line; there has, in consequence, been argument as to who the *quatuor* were. We consider that it is possible to show that Guy of Amiens lists four specific individuals, and that only the precise identities, and not the names of the third and fourth are in doubt.

In examining this passage, two things are immediately clear: four men are credited with killing Harold, and the fourth is called Gilfardus, from his father's soubriquet. The third, then, is the man named immediately before him, Hugo; and Hugo, in turn, is said to have accompanied at least two other men. As the total is four, it can be no more than two. An otherwise unidentified *Pontiui nobilis heres*, whether or not also *Alter ut Hectorides*, cannot stand alone as one of the missing pair, lacking either a verb or a copula. Each of these phrases (or both together) must modify one of the men otherwise shown to have made up the four.[1] Failing the

---

[1] The notion that the phrase *Pontiui nobilis heres* represented a separate member of the four seems to have begun with Freeman (*NC* iii. 499):

'The Latin poet of the battle describes this inglorious exploit with great glee. One of the four was Eustace . . . Nor are we amazed to find the son of Guy of Ponthieu . . . But one blushes to see men bearing the lofty names of Giffard and Montfort . . . taking a share in such low-minded vengeance on a fallen foe.'

'. . . Guy of Amiens (537) gives their names. Eustace has already been mentioned;

> Alter ut Hectorides, Pontivi nobilis haeres;
> Hos comitatur Hugo promptus in officio;
> Quartus Gilfardus patris a cognomine dictus;
> Regis ad exitium quattuor arma ferunt.'

By the omission from his footnote of vv. 535–6, Freeman concealed from his readers the grammatical impossibility of punctuating and interpreting the lines as he did.

noble heir of Ponthieu, the only two persons left for Hugh to accompany are the subject and object of *Aduocat*, the duke himself and Eustace of Boulogne. The beginning of the passage bears out this interpretation: William, who has seen Harold fiercely hewing down his Norman attackers, calls Eustace *to* him, seeking his aid. *Aduocare*, in the *Carmen* (v. 169) as elsewhere, does not mean 'to call to someone to do something', but rather 'to call someone to one's own presence'. Eustace was ordered to join the duke; that he himself was one of the four has never been questioned. On this ground too, then, the duke was the first of them.

Respecting Hugh, there are, at first sight, three possibilities: that all of v. 537 modifies this name; that *Pontiui nobilis heres* does but that *Alter ut Hectorides* does not; and that Hugh is undefined, the whole of v. 537 belonging to Eustace of Boulogne, who would then be the subject of *contulit* in v. 536. The last of these can be eliminated at once; Eustace was in no fashion heir to Ponthieu, nor is it anywhere suggested that he could have been. We show below that Hectorides apparently means Eustace and is used in place of his name at v. 563; here, therefore, *Alter ut Hectorides* must modify Hugh.[1] Eustace has already been shown to be an able and valiant warrior, and the newly introduced Hugh is succinctly characterized as his equal in valour. On this reading, the *Hos* of v. 538 falls late in the sentence, but no later than demonstrative and relative pronouns elsewhere in the poem (see the note to v. 256).

The royal confirmation of the foundation charter of Saint-Nicholas-des-Prés at Ribemont, dated 1084, is subscribed by Hugh, count of Ponthieu,[2] and although doubt has been cast on the name,[3] this is only because Hugh is otherwise unknown. The objection is considerably weakened by the fact that Enguerrand, son of Count Guy, is likewise known from but one document, even the date of which is unknown,[4] and

His reason was, apparently, a desire to dissociate the duke from such an ignoble deed, completely overlooking the fact that Guy of Amiens clearly did not think the deed anything but meritorious.

[1] We had had misgivings about this interpretation of the text, which would reduce the mention of Eustace to a single reference in the accusative case, for Guy has hitherto given him great attention. It has been pointed out to us, however, by Dr. L. J. Engels (see above, p. xxix) that Guy always carefully introduces new characters. Just as in vv. 519–22, William could be referred to simply as *dux*, while Eustace, on his first appearance in the poem, got two lines of description, so here Eustace, whose quality the reader by now knows well, is passed over in favour of Hugh of Ponthieu, the nephew or great-nephew of the poet.

[2] Preserved in the thirteenth-century cartulary of the church, Archives Nationales, MS. L.L. 1015, fol. 21ᵛ. Printed in *Gallia Christiana* x. 190.

[3] E. Prarond, *Les Comtes de Ponthieu—Guy Iᵉʳ, 1053–1100* (Paris, 1900), p. 49; Marquis Le Ver, Le Ver MS. 216, Bibliothèque d'Abbeville.

[4] Brunel vi, pp. 7 f. Note that the *Guido* and *Ivo* who are called *comites Ambiani* in the cartulary of Notre-Dame d'Amiens are probably not Guy of Ponthieu and

which, like the charter of St. Nicholas (and virtually all other documents for the house of Ponthieu in the eleventh century), is a later copy.

Count Guy had at least one younger brother whose name is unknown, and it is not impossible (though we think it unlikely) that he had a son old enough to fight at Hastings. Guy of Ponthieu's family had been established at Abbeville by Hugh Capet, who gave his daughter in marriage to the first of the house, also a Hugh. Thereafter, Hugh is one of the two most common names for the sons of the line, and it would be surprising had two generations of the family been without a Hugh. It would seem that they were not.

The charter of Saint-Nicholas-des-Prés bears no sign of being anything but an accurate copy of the original (e.g. the names and offices of other witnesses are, where verifiable, those of men who held those offices in 1084), nor is it likely that a thirteenth-century copyist would have substituted *Hugo* (a name that ceased to be used after Ponthieu passed to the house of Bellême in 1100) for *Wido* or *Guido* (a name borne by a twelfth-century count). Neither is it surprising that Hugh signed as count in the lifetime of Guy I. Heirs, apparent or presumptive, who sign as though already entered upon their heritage (after the usage of the Capetian house) are common at this period. Hence, it is by no means impossible, or even improbable, that the nearest male heir to Ponthieu in 1066 was a Hugh who survived to 1084 but predeceased Count Guy himself. The onus of proof to the contrary must fall upon those who would deny his existence.

The rare word *Hectorides*, which occurs here and at v. 563 of the *Carmen*, but which we have been unable to find elsewhere,[1] has further

yet another son, as the editors of *L'Art de vérifier les dates* believed (xii, Paris, 1818, pp. 190f.). See Ducange, *Histoire de l'état d'Amiens et ses comtes* (Rouen, 1840), pp. 226 ff., and the analysis of H. Hardouin, Ducange's editor, ibid., pp. xxxiv ff.

[1] No such word occurs in the files of the Committee for a Mediaeval Latin Dictionary in London or those of *Novum Glossarium* in Paris, and Dr. Otto Prinz has informed us that it is also lacking in those of *Mittellateinisches Wörterbuch*. Inquiries to a number of eminent medieval Latinists have been equally fruitless. The process by which such a word might come to be used of an eleventh-century count is not, in itself, far to seek. At least since the seventh century, the Franks had claimed Trojan descent (Fredegar's *Chronicle*, MGH SSRM ii. 45-7, 93), and, since Eusebius, Hector had been credited with sons other than Astyanax (*Chronicorum Canones*, ann. 864 post Abraham). Dictys Cretensis (*De Bello Trojano* iii. 20) names one as Laodamans. Thus any noble Frank might have been flattered with such a title. Similarly, any valiant warrior could have been so honoured, for the name Hector came early to be used as a synonym for 'hero' (Ovid, *Heroïdes* xiii. 65; Propertius 2. 22. 34). The name could even have been a genuine patronymic. Hector is found as a name in the Merovingian period (*Passio Leudegarii Episcopi Augustodunensis*, MGH SSRM v. 291; we owe this example to the kindness of Dr. J. M. Wallace-Hadrill); a Hector was bishop of Puy in the early tenth century; and a Hector, seigneur de Sassenage in Dauphiné,

obscured the identity of the four knights. Here it could on the face of it refer either to Eustace or to William (if Eustace is the subject of *contulit*). But in v. 563 it is used as a personal name to identify the leader of the night pursuit of the English, and we have already been told that William rested during the night (vv. 561–2). Hence, unless we are to assume that this very rare word is used of two different men within a space of twenty-five lines, Eustace must be the man referred to in both cases.

The only other early source that names those involved in a struggle with the surviving English is William of Poitiers (*GG*, p. 202), in whose account Eustace plays a sorry role by comparison with the duke. Yet if the opposing national prejudices of Guy of Amiens and William of Poitiers be allowed for, the identification of Eustace with *Hectorides* receives some support. A slighter indication, and inconclusive itself, but interesting, is that *Eustachius* (if followed by a word beginning with a consonant) and *Hectorides* have the same scansion. If Guy of Amiens himself coined this epithet in accordance with the classical practice for poetical pseudonyms, its absence elsewhere would be explained.

It has generally been assumed that Gilfardus, the last of the four, was Walter Giffard the younger; the misspelling of the nickname Gifart ('chubby-cheeks') is not a strong objection to this identification.[1] But is the phrase *patris a cognomine dictus* perhaps to be taken as meaning that this Giffard, unlike Walter, shared only a cognomen with his father? In v. 549 the fourth knight cuts off and carries away Harold's leg; William of Malmesbury, relating what seems to be the same incident,[2] claims that William was horrified and expelled the knight from his army forthwith. There is no evidence that William of Malmesbury had read the *Carmen*, nor has it influenced the Bayeux Tapestry, which has a similar scene.[3] The story is thus, apparently, not without foundation.[4]

---

died *c.* 1080. Hector impressed the medieval mind much more than Achilles. He became later one of the Nine Worthies of the World, and adjectives such as *Hectoreus* and *Hectorinus* are common. He gave his name to Sir Ector de Maris, and served as a sort of ghostly godfather to the hero of the Ektor Saga (cf. A. Loth, *Late Mediaeval Icelandic Romances* i (Copenhagen, 1962), pp. 81 f.). Yet this wealth of Hectoriana worsens rather than resolves the problem: why does the word not occur elsewhere?

[1] Giffard appears as Gifardus, Gyfardus, Vyfardus, Gifart, Giffart, Giffard (M. Fauroux, *Recueil des Actes des Ducs de Normandie, 911–1066, Mém. de la Soc. des Antiq. de Normandie* xxxvi (1961)), and Giphardus (*OV*, p. 174; ii. 148). For the intrusive 'l' cf. the writing Galfridus for Godfrey and Geoffrey.

[2] *GR* ii. 303: 'Jacentis femur unus militum gladio proscidit; unde a Willelmo ignominiae notatus, quod rem ignavam et pudendam fecisset, militia pulsus est.'

[3] *BT*, Pl. 72.

[4] The fact that Guy mentions no anger on William's part or disgrace of Giffard, while William of Malmesbury does not name the knight in question, is probably due to the different dates at which the two wrote. Guy, writing immediately after a near-run thing, finds the whole episode glorious. Giffard's disgrace

But in that case, Walter Giffard the younger can hardly have been the culprit, for he received an earldom from William. We incline, therefore, to see in Guy's Gilfardus a Giffard who was indeed disgraced, and whose family may have been glad to forget him.[1]

It is, admittedly, by no means certain that the *Quartus* of v. 539 is the *quartus* of v. 549, but it seems probable, because the order in which the four knights strike then fits their relative importance in the poem. William, the protagonist, gets two lines for his, the first blow; yet, if William's thrust be not immediately fatal, it will be Eustace's beheading of Harold that puts an end to him. Hugh and Giffard are left with less noble strokes.

may have come appreciably later, and his act on the field been seized upon as a pretext, in which case the *Carmen* would have been written before this happened. William of Malmesbury, living at a time when the Giffard family was of great power in England, would have hesitated to name one of them as the criminal.

[1] Part XII of *Heimskr.* ('Magnus Barefoot') preserves in chapter xvi an interpolation from the *Eirspennill* (ed. F. Jónsson, Oslo, 1916, pp. 121 f.), in which 'a foreigner named Gifford' seeks service with Magnus, and proves to be a coward. Freeman (*The Reign of William Rufus* ii. 451) suggested that this Gifford was a member of the Giffard family; certainly, the reduction of an otherwise unknown Giffard to the life of an incompetent mercenary would perhaps be explained were he the *quartus* himself (who may have been a mere youth in 1066) or his son.

I. THE ROYAL HOUSE OF ENGLAND[1]

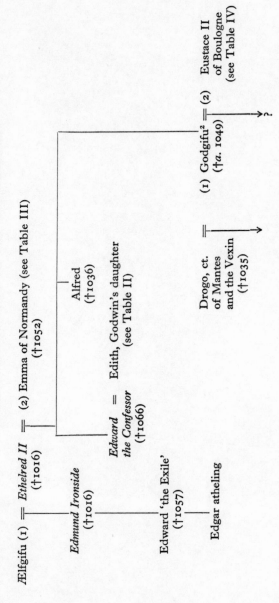

NOTES, TABLE I

[1] Kings of the English in italic.

[2] Godgifu has been assumed to have lived until at least 1051 on the basis of the *ASC*, MS. D, for that year, in which Eustace II of Boulogne is identified as, 'he who had married King Edward's sister'. The reference is, however, in the past tense. That Godgifu died before 5 October 1049 appears probable from the excommunication by Leo IX on that date of Eustace for incest. Godgifu and Eustace were fourth-cousins through their common descent from King Alfred, but in 1049 the definition of relationship within the seventh degree had not yet been altered to forbid the marriage of such distant relatives. Ida of Lorraine, on the other hand, the second wife of Eustace, was his first-cousin by marriage, her paternal aunt, Oda of Lorraine, having earlier married the maternal uncle of Eustace, Lambert II of Louvain. It seems much more likely that it was this alliance that gave the pope his pretext, for the house of Lorraine was in bad odour with Rome. Edmond Rigaux (see above, p. xxx n. 2) has adduced a number of arguments to show that Eustace must have married Ida before the date usually assumed, and that Godgifu's marriage to Eustace followed very quickly on the death of her first husband in July 1035. Perhaps the most telling of these is the statement that her brother, Alfred atheling, accepted from Eustace that aid for his ill-starred expedition to England in 1036 which he refused from the count of Flanders (*EE*, p. 42).

II. THE ROYAL HOUSE OF DENMARK[1]

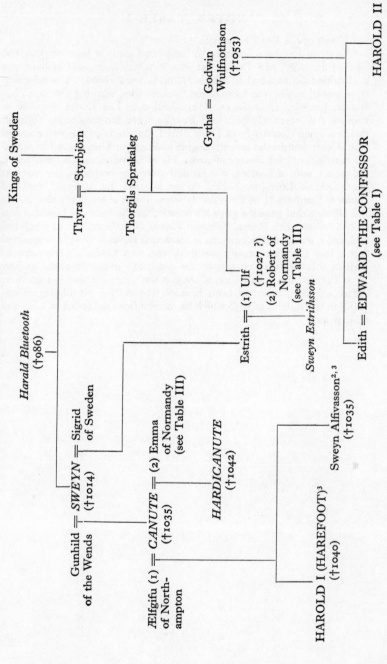

NOTES, TABLE II

[1] Kings of the English in capitals; kings of the Danes in italics; kings of both in italic capitals.

[2] King of the Norwegians.

[3] Chroniclers often referred to both Harold I and Sweyn Alfivasson as bastards, perhaps not even illegitimate sons, of Canute (cf. *ASC*, 1035; FW, 1035; *GR* i. 227), but monks tended to treat marriages *de more Danico* as mere concubinage, despite their undoubted standing in law, and vituperate their offspring. We give both kings the benefit of the doubt.

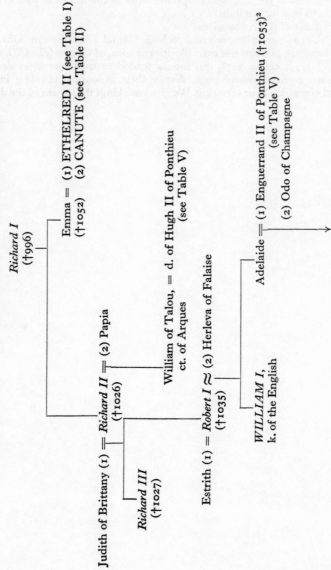

III. THE DUCAL HOUSE OF NORMANDY[1]

NOTES, TABLE III

[1] Reigning dukes in italics; kings of the English in capitals; duke-kings in italic capitals.

[2] The only evidence for a marriage of Adelaide with Lambert, count of Lens, in Artois (see Table IV), often named as her second husband, is the statement in the late and untrustworthy *Vita et Passio Waldevi Comitis* (*CAN* ii. 112) that Waltheof's wife, Judith, was the daughter of Lambert. Stapleton, though with some hesitation, accepted the marriage and this paternity for Judith (*Magn. Rot. Scacc. Norm.* ii, xxxi, note (i)), although he had earlier (*Archaeologia* xxvi (1836), pp. 350 f.) taken both Adelaide's daughters, Adelaide the younger and Judith, to be the children of Enguerrand II of Ponthieu. We support his earlier view for the following reasons: (1) Lambert of Lens was killed at the siege of Lille in July–August 1054; yet the endowment published by Stapleton in *Archaeologia* shows that Adelaide was still residing, at some time after the beginning of 1055, at Aumale, Enguerrand's maternal inheritance, of which Adelaide the younger was the heiress. (2) Adelaide the elder resided long enough in Aumale to be commonly described in later chronicles as 'comitissa de Albamarla' (despite her marriage at some time before 1070 to Odo of Champagne); she is nowhere called 'comitissa Lensensis'. (3) While Judith is associated with her mother and sister in the Aumale endowment, there is no mention of Lambert. (4) Lambert's lands passed to his older brother, Eustace II of Boulogne, and none were assigned to Judith, although an heiress normally inherited at least a portion of her father's property (as Adelaide the younger did), if not the whole (as Agnes/Anna of Ponthieu and Mathilda of Boulogne did).

IV. THE COMITAL HOUSE OF BOULOGNE[1]

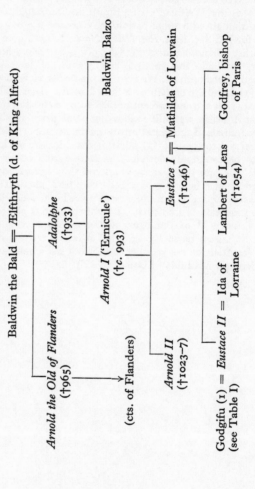

Baldwin the Bald $=$ Ælfthryth (d. of King Alfred)

Arnold the Old of Flanders (†965)

Adalolphe (†933)

(cts. of Flanders)

Arnold I ('Ernicule') (†c. 993)

Baldwin Balzo

Arnold II (†1023–7)

Eustace I $=$ Mathilda of Louvain (†1046)

Godgifu (1) $=$ Eustace II $=$ Ida of Lorraine
(see Table I)

Lambert of Lens (†1054)

Godfrey, bishop of Paris

NOTES, TABLE IV

[1] Based on the researches of E. Rigaux (see above, p. xxx n. 2). Ruling counts are italicized (Arnold the Old usurped from his nephews between 933 and 965).

V. THE COMITAL HOUSE OF PONTHIEU[1]

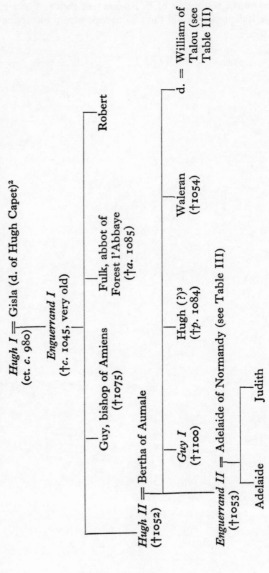

Hugh I ⚊ Gisla (d. of Hugh Capet)[2]
(ct. c. 980)

Enguerrand I
(†c. 1045, very old)

Robert

Guy, bishop of Amiens
(†1075)

Fulk, abbot of
Forest l'Abbaye
(†a. 1085)

Hugh II ⚊ Bertha of Aumale
(†1052)

Guy I
(†1100)

Hugh (?)[3]
(†p. 1084)

Waleran
(†1054)

d. = William of
Talou (see
Table III)

Enguerrand II ⚊ Adelaide of Normandy (see Table III)
(†1053)

Adelaide

Judith

NOTES, TABLE V

[1] Based on the researches of J. Delaîte (see above, p. xxx n. 2). Ruling counts in italics.

[2] Lambert of Ardres's statement that the houses of both Ponthieu and Boulogne were descended from a William, count of Ponthieu (Bouquet xi. 296 a–b), was discounted by so early a commentator as Malbrancq (*De Morinis* ii. 594); and, as Delaîte (op. cit., p. 33) has shown, William, count of Ponthieu, never existed. But it has subsequently been accepted that the *ci-devant* countess of Boulogne provided a link between the houses, as the grandmother of both Eustace II of Boulogne and Guy I of Ponthieu. This, as we have shown above, is, on the dates, impossible. If there is any truth at all in Hariulf's story, she was at best the aunt by marriage of Eustace and the step-grandmother of Guy (see above, p. xxxi). Yet, the obvious regard in which Guy of Amiens held Eustace of Boulogne and the flight of William of Talou and his wife, a daughter of Ponthieu, to Eustace's court after the siege of Arques suggest that some relationship that we cannot now trace may have existed. *Hugo miles*, the founder of the comital house of Ponthieu, married Gisla, daughter of Hugh Capet, probably at the time that he received Ponthieu from the latter, that is, between 965 and 980. We incline to postulate an early date within this period, as Hugh Capet would not have left a seat of power vacant there for any longer than needful after the death of the redoubtable Arnold the Old of Flanders (see Table IV). Although Hugh Capet himself did not marry his only known wife, Adelaide, before 970 (cf. F. Lot, *Les Derniers Carolingiens*, Paris, 1891, p. 74), he was by then almost 30, and Gisla could well have been the offspring of an earlier connection. Certainly, if she was old enough to bear children *c.* 975–80, a daughter of hers by Hugo could well have been by 995 the mother of the two sons of Arnold I of Boulogne; and it is pointed out by Rigaux (op. cit., p. 159) that tradition held that 'Ernicule' (Arnold I) had indeed married a daughter of a count of Ponthieu. This hypothesis leaves us, however, with the difficulty that Enguerrand I, in taking the widow of Arnold II of Boulogne as his second wife, would have been marrying the widow of his own nephew. Admittedly, there is no reason to assume that counts of northern France in the early eleventh century would have concerned themselves much with the canonicity of an otherwise desirable marriage. Equally admittedly, the two houses may have been connected by the marriage of younger sons and daughters of whose existence all record has been lost. By the suggested hypothesis, however, Eustace II of Boulogne would have been the first-cousin once removed of Guy of Amiens and the second-cousin of Guy of Ponthieu.

[3] On Hugh of Ponthieu see above, Appendix D, pp. 117 f.

SELECT BIBLIOGRAPHY

By the generosity of the Clarendon Press, we have been allowed to append a select bibliography. To keep its length to a minimum, we have confined ourselves in the main (but not exclusively) to listing those works cited in our edition, excepting those already cited in the 'Abbreviated References' (above, pp. lxxi f.) and a few others, mostly either of very specialized interest or well-known reference works. As the bibliography is meant primarily for the convenience of readers, whatever their location, we have not included manuscripts.

A full listing of works consulted would have duplicated to a great extent the comprehensive bibliographies of works bearing on the Conquest given by D. C. Douglas in his *William the Conqueror* (London, 1964) and *The Norman Achievement* (London, 1969), to which readers are referred.

PRIMARY SOURCES

Records and documents

Amiens: 'Cartulaire du chapitre de l'église cathédrale d'Amiens', in *Mém. de la Soc. des Antiquaires de Picardie; Documents inédits* xiv (1905).

—— 'Nécrologie de l'église d'Amiens', ed. Canon Roze, in *Mém. de la Soc. des Antiquaires de Picardie* xxviii (1885).

—— 'Sur une inscription du xie siècle provenant de l'abbaye de Corbie', by J. Corblet, in *Bulletins de la Soc. des Antiquaires de Picardie* ix (1867).

Coronation: *English Coronation Records*, by L. G. Wickham Legg. London, 1901.

—— *Laudes regiae*, by E. H. Kantorowicz. Berkeley, Calif., 1958.

—— *Le Pontifical romano-germanique du dixième siècle*, ed. C. Vogel and R. Elze. Vatican City (*Studi e testi* 226), 1963.

—— *Three Coronation Orders*, ed. L. G. Wickham Legg. London (Henry Bradshaw Soc. xix), 1900.

England: *Anglo-Saxon Charters*, ed. A. J. Robertson. Cambridge, 1939.

—— *Anglo-Saxon Writs*, ed. F. E. Harmer. Manchester, 1952.

—— *Councils and Ecclesiastical Documents relating to Great Britain and Ireland*, ed. A. W. Haddan and W. Stubbs. Oxford, 1869–78.

—— *Domesday Book* (in facsimile). London, Record Commission, 1861–3.

—— *Facsimiles of English Royal Writs to 1100 presented to V. H. Galbraith*. Oxford, 1957.

France: *Monuments de la monarchie française,* ed. Dom Bernard de Montfaucon, v. ii. Paris, 1730.

—— *Recueil des actes de Philippe Ier,* ed. M. Prou. Paris, 1908.

—— *Rouleaux des morts du IXe siècle au XVe siècle,* ed. L. V. Delisle. Paris, 1886.

Germany: *Jahrbücher des deutschen Reichs unter Heinrich III,* ed. F. Steindorff. Leipzig, 1874.

Ghent: Abbaye de Saint Pierre au Mont Blandin. *Chartes et documents,* ed. A. van Lokeren. Ghent, 1868.

Normandy: *Magni rotuli scaccarii Normanniae sub regibus Angliae,* ed. T. Stapleton (2 vols.). London, 1840, 1844.

—— *Recueil des actes des ducs de Normandie, 911–1066,* ed. M. Fauroux. Caen, 1961. (*Mém. de la Soc. des Antiquaires de Normandie* xxxvi.)

—— 'Observations on the history of Adeliza, sister of William the Conqueror', by T. Stapleton, in *Archaeologia* xxvi (1836).

Chronicles and narratives

Abbo. *Le Siège de Paris par les Normands,* ed. H. Waquet. Paris, 1942.

Adalbero of Laon. *Carmen ad Rotbertum regem,* ed. G. A. Hückel. Paris, 1901.

Adam of Bremen. *Gesta Hammaburgensis ecclesiae pontificum,* ed. B. Schmeidler. *MGH SSRG,* 1917.

Annales monastici, ed. H. R. Luard. London, 1864–9 (*RS* xxxvi, 4 vols.).

Balderic of Thérouanne. *Chronique d'Arras et de Cambrai,* ed. A. Le Glay. Paris, 1834.

Benoît de Sainte-Maure. *Chronique des ducs de Normandie,* ed. C. Fahlin. Uppsala (*Bibliotheca Eckmanniana,* vols. lvi, lx), 1951, 1954.

Brevis relatio de origine Willelmi Conquestoris, ed. J. A. Giles (in Giles, *Scriptores,* q.v.).

Caesar, Gaius Julius. *De bello civili.* Cambridge, Mass. (Loeb Library), 1961.

—— *De bello Gallico.* Cambridge, Mass. (Loeb Library), 1917.

La Chanson de Roland, ed. J. Bédier. Paris, 1960.

Chronicon monasterii de Bello, ed. M. A. Lower. London, 1846.

Du Méril, Édélestand. *Poésies inédites du moyen âge.* Paris, 1854.

Eirspennil, ed. F. Jónsson. Oslo, 1916.

Ermoldus Nigellus. *De gestis Ludovici Caesaris,* in *MGH PLAC* ii.

Eusebius of Caesarea. *Eusebii chronicorum canonum,* ed. A. Schoene. Berlin, 1866.

Excidium Troiae, ed. E. B. Atwood and V. K. Whitaker. Cambridge, Mass. (Mediaeval Academy of America publ. no. 44), 1944.

Flanders. *Recueil des chroniques de Flandres*, ed. J. J. de Smet. Brussels, 1837–65.

Flodoard. *Les Annales de Flodoard*, ed. P. Lauer. Paris, 1905.

Folcuin. *Gesta abbatum Sithiensium*, ed. O. Holder-Egger, in *MGH SS* xiii.

Fulco of Beauvais. 'Fulcoii Belvacensis Epistulae', ed. M. L. Colker, in *Traditio* x (1960).

Gaimar, Geffrei. *L'Estoire des Engleis*, ed. A. Bell. Oxford (Anglo-Norman Texts xiv–xvi), 1960.

Geoffrey of Rheims. 'Trois œuvres inédites de Godefroid de Reims', ed. A. Boutemy, in *Revue du moyen âge latin* iii (1947).

Hemingspattr Aslákssonar, ed. G. Fellows Jensen. Copenhagen (*Editiones Arnamagnaeanae*, series B, vol. iii), 1962.

Henry of Huntingdon. *Historia Anglorum*, ed. T. Arnold. London, 1879 (*RS* lxxiv).

Historia Eliensis, ed. E. O. Blake. London (Camden Third Series xcii), 1962.

Historia Ramesiensis, ed. W. Dunn Macray. London, 1886 (*RS* lxxxiii).

Jómsvikinga saga, ed. N. F. Blake. London (Nelson's Icelandic Texts) 1962.

Knighton, Henry. *The Chronicle of Henry Knighton*, i, ed. J. R. Lumby. London, 1889 (*RS* xcii).

Osbert of Clare. 'La vie de saint Édouard le Confesseur par Osbert de Clare', ed. M. Bloch, in *Analecta Bollandiana* xli (1923).

Ragnars saga. Volsunga saga ok Ragnars saga loðbrókar, ed. M. Olsen. Copenhagen, 1906–8.

Ralph de Diceto. *Opera historica*, ed. W. Stubbs. London, 1876 (*RS* lxviii, 2 vols.).

Richer. *Historia*, ed. J. Guadet, Paris, 1845; 2 vols.

Robert of Torigny. *Accessiones ad Sigebertum*, in *Chronicles of the Reigns of Stephen, Henry II, and Richard I*, ed. R. Howlett. London, 1889 (*RS* lxxxii, vol. 4).

Rodulf Glaber. *Francorum historia*, ed. M. Prou. Paris, 1886.

Stephen of Rouen. *Draco Normannicus*, ed. R. Howlett, op. cit., vol. 2. London, 1885. Also ed. H. Omont (*Le Dragon normand*). Rouen, 1894.

Symeon of Durham. *The Historical Works*, ed. T. Arnold. London, 1882–5 (*RS* lxxv, 2 vols.).

Theodulfus of Orleans. *Carmina*. In *MGH PLAC* i.

Vegetius Renatus, Flavius. *De re militari*, ed. C. Lang (as *Epitoma rei militaris*). Leipzig, 1869.

William of Apulia. *De gestis Normannorum in Sicilia, Appulia et Calabria*, in Muratori, vol. v.

William of Malmesbury. *Gesta pontificum Anglorum*, ed. N. E. S. A. Hamilton. London, 1870 (*RS* lii).

—— *Vita Wulfstani*, ed. R. R. Darlington. London (Royal Hist. Soc.), 1928.

William of Newburgh. *Historia rerum Anglicarum*, ed. R. Howlett, op. cit., vol. i. London, 1884.

SECONDARY WORKS

ADAM, R. J., *A Conquest of England*, London, 1965.

ANDRÉ, P., *Hugues Capet, roi de France, 941–996*, Berne (2nd edn.), 1941.

BAKER, T., *The Normans*, London, 1966.

BARCLAY, C. N., *Battle, 1066*, London, 1966.

BARING, F. H., *Domesday Tables for the counties of Surrey, Berkshire, Middlesex, Hertford, Buckingham, and Bedford, and for the New Forest*. London, 1909.

BARLOW, F., 'The Carmen de Hastingae Proelio', in *Studies in International History presented to W. Norton Medlicott*, ed. K. Bourne and D. C. Watt. London, 1967.

—— *Edward the Confessor and the Norman Conquest*. St. Leonards-on-Sea (Hastings and Bexhill Branch, The Historical Association), 1966.

—— *The English Church, 1000–1066*. London, 1963.

—— *The Feudal Kingdom of England*. London (2nd edn.), 1961.

—— 'A View of Archbishop Lanfranc', in *JEH* xvi (1965).

—— *William I and the Norman Conquest*. London, 1966.

BEELER, J., *Warfare in England, 1066–1189*. Ithaca, N.Y., 1966.

Belgium. Commission Royale d'Histoire. *Bulletins*, sér. 1. Brussels, 1839–50.

BERTRAND, S., *La Tapisserie de Bayeux et la manière de vivre au onzième siècle*. Paris, 1966.

BLAISE, A., *Dictionnaire latin–français des anciens chrétiens*. Strasbourg, 1954.

BLONDIN, C., *Mémoires pour l'histoire de Saint-Valery-sur-Somme*. Amiens, 1882.

BÖHMER, H., *Kirche und Staat in England und in der Normandie im xi. und xiii. Jahrhunderten*. Leipzig, 1899.

BOUREL DE LA RONCIÈRE, C., *Histoire de la marine française*. Paris, 1899.

BROOKE, C. N. L., *The Saxon and Norman Kings*. London, 1963.

BROOKE, Z. N., *The English Church and the Papacy, 1066–1200*. Cambridge, 1931.

BROWN, R. A., *The Normans and the Norman Conquest*. London, 1969.

BRUCE, J. C., *The Bayeux Tapestry elucidated*. London, 1856.

BRÜCKMANN, J., 'The Ordines of the Third Recension of the Mediaeval English Coronation Order', in *Essays in Medieval History presented to Bertie Wilkinson* (Toronto, 1969).

BUTLER, D., *1066: the Story of a Year*. London, 1966.

CHEVALIER, C., *Répertoire des sources historiques du moyen âge bio-bibliographe*. Paris (2nd edn.), 1905–7, 2 vols.

CURTIUS, E. R., *Europäische Literatur und lateinische Mittelalter*. Berne, 1954.

DAWSON, C., *Hastings Castle*. London, 1909, 2 vols.

DEANESLY, M., 'Roman Traditional Influence among the Anglo-Saxons', in *EHR* lviii (1948).

DELAÎTE, J., *Les Comtes de Dammartin en Goële et leurs ancêtres du VIIIe au XIIe siècle*. Liège, 1911.

DELARC, O., *Saint Grégoire VII et la réforme de l'église au XIe siècle*. Paris, 1889.

DÉVÉRITÉ, L. A., *Histoire du comité de Ponthieu*. London, 1767.

DODWELL, C. R., 'The Bayeux Tapestry and the French Secular Epic', in *The Burlington Magazine* cviii (1966).

DOUGLAS, D. C., 'The Ancestors of William FitzOsbern', in *EHR* lix (1944).

—— 'The Companions of the Conqueror', in *History* xxviii (1943).

—— 'Edward the Confessor, Duke William of Normandy, and the English Succession', in *EHR* lxviii (1953).

—— *The Norman Achievement*. London, 1969.

—— *William the Conqueror*. London, 1964.

DOZY, R., *Recherches sur l'histoire de la littérature de l'Espagne*. Paris, 1881, 2 vols.

DRÖGEREIT, R., 'Bemerkungen zum Bayeux-Teppich', in *Mitteilungen des Instituts für Österreichische Geschichtsforschung* lxx (1962).

DUCANGE, C., *Histoire des comtes de Ponthieu et de Montreuil*, ed. A. Le Sueur (*Mém. de la Soc. d'Émulation d'Abbeville*, sér. 4, viii (1917)).

—— *Histoire de l'état d'Amiens et ses comtes*, ed. H. Hardouin. Rouen, 1840.

DUPONT, E., *La Participation de la Bretagne à la conquête de l'Angleterre par les Normands*. Paris, 1911.

DUSEVEL, H., and SCRIBE, P.-A., *Description historique et pittoresque du Département de la Somme*. Amiens/Paris, 1836.

ENGELS, L. J., *Dichters over Willem de Veroveraar: Het Carmen de Hastingae Proelio*, Inaugural Lecture, University of Groningen. Groningen, 1967.

FARAL, E., *Les Jongleurs de France*. Paris, 1910.

FLICHE, A., *Le Règne de Philippe Ier, roi de France*. Paris, 1912.

FOREVILLE, R., 'Aux origines de la légende épique. Les "Gesta Guillelmi ducis Normannorum et regis Anglorum" de Guillaume de Poitiers', in *Le Moyen Âge* lvi (1950).

FREEMAN, E. A., *The Reign of William Rufus*. Oxford, 1882.

FURNEAUX, R., *Conquest, 1066*. London, 1966.

GANSHOF, F., *La Flandre sous les premiers comtes*. Brussels (3rd edn.), 1949.

GEORGE, H. B., *Battles of English History*. London, 1904.

GODEFROY, F., *Dictionnaire de l'ancienne langue française et de tous ses dialects du IXe au XVe siècle*. Paris/Abbeville, 1880–1902.

GRIERSON, P., 'A Visit of Earl Harold to Flanders in 1056', in *EHR* li (1936).

—— 'The Relations between England and Flanders before the Norman Conquest', in *Transactions of the Royal Hist. Soc.*, ser. 4, xxiii (1941).

GRIMM, J., and SCHMELLER, A., *Lateinische Gedichte des X. und XI. Jahrhunderten*. Göttingen, 1838.

HARDY, T. D., *Descriptive catalogue of manuscripts relating to the history of Great Britain and Ireland*. London, 1862–71 (*RS* xxvi, 3 vols.).

HASKINS, C. H., *Norman Institutions*. London, 1960.

HAUTEVILLE, A. d', and BÉNARD, L., *Histoire de Boulogne-sur-Mer*. Boulogne, 1860.

HÉLIOT, P., *Histoire de Boulogne et du Boulonnais*. Lille, 1937.

HOLMES, U. T., 'The Houses of the Bayeux Tapestry', in *Speculum* xxxiv (1959).

HONEYBOURNE, M. B., 'The Pre-Norman Bridge of London', in *Studies in London history presented to Philip Edmund Jones*. London, 1969.

KÖHLER, G., *Die Entwicklung des Kriegswesens und der Kriegführung in der Ritterzeit von Mitte des XI. Jahrhunderts bis zu den Hussitenkriegen*. Breslau, 1886.

KÖRNER, S., *The Battle of Hastings: England and Europe, 1035–1066*. Lund, 1964.

LAPORTE, J., 'Rapports de l'abbaye de Saint-Riquier avec l'Angleterre', in *Revue Mabillon* xlix (1959).

LARSON, L. M., *The King's Household in England before the Norman Conquest*. Madison, Wisc. (Univ. of Wisconsin publ. no. 100), 1904.

LAUER, P., *Annales de l'histoire de France à l'époque carolingienne: Robert Ier et Raoul*. Paris, 1910.

LEFILS, F., *Histoire de Saint-Valery et du comté de Vimeu*. Abbeville 1858.

LEMMON, C. H., *The Field of Hastings*. St. Leonards-on-Sea (4th edn.), 1970.

LLOYD, A., *The Year of the Conqueror*. London, 1966.

LOT, F., *L'Art militaire et les armées au moyen âge*. Paris, 1946.

—— *Les Derniers Carolingiens*. Paris, 1891.

—— *Études sur la règne de Hugues Capet et la fin du Xe siècle*. Paris, 1903.

LOYN, H. R., *Anglo-Saxon England and the Norman Conquest*. London, 1962.

—— *The Norman Conquest*. London, 1965.

LUCHAIRE, A., *Histoire des institutions monarchiques de la France sous les premiers capétiens*. Paris, 1891.

MACDONALD, A. J., *Lanfranc*. Oxford, 1926.

MACLAGAN, E., *The Bayeux Tapestry*. London, 1953.

MANITIUS, K., 'Eine Gruppe von Handschriften des 12. Jahrhunderts aus dem Trierer Kloster St. Eucharius-Matthias', in *Forschungen und Fortschritte* xxix (1955).

MANITIUS, M., *Handschriften antiker Autoren in mittelalterlichen Bibliothekskatalogen*. Leipzig, 1935.

—— *Geschichte der Lateinischen Literatur des Mittelalters*. Munich, 1911–31.

MARGARY, I. D., *Roman Ways through the Weald*. London, 1949.

MARSDEN, P. R., 'The Riverside Defensive Wall of Roman London', in *Transactions of the London and Middlesex Archaeological Society* xxi (1967).

MATTHEW, D. J., *The Norman Conquest*. London, 1966.

—— *The Norman Monasteries and their English Possessions*. Oxford, 1962.

MERRIFIELD, R., *The Roman City of London*. London, 1962.

Mittellateinisches Wörterbuch, ed. Dr. Otto Prinz. Munich, 1959– .

MOHRMANN, C., 'Le dualisme de la latinité médiévale', in *Revue des études latines* xxix (1951).

MONTEBAUR, J., *Studien zur Geschichte der Bibliothek der Abtei St. Eucharius-Matthias zu Trier*. Freiburg im Breisgau, 1931.

NAMUR, J. P., *Histoire des bibliothèques publiques de la Belgique*. Brussels 1840–2.

NIERMEYER, J. F., *Mediae Latinitatis lexicon minus*. Leyden, 1954– .

OAKESHOTT, R. E., *The Archaeology of Weapons*. London, 1960.

PAYNE-GALLWEY, Sir R., *The Crossbow*. London, 1903; 1958.

PRAROND, E., *Les Comtes de Ponthieu—Guy Ier, 1053–1100*. Paris, 1900.

PRENTOUT, H., 'Le mariage de Guillaume', in *Mém. de l'académie nationale . . . de Caen*, N.S. vi (1931).

RABY, F. J., *A History of Secular Latin Poetry in the Middle Ages*. Oxford (2nd edn.), 1957.

RAMSAY, Sir J., *The Foundations of England*. London, 1898, 2 vols.

RENN, D., *Norman Castles in Britain*. London, 1968.

RICHARDSON, H. G., 'The Coronation in Mediaeval England: the Evolution of the Office and the Oath', in *Traditio* xvi (1960).

—— and SAYLES, G. O., *The Governance of Mediaeval England from the Conquest to Magna Carta*. Edinburgh, 1963.

RIGAUX, E., 'Recherches sur les premiers comtes de Boulogne', in *Bulletins de la Soc. Acad. de l'arrondissement de Boulogne-sur-Mer* v (1894).

ROUND, J. H., *The Commune of London and other studies*. London, 1899.

—— *The King's Sergeants and Officers of State with their Coronation Services*. London, 1911.

—— *Studies in Peerage and Family History*. London, 1901.

SACHY, J. DE, *Histoire des évesques d'Amiens*. Abbeville, 1770.

SCHLECHTE, H., *Erzbischof Bruno von Trier. Ein Beitrag zur Geschichte des geistigen Strömungen in Investiturstreit*, Inaugural Dissertation, Leipzig University. Leipzig, 1934.

SCHNITH, K., 'Die Wende der englischen Geschichte im 11. Jahrhundert', in *Historisches Jahrbuch* lxxxvi (1966).

SCHRAMM, P. E., *Herrschaftszeichen und Staatssymbolik*. Stuttgart, 1954–6, 3 vols.

—— *A History of the English Coronation*, transl. by L. G. Wickham Legg. Oxford, 1937.

SOUTHERN, R. W., *The Life of Saint Anselm by Eadmer*. London, 1963.

SOYEZ, E., *Notices sur les évêques d'Amiens*. Amiens, 1878.

STENTON, Sir F., *Anglo-Saxon England*. Oxford, 1943.

THIERRY, J. N. A., *Histoire de la conquête de l'Angleterre par les Normands*. Paris, 3rd edn., 1830.

WALEY, D. P., 'Combined Operations in Sicily, A.D. 1060–1078', in *Papers of the British School at Rome* xvii (1954).

WALLACE-HADRILL, J. M., *The Barbarian West, 400–1000*. London, 3rd edn., 1967.

—— *The Long-haired Kings and other Studies in Frankish History*. London, 1962.

WARD, P. L., 'The Coronation Ceremony in Mediaeval England', in *Speculum* xiv (1939).

WHITE, G. H., 'The Battle of Hastings and the Death of Harold', in *The Complete Peerage* xii, Appendix L. London, 1953.

WHITE, G. H., 'The Companions of the Conqueror', in *The Genealogists' Magazine* ix (1944).

WHITELOCK, D., and others, *The Norman Conquest: its Setting and Impact.* London, 1966.

WILLIAMSON, J. A., *The English Channel.* London, 1959.

—— *The Evolution of England.* Oxford, 2nd edn., 1944.

INDEX

Names are given in their modern English forms, where these exist, otherwise in the forms that we have found most frequent in the literature. Italicized page numbers refer to the text either of the *Carmen* (pp. 2–52) or of it and other eleventh-century sources printed on pp. 84–90 and 98–109.